Diana, A Cultural History

Also by Jude Davies

GENDER, ETHNICITY AND SEXUALITY IN CONTEMPORARY AMERICAN FILM (*with C. R. Smith*)

Diana, A Cultural History

Gender, Race, Nation and the People's Princess

Jude Davies
Senior Lecturer
School of Cultural Studies
King Alfred's College
Winchester

palgrave

First published 2001 by
PALGRAVE
Houndmills, Basingstoke, Hampshire RG21 6XS and
175 Fifth Avenue, New York, N. Y. 10010
Companies and representatives throughout the world

PALGRAVE is the new global academic imprint of
St. Martin's Press LLC Scholarly and Reference Division and
Palgrave Publishers Ltd (formerly Macmillan Press Ltd).

ISBN 0–333–73688–5 hardback
ISBN 0–333–73689–3 paperback

This book is printed on paper suitable for recycling and
made from fully managed and sustained forest sources.

A catalogue record for this book is available
from the British Library.

Library of Congress Cataloging-in-Publication Data
Davies, Jude, 1965–
    Diana, a cultural history : gender, race, nation, and
    the people's princess / Jude Davies.
        p. cm.
    Includes bibliographical references (p.) and index.
    ISBN 0–333–73688–5
    1. Diana, Princess of Wales, 1961——In mass media. 2. Mass
media and public opinion—Great Britain—History—20th
century. 3. Popular culture—Great Britain—History—20th
century. 4. Princesses—Great Britain—Biography. 5. National
characteristics in mass media. 6. Race relations in mass media.
7. Sex role in mass media. 8. Women in mass media. I. Title.

DA591.A45 D531216 2001
941.085'092—dc21
[B]
                                        2001021550

10   9   8   7   6   5   4   3   2   1
10   09 08 07 06 05 04 03 02 01

Printed in Great Britain by Antony Rowe Ltd, Chippenham, Wiltshire

Contents

Preface

Contrary to the tenor and scope of some accounts, Diana, Princess of Wales did not spring fully formed into popular consciousness on 31 August 1997. While the unpredicted and, to many, astonishing global public mourning for Diana decisively changed and intensified her significance, it built upon ideas and assumptions about femininity, whiteness, royalty, national identity and media society with a long history in representing Diana, and others to whom the word 'princess' has been applied. Diana both shaped the meaning of these terms and was shaped by them.

For someone who was not known much for speaking, Diana has attracted a lot of verbiage. Her career in itself made a strong case against the priority of words, privileging what some call 'affectivity', and others see as 'reaching out' to others. There are good reasons for being wary of projects of explaining Diana. But whatever her emotive and inspirational status, Diana always did *signify*.

What she signified is the subject of this book. The Diana we knew was a real person, but we knew her for the most part through her representation in mass media. This, then, is an attempt to chart the history of such representations. In doing so, it aims to show how Diana came to stand for transformation, and how it came about that in thinking about Diana we thought not only about ourselves, but also about others.

Acknowledgements

I am grateful to King Alfred's College, Winchester, for supporting this work through a research grant, teaching relief and sabbatical leave.

I would like to thank Clive Bloom, whose guidance, advice and insight have been extensive and indispensable. I am also very grateful to Sandra Kemp, Heather Nunn, Nick Couldry, Jeremy Gilbert, Mick Jardine and Carol R. Smith, for their comments on drafts of various sections at various stages of development.

This book has also benefited from the intelligence, assistance and sometimes critique of the following: Maggie Andrews, John Arnold, Victoria Howell, Fan Carter, Mary Condé, Ian Crook, Pamela Ezell, Patrick Hagopian, Ann Kaloski-Naylor, Erna Kelly, Margaret Leah, Karen Loeb, Alison Pearce, Louise Stimpson, Agnes Smith and Michael Thomas. During its composition I have been sustained by the intellectual fellowship centred on the Birmingham Urban Cultures reading group, and especially Maria Balshaw and Liam Kennedy, who combine intellectual and inspirational gifts in ways that are rare indeed.

My greatest debts of gratitude are to Agnes and Carol R. Smith, who both inspired this project and enabled its realization. It is to Carol, who continues to teach me much about gender, race and representation, that this book is dedicated.

Portions of chapter 2 draw upon work previously published in somewhat different form, in *History and Heritage: Consuming the Past in Contemporary Culture*, edited by John Arnold, Kate Davies and Simon Ditchfield, and as 'Princess: Diana, Femininity and the Royal', in *New Formations* 36, edited by Jeremy Gilbert, David Glover, Cora Kaplan, Jenny Bourne Taylor and Wendy Wheeler. My thanks to all the editors for their advice and support.

Introduction: Why a Cultural History?

The aim of this book is to trace a critical history of the representation of Diana, Princess of Wales in the mass media. Its concern is with 'Diana' the emblem, symbol, icon and sign: cultural productions which not only signify different modes of being in the world, but are also sites of contest and debate. Representations of Diana as media saint and arch manipulator, celebrity victim and successful campaigner against land-mines, feminist icon and romantic heroine, princess and everywoman, testify to the continuing historical contentiousness of gender, nation, race and self. This book investigates the processes through which the figure of a young Englishwoman of aristocratic stock came to crystallize such conflicts over identity, and evaluates the significance of Diana's ambivalent status.

Despite the trivial status often accorded to mass media representations of Diana, it is not hard to see how they have played an active part in marking the boundaries between culture, politics and identity. Diana representations raised and continue to pose a series of vexed questions, the most salient of which can be summarized under notions of (post)modern selfhood, gender and the nature of society. From the moment of her 'discovery' by the British press late in 1980, images of and information about Diana's life dramatized the production of a self through processes of affective and familial bonding, acts of consumption and display, and highly mediated self-presentation. Moreover, shifts in the scope and significance of such representations reflect a variety of historical investments. For example, after Diana's death in August 1997, the privatized biography of romance, marriage, parenthood, separation and divorce has often been re-narrated in terms of the struggle for emotional authenticity under conditions of modern anomie, patriarchal subjection and postmodern fragmentation. In ways

1

that overlap and interlock with this, Diana is taken to exemplify femininity, both with respect to the lived experience of female gender identity and as the embodiment of 'feminine values'. At still another level, she has become a focus of sociality, the 'glue' that holds together human communities. The figure of Diana emblematizes familial, romantic and affective ties, and offers an historical connection with the social fabric of the past. Sometimes elaborated in religious or quasi-religious terms, this has global scope, but has been particularly marked in British culture by notions of national identity and Englishness.

Less obviously, these significances are themselves configured by notions of monarchy and the royal family, by racialized ideologies of whitenesss and through forms of gender symbolism. It is therefore necessary to uncover the function of these contexts in producing Diana's iconicity before we can assess the historical significance and potential of Diana's example. Not that the location of origins is sufficient by itself to define the significance of 'Diana'. Rather, the project of historicizing Diana representations is aimed at evaluating the claims of newness associated with the impact of her death, and the possibilities opened up by Diana's signification for a postcolonial Britishness and for a whiteness reconstructed 'in the feminine'. The goal here is neither the fixing of an historical subject by means of biographical revelation, nor the description of posthumous appropriations of Diana's significance. This is a cultural history, not a true story.

The ambivalence of the cultural meanings put into circulation around Diana has its own popular history and historiography, which can be illustrated by reference to two descriptions of Diana as icon by the journalist Anthony Holden. Once a sympathetic biographer of the Prince of Wales, Holden became a critic of the monarchy and supporter of Diana. It was from the latter position that he contributed the following to a debate entitled 'Diana: Monster or Martyr?' published in *Tatler* magazine late in 1993:

> A vandalised icon, a betrayed innocent, a manipulative hysteric: Diana, Princess of Wales is many things to many people. The diverse Dianas who pour forth from biographers and newspaper columnists, 'sources close to' and other pub bores are all, in the end, mere reflections of their creators. Just as the British have an umbilical need for their monarchy, like a pricey national nanny or a golden dummy to suck, so every kitchen table in the land needs its own private Diana to perk up its own private soap opera. She's right,

he's wrong; hate him, love her. The people's princess is pawn to K-4 in any conversational gambit.[1]

Four years later, in the wake of widespread public grief at Diana's death, Holden returned to the issue of her multiple significance in his laudatory biography *Diana: A Life and a Legacy*:

As darkness fell ... ten days after her death had convulsed the nation she loved, just who lay buried on that island? As it falls again tonight, who lies there now? A beautiful young mother, cruelly cut off in her prime? An incarnate idea whose time had come, inspiring Britain to cast off its post-imperial shackles and look to its European future? A martyr to the media age? Or a saint in the making, who by her own example has turned us all into better people?[2]

Both these passages indicate the constant proliferation of meanings associated with Diana. What had changed between 1993 and 1997 was the framework in which contests over Diana's significance took place, from soap opera star to national saint. First a modern Cinderella, later a celebrity victim and then empowered woman, icon and England's rose, Diana's life was seen as a series of transformations of femininity. The popular response to her death established Diana as the inspiration for social and cultural 'feminization'; transformation (of Britishness, of whiteness) by femininity. But questions remain as to what kinds of femininity, and what kinds of feminization?

Holden's lists demonstrate the ways that Diana's ambivalent femininity, rendered in terms of ideal or abject, inspirational or disenchanting, was itself made complex by a range of identities which intercut and overlap with gender. He cites the salience of heterosexuality, motherhood, youth and, sidestepping notions of royalty, Diana's status as national emblem. Equally important, if usually more implicit in configuring 'Diana' are white racial identity, English/British ethnicity and various codes of class – social and economic, aristocratic and middle-class. In combination with Diana's many-faceted femininities, these forms of identity call up a seemingly endless series of figurative and symbolic meanings, suggesting powerful but inconclusive formulations from the 'English rose' of the early 1980s to a 'fantasy of our own potential' or 'simpering Bambi narcissist'.[3] It is no accident that the most popular epithet for Diana, the 'people's princess', is an unstable term that yokes together multiple definitions of royalty, femininity and populism.

Representations of Diana have emerged historically and unevenly, piled on top of one another like Holden's lists, in which each term partially displaces its predecessors but also draws significance from them. Hence the combination of stasis and movement in the sequence 'vandalised icon … betrayed innocent … manipulative hysteric' and the intensifying progression from 'mother' to 'incarnate idea', to 'martyr' to 'saint'. It is these processes of contestation, accumulation and sedimentation that have produced 'Diana' as a multifaceted and complex sign of identity. Royalists and republicans, feminists and patriarchs, revisionists and traditionalists, patriots and internationalists all have found elements in Diana's media iconicity to celebrate.

Writing in the journalistic mode, like that of Holden, tends to foreclose or forget these tensions. To historicize Diana representations is to pay attention to the complexities of their function in crystallizing competing definitions of gender, 'race' and ethnicity, national identity, sexuality and human relations in a mediated world. At the same time, such directly analytical work must be shaped by a sense of the dynamism of Diana's cultural meaning. It is not simply a matter of showing how representations of Diana have helped to define British identities from 1981 to the present. This is not a linear history, but one sundered by breaks and reversals, transformations achieved and recuperated, and possibilities as yet unrealized.

This book as a whole seeks to negotiate between contrasting impulses to demystify and to re-imagine the people's princess. An important strand attempts to unmask mythic constructions of 'Diana', ranging from the aristocratic yet ordinary 'English rose', to inspirational narratives of Diana's trajectory as a story of female empowerment that redefined whiteness and Englishness, or transcended class and nation. Yet it is also important to retrieve, or better, re-imagine the possibilities for remaking identity opened up by the personal example of Diana and the reaction to her death. Where once the act of marrying the heir to the British throne provided the symbolic resources for a national identity, later Diana's close relationships with non-British Moslems such as Hasnat Khan and Dodi Fayed suggested to many people possibilities of transforming conservative white English attitudes to racial and national 'others'. The ambivalent cultural meanings called up by these repeated romance narratives typify how the figure of Diana requires a multifaceted response.

By evaluating the production of 'Diana' as a site of contest over identity, this book creates a contextual and material history of Diana representations. Beginning with an historical overview of Diana as a sign, subsequent chapters trace in detail the importance of gender, monarchy and race in determining her cultural meaning. The final chapter considers the implications of re-imagining national identity by reference to the gendered, class and racial identities associated with Diana. Three themes come into focus repeatedly: the relations between royalty, national identity and popular culture; interlocking questions of agency, personal and social transformation and gender symbolism raised most pertinently in feminist critical traditions; and the crucial but often subterranean discourses of white racial identity. This introduction will show how the ambivalence of Diana is directly related to these themes, and in doing so will provide critical contexts for understanding Diana representations.

The status of Diana as (re)configuring national identity stems directly from her connection with the British royal family. The 'Diana events', the popular responses to Diana's death and funeral, highlighted the important role played by the British monarchy in making visible national identity, even as the Windsors' performance was compared unfavourably with the example of the late Princess. Never fully royal, but certainly not consigned by her divorce to the status of the merely ordinary, Diana occupied a pivotal position combining the mystique of monarchy with the appeal of the everyday. The synthesis of ordinary and extraordinary is so central to the modern constitutional monarchy that it is the stuff of cliché, but Diana's iconicity combined the two with unique force. Historically and symbolically, Diana comes between royal predecessors such as Victoria and Elizabeth II, and the considerably less auratic figures identified in the popular media as her successors, the late television presenter Jill Dando, and Sophie Rhys-Jones, created Countess of Wessex after marrying into the monarchy in June 1999.* As well as possessing a certain physical resemblance to Diana, both Dando and Rhys-Jones have been represented in ways that reiterated the elements of Diana's iconicity that exemplified the ordinary. Yet neither has come close to emulating the intensity associated with Diana, in part because their personae lacked the element of the extraordinary that had allowed Diana's iconic meaning to transcend class. Flanked on one side by Elizabeth's regal status and on the other side by the middle-class ordinariness of Sophie

---

* Dando, perhaps best known for presenting the BBC's *Crimewatch UK*, was shot dead on the doorstep of her London home in April 1999. Rhys-Jones married Edward, fourth child of Elizabeth II, in June 1999.

Rhys-Jones, the figure of Diana can thus be seen as simultaneously real-izing, negating and superseding the project of royalty. The epithet 'people's princess' has stuck because it encapsulates this ambivalence. Viewed clearly, Diana's unique iconicity is a particularly intense term in a series of historical accommodations between monarchical deference and populism.[4]

This continuity is registered even in the epochal 1992 *Modern Review* article in which the journalist Julie Burchill hailed Diana as 'the one and only People's – and Pop's – Princess'.[5] In a typically Burchillian reversal of received wisdom, the essay inverted the then dominant per-ception of Diana as poorly educated and an avid consumer of popular culture, which had been disseminated by the popular press. It reversed the elitist trajectory of monarchism, revitalizing the royal project of emblematizing national identity, but in the name of Diana and her populist tastes. Significantly, Burchill's disaffection with the Prince of Wales, whom she portrayed as a pretentious snob, did not extend to the royal family at large. Identifying Victoria and 'the present Queen in the Sixties' as previous royal modernizers, Burchill's essay made a key connection, suggesting the mutual dependence of the British monar-chy and mass media which had been temporarily obscured by the hos-tility of the Murdoch-owned press, and 1980s Thatcherite culture more generally.[6] In ways left unconsidered by exceptionalist accounts of the 'people's princess', the significance and status of the British monarchy have long been powerfully shaped by its reproduction in mass media. First published in 1868 and hugely popular in cheap editions, Queen Victoria's edited diary, *Leaves from the Journal of our Life in the Highlands*, is part of a numerous and diverse tradition, which extends to the present.

Critics such as Judith Williamson and Margaret Homans have emphasized how popular forms have portrayed the British monarchy in terms of the specifically middle-class family.[7] Their work identifies the crucial importance of such royal representations in validating middle-class values. What has attracted less attention are the multiple ways in which images, memorabilia and the sheer physical presence of the royal family have been disseminated in ways that engage working-class consumers. Homans describes significant phases in the mediatiz-ation and commodification of the monarchy, as for example the reduplication of thousands of images of Victoria and Albert in the form of *cartes de visite* 'for ordinary subjects to purchase and collect'.[8] Other historians have estimated that in the weeks immediately following Albert's death, 70,000 such photographs were sold. Later in Victoria's reign, growing literacy and the availability of cheap, printed texts and images facilitated what has been called 'a new sense of working-class involvement with the Queen and the Royal Family ... a new personal interest', which centred on royal personages as members of a family. By the time of Victoria's Diamond Jubilee in 1897 technological developments allowed not only the sale of illustrated newspaper supplements at a half penny, but also the making of a film of the Thanksgiving Procession.[9]

Mass media representations of the royal family further proliferated in the twentieth century. A 1941 biography of Edward VII stated that immediately after his accession in 1901, 'England was flooded with illustrated supplements and books of photographs, which pursued him through every phase of his career'.[10] The post-war period has seen the marketing of inexpensive souvenirs of Elizabeth's coronation and the royal weddings, books and magazines utilizing cheap colour reproduction, and of course heavy and sustained coverage in the popular press and on television. Television and newspapers have emerged as popular counterparts to the realist discourse of documentary portrait photography which in the nineteenth century ensured the reproduction of Victoria by reference to middle-class norms.[11]

Shifts in social and cultural attitudes since the war, signalled most obviously in the increasingly intrusive and hostile coverage of the royal family found in the Murdoch-owned popular press in the 1980s and early 1990s, have given rise to a common-sense view that positions the monarchy and popular media in antagonism. A succession of *causes célèbres* has overshadowed the mutual dependence of the post-war monarchy, press and television. These most frequently involved Diana, pregnant in a swimsuit, exercising in a private gym, walking in the street, but also include the 1992 publication of intimate photographs of Sarah Ferguson, Duchess of York, with her financial adviser, and extend to the plea for privacy issued on behalf of the Princes William and Harry on the first anniversary of Diana's death. In all these examples, whatever the varying judgements on individual morality, media intrusion into the personal lives of individuals is understood to undermine the mystique thought necessary for the cultural work of royalty. Even before Diana came on the scene, things were never so simple.

Especially since the 1950s, it is their association with populist media that has in large measure underwritten the claims of monarchy to represent both the specifics of national identity and the 'universal' elements of the human condition. Even when we might feel that they do not reflect ourselves directly, members of the royal family provide a continuous, widely followed narrative, similar to a soap opera that everyone watches and discusses.[12] Mass media's preoccupation with spectacle allows for a synergy with monarchical aura which contains the potentially corrosive effects of revelation. For most of the twentieth century, royal reportage in the press and on radio and television continually and unthinkingly juxtaposed monarchical mystique with material that portrayed the royal family as ordinary people. Even upmarket royal souvenirs sustain this ambivalence, overtly combining feudal deference with capitalist modes of production, industrial techniques with hand-painting, mass production with limited editions, saturation marketing with 'by royal appointment' or formal royal approval. Perhaps most tellingly, advertisements for 'heirloom quality' royal plates and figurines, whose premium prices are payable in instalments, appear primarily in the most populist and transient of contexts, satellite and cable listings magazines, the popular press and television shopping channels. This is not to deny the links between intrusive media coverage and shifts in monarchical prestige, but it is to negate the sense of monarchy and mass media as antithetical institutions of feudalism and modernity. While monarchy and soap opera are often posed as antitheses, they are consumed in much the same way. It is their very similarities that sustain the continual framing of royal reportage as newsworthy. Banner headlines asking questions such as 'What do we want: THE MONARCHY OR SOAP OPERA ??'[13] posit a very safe kind of crisis, whose bottom line is that 'we' can continue to enjoy both. Post-war debates on the demystification of monarchy by media intrusion are best understood, therefore, in terms of ongoing negotiations over control of representation. The royal family's appeal across class differences depends upon deference, projection, fantasy and fascination with narrative and images in ways that are continually being negotiated by producers and consumers. The contemporary monarchy is a necessarily highly mediated institution, whose ability to represent the nation is sustained, or challenged, as much by the observation of formal and generic conventions as by overtly political debate.

The highly mediated embodiment of identity in a royal family is unthinkable without gender difference. The monarchy is habitually understood as transcending class by reference to supposedly universal female identities and interests. Whether stigmatized as gossip, commodified in the commemorative royal plate or ceramic figurine, or in the gift of a royal picture book to a beloved grandmother, consuming the monarchy is widely understood as what women do. Household ornamentation, watching television and the discussion of soap operas and the lives and loves of the royal family are stereotyped as female activities. At first sight, this transcendence of class difference relies upon defining femininity within the symbolically private realm of the family. This is due in large part to the historic shift initiated by Queen Victoria's deliberate performance and dissemination of the domestic life of her family. In Victorian spectacles of royalty as a domestic family, differences of social hierarchy were transcended by reference to notions of supposedly classless female identity, which was of course neither natural nor universal, but specifically produced as desirable by and for the emergent middle class boosted by imperial expansion. Whether conscious or not, Victoria's performance of queenship as household management played a major part in naturalizing a shift in dominant notions of national identity from the aristocratic and rural to the middle-class and industrial. What had been satirized in *Punch* in the 1840s as Prince Albert's Teutonic arrogance in attempting to bring 'Germanic' efficiency and technological development to farming[14] was softened and domesticated in relation to the Queen, enabling the formation by the century's end of a national self-image as the 'workshop of the world'.

This could work only too well, as a contemporary (1868) reviewer of *Leaves from the Journal of our Life in the Highlands* noted, with the comment that, 'the queen is lost in the woman'.[15] The phrase suggested both the success in cohering the nation and the tensions involved in Victoria's production of spectacles and narratives of family life at Balmoral, registering mid-Victorian anxieties over a potentially lost or absent queen. Such tensions highlight how the strategic deployment of gender difference in the service of remodelling national identity is a matter of continual performance and negotiation. It is neither determined nor exhausted by its origins in the Victorian middle-class 'separate spheres' gender ideology which has persistently identified femininity with the domestic. Moreover, as two generations of scholars have shown in the comparable contexts of romance reading, female-oriented television and film genres, women's magazines and the organization of domestic space, the consumption of such material can result in the production of dynamic and communal meanings.

The sense that Diana was different from the rest of the royal family, given decisive form in Andrew Morton's 1992 biography *Diana: Her True Story*, and intensified posthumously, challenged the patriarchal family in the name of a female-centred narrative of liberation and empowerment. Yet the continued importance of symbolic and actual

femininity in sustaining the cross-class appeal of the monarchy complicates Diana's trajectory. From Victoria to Elizabeth II, femininity has
been deployed in the service of monarchical projects of national
embodiment. Morton showed Diana bearing the personal cost of this
arrangement, and reversed the order of priority by presenting her
gender identity as more important than her role as exemplar of
Britishness. However, this remains a partial and uneven development,
on the one hand heavily dependent on monarchical structures to position Diana as symbolically transcending her own class position, and on
the other hand invoking somewhat essentialist notions of femininity
and Englishness. A sense of royalty as similar-but-different, the mainstay of popular royal talk,[16] is placed somewhat disadvantageously
against the promise of self-identity held out by Diana as
Englishwoman. In this sense Morton's Diana represented a refusal of
the logic of performance by which a branch of German royalty had for
150 years embodied Britishness. The configuration of a liberatory narrative in these somewhat essentialist terms constitutes a fundamental
obstacle to linking Diana's gendered biographical trajectory to a
putative transformation of national identity.

The multiple registers in which Diana is understood in terms of
transformation narratives gives rise to the second recurring theme in
the history of Diana representations. Her life has been elaborated in
terms ranging from the Cinderella narratives of the 1980s, to feminist
and quasi-feminist accounts of virgin, victim, survivor and world-
renowned humanitarian. At another level, competing investments
have been made in Diana as the saviour, then the nemesis, then potentially the saviour again of the British monarchy. More widely, Diana
has been hailed as the archetype of a range of possible futures. Thus
she has been described not only as the 'fantasy of our own potential',
but also as embodying the principles of instinct in a mechanistic world
and intimacy in a cynical one, and as the representative of a de-
alienated (post)modern society building 'personal' relationships with
people she never met, via the mass media.[17] These various and contradictory versions of transformation produce Diana's trajectory as one
in which inspiration and disenchantment are inextricable. 'Diana'
continually encodes and decodes femininity.

This doubling, which produces a potentially infinite regression, is
responsible in part for the combination of uncertainty and hyperbole
that was characteristic of much journalism in the immediate aftermath
of Diana's death. Even when the popular response within Britain was
described as 'revolutionary', the term was usually hedged around with

perhapses and adverbial or adjectival qualifiers, or grammatically contained within relative clauses.[18] It continues to trouble the celebratory discourses which link Diana to social, cultural and national transformation. These include understandings of Diana as the epitome of 'feminine values', as unsettling the boundaries between humanitarianism and politics, and between the public and private spheres; and the mourning for her as 'final proof that Mrs Thatcher was wrong: there is such a thing as society'.[19]

The centrality of competing gender formations to Diana's iconicity works against a direct resolution of its ambiguity. It suggests the limitations of diagnostic explanations for the Diana phenomena as, say, constituting an absolute break in the history of media, or in terms of holistic categories such as alienation and ideologies of conservative modernization. Rather, the meanings put into circulation by Diana's life and its representation are politically and culturally multivalent, deriving as they do from the collision of a variety of discourses about gendered, national, racial and familial identity, associated with a range of positions with sometimes contradictory objectives.

Paradoxically, this complexity intensifies and frustrates the desire to fix Diana's significance. This wish for resolution is evident in the posthumous explosion of press coverage and illustrated memoirs which promised inside information derived from personal contact with Diana herself. Such material intensified a trope that was already common in popular writing about Diana, which works by noting, enumerating and regretting the proliferation of myth before moving to contain it by offering direct knowledge of Diana's personality.[20] But to re-enact the myths is to reiterate them, not least because it is Diana's emblematic and symbolic significance which generates interest in the person. While Anthony Holden is one of Diana's more perceptive biographers, there are good reasons for rejecting his injunction that 'We must remember her as the gentle, caring, confused, at times infuriating human being'.[21] No doubt the proper function of the biographer is to seek closure in analysis of the person, but the cultural significance of Diana cannot be reduced to her personal qualities. Even assuming that her personality could be described definitively, the significance of Diana is produced culturally by discursive processes, and hence cannot be explained by reference to her actual selfhood. Diana's life, as Jenny Kitzinger reminds us, 'was not a script',[22] but it is made meaningful through fictive genres such as romance, tragedy, soap opera and *bildungsroman*, as well as the multiple forms of visual representation, and in relation to discourses of gender, the royal, national identity and others. This is not to deny the importance of Diana as an historical figure, but to insist that this importance can only be understood textually, via a focus on the images and narratives through which she was known, and of which she was, in complex and partial ways, author.

To emphasize the pre-eminence of textual and visual mediation is to invoke a highly influential paradigm within cultural studies which asserts the difficulty of separating subjectivity from representation. But it is also, and more significantly, a strategic response to the ambivalence of Diana as an icon. Questions of agency are not evaded by this approach, but resituated from biographical speculation over intentions, which refuses to admit its own fictive status, to explicitly speculative (re)construction. What matters is not the extent of Diana's actual authorship of her iconic meaning, which in any case must always remain conjectural, but the multiple identities signified by her representation.

The drive to resolution is also apparent in more sophisticated analysis, including both journalistic commentary and academic work, which reflects the importance of gendered identity. Diana's pre-eminent status as a representative female yields a compelling narrative of personal transformation from victimization to empowerment. Yet the complex and conflicted relations between Diana herself, and the producers and consumers of images and stories about her, throw into relief the complicated and gendered power structures behind representation itself. The uneasy connections between Diana, paparazzi and the millions who bought images of Diana out of an identificatory investment in her life are the most striking but by no means the only example of this. It is also visible in the ambivalent significance of those most intensely revelatory texts, the Andrew Morton biographies and the 1995 interview given to BBC television's *Panorama*, both of which, it is said, Diana herself came to regret. At another level, Diana's exemplarity is understood in terms of a gender symbolism whereby the transformative potential suggested by her example is almost universally (if not always overtly) identified with femininity, of various, often very different kinds. The indebtedness of Diana's iconicity to ideological formations of royal femininity intensifies this ambivalence. As argued above, the forms of royal femininity disseminated in the post-war era simultaneously cancel and preserve 'separate spheres' gender ideology through the staging of domestic virtue as public symbol. Although in several ways Diana's trajectory can be read as breaking with exactly this structure, many important elements of her iconicity remain embedded within it, including the imputed expressivity of Diana images, her status as typical and exceptional, her transcendence of class status and her public performance of 'caring'. Hence Diana is continually read in terms of conflicting discourses of femininity. Her significance pivots between feminization as a deliberate transformation of politics and the feminine defined as the non-political.

Therefore, debate over Diana's cultural meaning reposes a central theoretical question of second-wave feminism; how to contest the male and masculine domination of culture and politics, and bring to power values, priorities and aptitudes associated with femininity, whilst simultaneously contesting essentialist and unitary constructions of gender and other forms of identity. Across the variety of representations, Diana's exemplary femininity has been worked through in ways that produce contradictory effects. The presence of elements of second-wave feminism in the construction of Diana as media icon, albeit largely mediated through therapeutic discourses, serves to authenticate a transformative project in which gender functions as a dynamic category. The separation of public and private life, and the direction of 'feminine' values and aptitudes such as caring and humanitarianism away from the political sphere are challenged in the name of an emergent cultural and social feminization. Yet conversely, an insistence on the primary importance of Diana's femininity can also function powerfully against transformation, by constraining the values associated with women as the other of a masculinized worldly politics.

This problematic is expressed through Diana's own words, in the contradiction between her reported wish 'to do, not just to be', and her insistence, at the moment when for many she was being her most politically active, that 'I am not a political figure. The fact is I am a humanitarian – always have been, always will be.'[23] Critics have responded productively to this apparent impasse by focusing on the ways in which Diana as exemplary female troubled the rigid categorization of political/humanitarian, private/public.[24] In order fully to realise these possibilities, such arguments must be revised and extended by reference to the range of identity formations encoded in Diana's iconicity.

Homans's exemplary work on Victoria and British culture has demonstrated the contemporary relevance of discussing royal femininity. In particular, she points to the reciprocity between middle-class femininity, defined according to separate spheres ideology, and the forms of royal identity performed by Queen Victoria. As Homans puts it:

> The terms through which Victorian culture defines and contests woman's 'sphere' uncannily echo the distinctive discourse of constitutional monarchy: passivity, moral power, duty, and being and appearing in lieu of originating or executing politically engaged action.[25]

The homologies between patriarchally defined femininity and constitutional monarchy thus constitute a major reason for a critical interest in royal women. Yet, as Homans suggests, the importance of contemporary considerations of gender and power can tend to overdetermine such critical enquiry. Thus for Homans considerations of the power and privilege conferred or denied by class (and, we might add, race) tend to be obscured by what she calls 'an oppositional vocabulary of free self-creation and constraint'.[26] Homans deals with this problematic by insisting on the variability of Victoria's agency and its reciprocal relation with the representational activity of the nation, both made visible by reference to local and specific examples.[27] On the one hand, this allows her to demonstrate the crucial importance of notions of gender in facilitating shifts in national identity, making good the claim that 'the monarch of nineteenth-century Britain had to be a woman, and a married woman'.[28] On the other hand, Homans simultaneously utilizes and constrains validating discourses of female agency by connecting the Queen's performances-of-absence and performances-of-reluctance-to-perform with contemporary political debates over numerical and symbolic representation.

In employing this double strategy, Homans's work suggests powerful critical approaches to the cultural meaning of Diana. However, despite its influence on this book, for a variety of reasons it is not possible to recycle her methodologies exactly. Obviously, there are significant differences between Diana and Victoria, due to both the historical shifts in gender politics and monarchical power and to their different positions in the royal hierarchy. Victoria's performances of queenship were legitimated by the constitutional structures that also enforced the gender hierarchy; from 1995 Diana was officially 'semi-detached' from royal status and more overtly dependent on media representation. At the same time, Victoria exercised far greater control over the dissemination of royal spectacle than Diana ever did. Both these differences render mechanisms of authorship and agency somewhat more transparent for Victoria. Moreover, the emancipation of women as political agents renders obsolete the metaphorical 'fit' discussed by Homans between womanly and political influence. Hence despite the plangent criticism of the anti-democratic nature of the mourning for Diana, when debates over political representation resurfaced during debate over the Labour government's reform of the House of Lords in 1999, few points of contact with gender politics or the example of Diana emerged.

Most importantly, Diana's biography is usually seen in ways that reiterate and resolve the critical problematic that informs Homans's work. The feminist trajectory characterized by Homans in terms of 1960s and 1970s projects of unmasking female victimization, followed by 1980s and 1990s celebrations of female agency, is played out – and perhaps emptied out – in dominant accounts of Diana's own victimization and fulfilment. This issue poses difficulties which are difficult to resolve. My own response has been to concentrate largely on the emblematic and symbolic structures that continue to prove crucial for Diana's cultural meaning. This has involved a conscious bracketing of the lived experience of femininity and my own lived experience of masculinity, except in connection with these semiotic structures. These limitations ensure that this book must be read as supplementing, rather than displacing, the work of critics who relate Diana to gender as lived experience.[29] Clearly, still, this does not release one from the obligation to engage with such work.

To be concerned with Diana's exemplary status is fraught with difficulty. First, there is the danger of installing a very privileged and somewhat unusual identity as typifying femininity. Even rehearsing the centrality of femininity to the various symbolic resonances of 'Diana' risks collapsing a range of racial, ethnic, sexual, generational and other modes of difference behind the category of gender. The prime importance of gender difference for the cultural meaning of Diana must not be allowed to reinforce the ways that her iconicity confers privileged status upon whiteness and heterosexuality. In a different context, to take the example of Diana at all seriously risks complicity with a 'bad' cultural populism in which an explicit engagement with politics is displaced by a symbolic reading of lifestyle and cultural resistance. A focus on Diana – and cultural politics – should supplement and invigorate political engagement; it is not a substitute. Not for the first time, the absorption of certain feminist discourses within popular culture takes forms which reverse the significance of the second-wave slogan that 'the personal is the political'.

For all these reasons, Diana's cultural significance must be understood by reference to multiple, interlocking and sometimes contradictory discourses of identity. In turn, the most useful ways of approaching these representations are those which are organized around a sense of identities-in-relation, rather than the privileging of one set of identity constructions (heterosexual femininity, whiteness, royalty), as a master-code. It is this sense of the complex interlocking of identities in the iconicity of Diana that is the key to understanding the multiple and sometimes contradictory meanings associated with her, and therefore it constitutes the central problematic discussed in this book. Importantly, however, it would be wrong to displace an insistence on specificity by talk of Diana as 'floating signifier', whose meaning is perpetually deferred. Interest in Diana is plainly focused on investments in her as realization, embodiment, performer; as arresting the slippage of signification and re-marking boundaries. What becomes important is to distinguish between the different kinds of exemplarity constructed by reference to, for example, ideologies of royalty, of anti-feminist, feminist and post-feminist notions of gender. Most productively, Diana's emblematic femininity and its relation to the transformation of Britishness needs to be rethought by reference to the representation of white racial identity.

Continuing to write about Diana risks perpetuating the centrality of white racial identity to British culture, but it also promises to help redefine whiteness. In any case, the continuing prominence of Diana in popular media, the at least partial regeneration of the British monarchy, and the publication of several academic studies, all suggest that Diana's cultural importance is not going to go away. Despite a sense of media saturation and the exhaustion of popular interest, Diana casts a long shadow, made visible again by the invocation of her paradigmatic status in media coverage of the 1999 wedding of Prince Edward and Sophie Rhys-Jones. This work is therefore offered not as a direct intervention in gender politics, constitutional debate or politics itself, but as cultural analysis of the ways in which codes of femininity have been played out in relation with other identities to produce notions of transformation.

Hence Chapter 1 provides an overview of the historical development of Diana's cultural significance which traces the shifting investments made possible by her biographical trajectory as represented in mass media. The construction of Diana as primarily exemplifying the condition of being female is shown to be complexified in two main ways: first by the imbrication of codes of gender with other forms of identity, such as 'race', ethnicity, sexuality and generation; and then by the placing of Diana's emblematic femininity within overarching symbolic structures of national identity, royalty and humanitarianism. This discussion makes clear that Diana's media iconicity is heavily influenced by the forms of femininity developed in conjunction with the post-war production and consumption of the British royal family in mass media. Chapter 2 focuses specifically on the construction of 'royal femininity' as a set of historically developed and highly mediated ways of representing identity. Here the aim is to substantiate the claims made above for the role of gender formations in allowing the royal family to be read as icons of national identity, during a period of increased media exposure of the 'private' and domestic lives of its members, and in turn for the ambivalence of royal femininity in bridging between public and private. This chapter contextualizes the representation of Diana in the 1980s and early 1990s with respect to traditions of royal representation visible in the portrayal of the present Queen Mother, Queen Elizabeth II and the Prince of Wales in mass media. The trajectory of Diana representations is mapped by reference to the poles of idealizing 'royal femininity' and putting it in crisis. The examination of material here suggests that even when Diana comes to be represented in opposition to or transcending royalty, her media iconicity remains powerfully inflected by formations associated with the monarchy.

Chapters 3 and 4 extend and widen the focus to trace the development of, respectively, narratives and images of Diana from 1980 to the posthumous material of 1997–99. The concern here is initially with the terms in which 'Diana' was constructed as an icon of victimized, surviving and finally empowered femininity, as exemplified in the biographies by Andrew Morton published in 1991–8, and Diana's *Panorama* interview in November 1995. Chapter 3 aims to make clear the class-bound nature of this trajectory in its popular forms, and to show how it remained highly ambiguous through its invocation of pre-feminist, anti-feminist and feminist notions of gender. Evidence for these transformations was sought above all in photographs of Diana. The following chapter considers the pre-eminent status of visual images in signifying 'Diana', balancing a sense of the power of emblematic status with the persistence of objectification in the continued assumption that Diana's appearance was revelatory of her feelings and her self. It closes with a consideration of the possibility that media coverage of Diana's involvement in the campaign to ban anti-personnel land-mines in 1996–7, and the sale of 79 of Diana's dresses in June 1997, to some extent broke with these objectifying structures, albeit in ways that continue to pose difficulties for progressive readings of Diana's life.

The fifth and final chapter continues this broadly chronological trajectory by considering Diana's posthumous significance, concentrating on the self-consciously revisionist elaborations of Diana as an alternative focus of national identity. Building upon the more critical and analytical registers of the rest of the book and moving on from them, here a more thematic argument is launched. In the struggle over memorializing Diana, I argue for a double move which narrowly circumscribes Diana's status as exemplary female while highlighting the dynamics of the performance and embodiment of identities associated with her mediated images and narratives. Reflecting recent developments in cultural studies, a key term here is the deployment of white racial identity in Diana's media iconicity. This chapter therefore evaluates, particularizes and deconstructs the kinds of white identity associated with Diana, arguing that the rethinking of whiteness via an acknowledgement of its specifics, a sense of its transformation and its position on the one hand within the structuring of racial difference, and on the other hand inside multicultural polities, nations and worlds, is the most progressive way of remembering Diana.

Enough time has elapsed since Diana's death and the extraordinary public response it elicited to put into proportion the undoubted excessiveness of contemporary reactions. It is now possible to analyse the processes behind the intense feelings prompted by Diana's life and death, and to understand the reciprocal relations between affective responses and mediated representations of Diana and of the various mourning practices. The emotional intensity associated with Diana by people with whom (like myself) she had no personal contact, yet who loved, loathed or professed indifference towards her, still requires explanation. While other viable approaches bring to bear sociological and cultural analysis of the mourning or so-called 'Diana events', or suggest explanations from psychoanalysis for popular investment in celebrity lives[30] this book seeks answers by investigating her media iconicity since Diana first appeared in British newspapers and on television in September 1980. The nature and significance of the affectivity associated with Diana is understood here in terms of a cultural meaning composed of transformations, transcendences and iconicity. These are best understood, it is claimed, by paying attention to the names in which they are invoked, or put another way, their construction in discourses of gender, race, national identity, the family, sexuality and more. In other words, one task of this book is to rewrite both abjection and transcendence in the discourse of difference.

It goes without saying that this book takes up the concern with constructions of identity in contemporary film, popular music culture and television originated by women, people of colour, lesbians and gay men. One effect of such material has been to put at stake the 'default position' of heterosexual white masculinity. The present work is offered from one of the subject positions of straight white masculinity. I have already indicated some of the limitations this imposes: little attempt is made to relate Diana, Princess of Wales to the lived experience of femininity, or come to that of whiteness, aristocratic class position and heterosexuality. Instead, I have been concerned throughout with the discursive and semiotic analysis of representations. Perhaps, it may be objected, such an approach predisposes this work towards a negative critique rather than a positive response. Certainly, the overall argument here places more emphasis on unmasking the continued symbolic appropriation of femininity to police distinctions between public and private than on reading Diana in the context of the productive deployment of 'feminine values' in the public sphere. However, this is balanced, I hope, by a continued attention to the ways that the very mixed and ambivalent example of Diana may be read to help envisage genuinely progressive kinds of transformation.

1
Historicizing the Signs of Diana

princess n. 1.1 a female sovereign or ruler (*arch.*)
II.5.a Applied to a female or anything personified
as feminine, that is likened to a princess in pre-
eminence or authority ...
b. Used as a form of addressing a woman or girl
(*colloq.*)

OED

2. a nonreigning female member of a sovereign
family
3. the wife and consort of a prince
4. any very attractive or outstanding woman

The Collins English Dictionary[1]

The princess and the people

The epigraphs to this chapter – entries from the most authoritative and
the most popular British dictionaries – illustrate how hard it can be to
pin down the meaning of a princess. The word defines female identities through independent sovereignty (*OED* 1.1; *Collins* 2) and by marriage (*Collins* 3). In each of these it stands at the conjunction of
femininity and monarchy, though the latter can be understood
metaphorically (*OED* II.5.a), even so far as to imply meritocratic
democracy (*OED* II.5.b; *Collins* 4). To complicate matters further,
Diana's biography is often seen as narrativizing these combinations
twice over, the first time in the realm of fantasy (the 'girl next door'
who married the Prince of Wales); the second time for real (the
'people's princess'). One way of conceptualizing the distinction

between these repetitions has been to distinguish between Diana's 'iconic' status, shared with the royal family, in which the gap between 'them' and 'us' is closed by resemblance, and her 'indexical' significance, in which Diana's life and image measured the democratic aspirations of the average person for personal and professional fulfilment.[2] Such a distinction sheds welcome light on the very mixed meanings put into circulation by the figure of Diana, but can never provide watertight categories, not least because, as these definitions show, a slippage between the iconic and the indexical is already discursively built into the term princess.

This chapter traces the ways in which this slippage has been made meaningful historically. Diana took on many of the significances listed above and more, from prince's bride to 'queen of hearts', from 'fashion icon' to epitome of female empowerment, from 'trash icon' to avatar of a new Britain.[3] Images and narratives evoked on different levels an actual person and a dynamic series of emblematic, symbolic and mythic significances. These plural and often contradictory conceptions can be evaluated by means of an historical overview of Diana representations and popular investments in them. The point here is not to present an authoritative singular reading of Diana's cultural meaning. Rather, it is to try to explain in detail the historical and discursive generation of a deeply ambivalent figure.

The 'Diana events' played out this ambivalence overtly in terms of the production and consumption of representation. Even as the popular authoring of tributes in flowers, shrines, poetry, donations and charitable work set the seal on the reciprocity of Diana's relation with her public, so it underlined the importance of representations in mediating this relationship. If the *volte face* of the press over the use of paparazzi photographs seemed hypocritical, ordinary people could not remove themselves from a similar paradox. Was it not the intensity of popular fascination that created the market for the photographs that contributed to Diana's death? Memorial offerings left at the gates of Kensington Palace and at the place de l'Alma, Paris, called for a boycott of intrusive journalism, and were illustrated with photographs cut out of newspapers and magazines, in many of which the figure of Diana registered distress at media intrusion.

These are not simple contradictions which enable popular interest in Diana to be contemptuously dismissed. Instead, they make visible tensions within the notion of the popular, around the construction of human community with the materials of mass culture. To the vast majority of those affected by her death, Diana had only even been known via the mass media. Suddenly, for many people, representations became crucial but insufficient: one had actually to take flowers and artefacts to Kensington Palace, to go to London for the memorial service, to sign a condolence book in person, to visit the shrines at the place de l'Alma and elsewhere. The sense of loss sharpened the need to recover Diana as person. But there never had been any unmediated access to Diana's personality and intentions. In any case, since 1980 what Diana means has always been in excess of who she is. This is not to deny the significance of the fact that Diana was a real person, nor to do away with any sense of intentionality on her part. Indeed, it will be important to insist on reading representations of Diana as bearing the traces of attempts at self-presentation, as a means of countering wide-spread assumptions about their expressivity. Rather, this is to empha-size the complex production of Diana's meaning through the combination of intention, visual images, linguistic and semiotic struc-tures, and practices of reading. In particular, it is to call attention to the ways in which narratives and images of Diana are inflected by various discourses of identity, and are embedded within symbolic frameworks that crystallize ideas about such things as community, Britishness and the human condition of modernity.

Stardom, self-realization and spectacles of presence

A useful way of conceptualizing the relations between Diana and iden-tity formations is suggested by Richard Dyer's notion of stars as 'articu-lat[ing] what it is to be a human being in contemporary society'.[4] In many ways her iconicity replays familiar forms of tragic celebrity. Her early death, dysfunctional personal relationships, glamorized sexuality and love/hate relationship with the media all recall elements found in the myths of Marilyn Monroe and Judy Garland. That Diana herself sought to break with the limitations of her symbolic role is comparable with other stars who have articulated frustration at the restrictions of their mediated personae. Like Monroe also, Diana's continued manipu-lation of ambivalent gender discourses meant that for the most part gender progressives engaged with her example only retrospectively.[5]

In fact, Diana was a particular kind of star, whose iconic status was heavily inflected by her membership of the British royal family. For her, 'being' was, in several overlapping ways, a kind of 'doing'. Diana's stardom is unusual both in its intensity and in its relation to narratives of self-realization. Surely few others can have been required to play themselves for so long, with so little power over maintaining a distinction between private and public; few have carried quite such a range of symbolic significance and been the subject of such intense fantastic investment. Most exceptional is Diana's status as icon of national identity, which after her death promised to enable a transformation of nationhood in the name of the feminine. But what also distinguishes Diana is the way that her biographical trajectory became a spectacle of self-realization. Typically, the life of a star is understood as a process of the dissolution of an authentic self by the 'hall of mirrors' effect of mass mediation. Diana is readily understandable in these terms. Yet her biography also reverses this trajectory, as the story of the winning of true selfhood by a hard process of rejecting the false personae foisted upon her by others, her in-laws, the media and her public. As her life went on, it became increasingly difficult to separate person and persona, yet that life is understood as a succession of transformations, in each of which the real Diana emerged from unwanted symbolic forms.

This reflexivity between images of Diana and narratives of transformation takes in opposite directions the star's performance of 'the promise and the difficulty that the notion of individuality presents' noted by Dyer.[6] As Lisa Blackman has remarked, Diana stood for 'the self-made individual', while she also 'captured the costs of living this "fiction of the autonomous self" and the means through which such transformations could be effected'.[7] This double significance is made explicit in the notion that Diana's life was a continual battle for control over her representation, in which the symbolic and the fake are eventually supplanted by the actual and the personal. Popular investment in these conflicts took the forms not only of affiliations with the various meanings activated by Diana's image, but also of the impossible wish that images could become perfect windows on Diana's self. In this symbolic economy the patriarchal discourses that embed femininity within visuality and emblematic meaning are contested but not entirely displaced. At the same time, Diana is positioned as experiencing in intensified form a (post)modern, mediatized selfhood in process, where individual identity is derived from sequential acts of consumption, and the blurring of boundaries between performance and interior selfhood. This iconicity forms a bridge between two contrasting histories of representations of women. On one side is the tradition of female statuary and figuration described by Marina Warner, in which the social and historical actualities of femininity are evacuated by symbolic discourses. On the other is Nancy Armstrong's account of the formation of contemporary notions of the self by reference to femininity, domesticity and moral action, such that 'the modern individual was first and foremost a woman'.[8]

The complex interaction between these two sets of discourses can be demonstrated by looking at one of the best known and most iconic images of Diana alone, the photograph first published in 1992 on the front of Andrew Morton's book *Diana: Her True Story*. The covers of this epochal text, its 1993 reissue in paperback, and the revised hardback edition that claimed itself to be the best-selling book of 1997, all bear the same black and white image by the fashion photographer Patrick Demarchelier. Diana is shown from the waist up, against a white background. Her image fills the frame. She is wearing a very dark blazer-style jacket, stylishly cut off at the waist with long sleeves that extend to the photo's bottom edge, over a high-necked blouse of slightly lighter hue. Jacket and blouse together form a strong block of blackness which takes up more than half the photograph, leavened only by two rows of shiny buttons on the jacket, and white polka dots on the narrow strip of blouse visible underneath. Visible at the lower edge of the image are a few inches of what might be a skirt or trousers, in a lighter shade. Diana's head is level, and she looks directly at the viewer. Her half-smile, the strong outline of her body, and returned gaze all signal the direct presentation of a real person without pretence or affectation or symbolic significance. There are no flags, no signals of royal or national identity, no children. Diana's body is lit flatly, with slightly more light falling on the right side of her face. She does not glow.

All this was in stark contrast to what had been until this point the most plangent still images of Diana, the September 1980 press photographs of her outside the Young England kindergarten, with sunlight streaming through her dress, silhouetting her legs. The cover of *Her True Story* showed a very different kind of embodiment: bold, solid and self-assured in comparison to the insubstantial semi-transparency of the kindergarten images. As such, it gave visual form to the two basic ideological propositions made in the book: that it was a story of self-realization, and that Morton's mode of representation was sympathetic to female empowerment, in contrast to the symbolic and appropriative discourses through which Diana had previously been portrayed.

On the covers of the 1992 and 1993 editions, the words of the title occupy the same space as the photograph, with 'DIANA' partially obscuring the head of its referent, and the words 'Her True Story', appearing just above Diana's right shoulder. The image reiterates the promise of this title, making Diana present to readers. On the front of the 1997 revision, the same photograph is shrunk and bordered with black and gold. This framing both enacts mourning through its resemblance to a funeral card, and reiterates the promise that the now dead princess is made present within the book. Inside, Morton substantiated this further, explaining that the photograph had been selected by Diana herself from her private study.[9] This cemented the notion that the book was part of a deliberate process of making public what had remained private, adding the claim that this was in important respects a self-revelation. Yet even before Diana's active collaboration with the project was made known in this posthumous edition, the image was already enacting the narrative of Diana's liberation from containment in symbolic forms (model wife, national mother, princess), and coming to self-fulfilment. As such, the photograph plays out a central element of her iconic significance which compels belief across a wide range of perspectives, among those who celebrate and revile Morton. It is also deeply problematic.

The considerable effectiveness of the photograph in securing this meaning is dependent upon persuading viewers to forget its own textual status, and that of the biography it introduces. Its highly attractive and persuasive message – Diana's emergence from false consciousness, victimization and oppression, to self-presence – is itself an ideologically inflected recoding. What is going on here is not a linear process of demystification, but the continual generation of symbolic meanings. Moreover, rather than simply charting the emergence of a 'progressive' femininity, the continued production of Diana representations in emblematic terms as here draws upon a combination of conflicting discourses of identity and representation.

In part because of Diana's collaboration with it, the work of Andrew Morton has accrued special status, successfully defining itself as being 'as close as we will ever get to her autobiography'.[10] Yet Morton's decoding of the gendered hierarchy behind Diana's royal status was accompanied by a highly loaded mythic recoding. At the moment that it liberated Diana from her position within the ideological structure of royalty, the written text of *Diana: Her True Story* reincorporated her into a gendered symbolic, as the epitome of 'feminine' caring and warmth against the cold indifference presented as the dominant Windsor family characteristic. A detailed analysis of how Morton accomplished this follows in Chapter 3. The focus here is on how the cover image both draws upon and reinforces this biographical trajectory by making a spectacle of Diana's self-realization.

The cover photograph simultaneously presents Diana as having emerged as her own person, and as being available to the viewer's gaze. Purified of the trappings of royalty and location within a family, her smart but casual clothing does not seem to say much, except by what it is not. This is the real Diana stripped of the signs of the regal, of glamour, of motherhood. She is further made present by privileging her frank, level gaze, which stands out against the black jacket and white background, contrasts which are emphasized by reproduction in black and white. Not shown – in fact, cut off by the cropping of the image – are Diana's hands. After her death, these would become the most symbolically important parts of her body, as Diana's practice of touching came to be celebrated in terms of 'reaching out' to others with an ethic of care.[11] Their absence here could be seen as indicating the flawed nature of a pseudo-autobiography that symbolically and actually negates its subject's ability to write. Though *Her True Story* was based in part on Diana's tape-recorded responses, they are seamlessly incorporated into the text which remains under Morton's sole control. Even when 'her own words' do appear in the posthumous editions, they are decontextualized and heavily edited. But there is little evidence that readers noticed Diana's missing hands, nor that if they did, this undermined the book's narrative of self-realization. It does not jar because the photograph privileges instead the expressivity of Diana's face. By doing so, the cover enacts visually the way that the written text of *Her True Story* subjugates the representational modes of autobiography to the logics of visibility and symbolic action.

The power of Demarchelier's image lies in shaping and circumscribing Diana's performativity, such that she is understood as authoring not her representation but her actual self, and that this is in itself her triumph. This embedding of Diana in a spectacular production of selfhood lays the groundwork for the ideological manoeuvres in the written text whereby Diana is constructed as exemplary female through her embodiment of warmth, caring and human affectivity. The pared-down neutrality of Diana's image in the cover picture also helps to facilitate this. However, complications arise due to Diana's relation to notions of royalty. How to ensure that in placing Diana in opposition to the Windsor family, she is read not as simply reverting to the aristocratic position of her birth, but in terms of ordinariness and commonality that transcend class? The *Her True Story* cover design addresses this difficulty by using a second Demarchelier image on the back, in which Diana is overtly de-classed. In what appears to be a studio shot, again with a blank white background, she wears a plain black polo-neck, trousers and court shoes, a ubiquitous ensemble later deployed by Hillary Rodham Clinton during her transition from First Lady to political candidate. But Diana's princess-hood in the sense of rank and privilege remained a major part of her appeal. Hence the studio shot was relegated to the back, while the front cover image sporting the black jacket with its unmistakable designer cut, gently confirmed Diana's status. This was emphatically not the fairy-tale princess, but neither was it the girl next door. Taken together, the images ensured that Diana was regarded as combining everywoman status with the glamour conferred by rank. Her aristocratic lineage is affirmed and at the same time abstracted. By being signified through personal style, wealth and privilege are rewritten through the discourse of Diana's exemplarity, whereby she is accorded the double status of the best and the most typical, as in the dictionary definitions of princess as both 'any very attractive or outstanding woman', and a 'female member of a sovereign family'.

This abstraction of Diana's class identity is thrown into relief by comparison with the cover design for the publication of *Diana: Her True Story* in the United States. Here more emphasis was placed on Diana's uniquely glamorous and elevated social status by the use of another Demarchelier image, this time of Diana in an ostentatious white chiffon evening gown. The off-the-shoulder dress was, in the words of one commentator, 'fairy-tale ... early Diana', but Diana's gaze, level and unsmiling, is as piercing as ever.[12] Here Diana appeared more as epitome of female perfection than as example of a common gender identity. To identify with her was presented more markedly in terms of fantasy. Yet as Camille Paglia's memorable description of the gown as resembling 'a stripped-down wedding dress from which every adornment has been torn, after battle on the field of love' indicates, even this exceptionalism could call up themes of ostensibly universal relevance.[13] Paglia's terminology of stripping also hints at the higher degree of eroticism engaged by this image. Diana's bare arms and shoulders contrast markedly with the way in which, on the UK cover, her blazer's darkness acts as a kind of protective armour to absorb the potentially sexualized or voyeuristic gaze. The American cover thereby links Diana's self-realization with erotic enfranchisement, somewhat ironically given that, as we will see, Morton's 1992 text rigorously sub-limated Diana's sexuality. However, even this positive reading is poten-tially undermined by the voyeurism entailed by the image as spectacle.

These choices of image imply the somewhat different cultural work associated with Diana by different national audiences.[14] For British consumers, both the possibility of individuated fantasy identification with Diana and the sense of her aristocratic identity were inhibited by her royal status, and hence her continued importance in performing national identity. Hence, rather than selling the glamour of rank *per se*, the cover of the UK edition authenticated both Diana's emergence as a private individual and an overtly feminized and incipiently 'modern' sense of the monarchy itself. Even Diana's jacket is readable as symbolizing this. Its high waisted, long-sleeved cut and its parallel rows of large shiny buttons, much too far apart to be anything other than decorative, suggest a self-conscious reworking of military dress. It is a low-key counterpart of the white Royal Hussar style suit designed by Catherine Walker and worn by Diana while inspecting soldiers on parade at Sandhurst in April 1987. Complete with gold braid and frogging, this outfit clearly did more to ironize military uniform than to complement it, earning disapproving press description as a 'Sergeant Pepper uniform'.[15] The more subtle design on the *Her True Story* cover might be read as appropriating symbolically masculine elements of military dress exactly in the service of re-imagining the monarchy in terms of femininity. Gender difference is invoked to distinguish between militaristic, imperialist, hidebound and antiquated monarchy (Charles and the Windsors), and the possibilities of regeneration and modernization held out by Diana. While it may seem somewhat tendentious to see such significance in a few shiny buttons, in fact this meaning is eminently readable within the context of Diana's visual representation before 1992, which had drawn heavily on the discourse of white femininity as 'light of the world' described by Richard Dyer.[16] As a revisionist take on this tradition of iconography, the front-cover image presented the ideal white female not as the legitimating emblem whose need for protection justified Imperialism, but as the antithesis of, and replacement for, a corrupt Establishment.

The cover photograph of *Her True Story*, then, accomplishes some complex ideological work. Diana's self-realization is presented in contradistinction to the monarchy, yet she is signalled as a different kind of royal as well as being a private person. This is achieved by deploying markers of class while simultaneously erasing class specificity in the name of emblematic femininity. Moreover, the appeal to an abstract, universal notion of femininity is made within a racially defined discourse of whiteness.

While in some ways the Demarchelier photographs and Morton's work belong to an historical moment eclipsed by Diana's death and its aftermath, their continued popularity suggests that they remain to a large extent symptomatic of representations of Diana in general. The challenge set by this material for those interested in progressive ideas about identity lies in the ways that a positive trajectory of personal liberation remains embedded within mythic discourses. What is at stake here is not merely a structuralist or poststructuralist suspicion of myth, transcendental signifiers and metaphysics of presence, or theoretical objections to the naturalization of the ultimately arbitrary arrest of the slippage of signification. The point is that the mythic framing of Diana's trajectory as one individual's emergence to self-presence ultimately reinforces traditional social, gendered and racialized hierarchies. Thus, for example, the cover image of *Diana: Her True Story* makes Diana's own words superfluous, since it reinforces the objectifying notion that images of Diana are where her true self is most directly expressed. This is typical of many celebratory Diana images. It offers to make bearable the condition of femininity as being seen and not heard, rather than contesting it. In turn, the containment of femininity in discourses of visuality also circumscribes the use of Diana to rethink national identity and racial difference 'in the feminine'.

While the Demarchelier Diana is no less ideologically loaded than the pointedly sexist discourses that created 'Shy Di' in the 1980s, it is unarguably a more 'positive image' of empowered femininity than, for example, the September 1980 photographs of Diana holding children with the sun shining through her dress. Yet, the more Diana is celebrated for her figuration of symbolic and exemplary femininity, the more femininity may be confined to the 'merely' cultural realm of the performative and the visual, leaving the political arena untransformed. Recognizing this double bind in various ways, several feminist critics, among them Rosi Braidotti, Sally Begbie and Zoë Sofoulis, have been at pains to conceptualize the cultural importance of Diana in ways that go beyond a static sense of the embodiment of gendered identity. In an essay which appeared a few months after Diana's death, Sofoulis begins to pursue this aim by attending to what might be seen as the penetration of popular culture by feminist desires. According to her contribution to the collection *Planet Diana*, entitled 'Icon, Referent, Trajectory, World',

> It was not a desire for idealised and perfect heroes that prompted audiences to follow the stories of Diana and her death, but interests in love, sex, emotions, self-disclosure, personal growth, and the

personal and social relevance of this woman's story. While these interests have arguably, via the paparazzi, killed her, they are not merely expressions of voyeurism, for they make an implicitly feminist claim that the familial, sexual and emotional dimensions of life that bourgeois ideology once consigned to the domain of the 'private' and the 'personal' be re-acknowledged as proper concerns for the public and political sphere.[17]

While Sofoulis perhaps underplays the cultural work necessary to realise the feminist potential of consuming Diana culture (much is riding on the word 'implicitly'), these comments suggest a useful point of entry into the overlapping mythic and feminist registers of Diana's cultural meaning. Sofoulis directs our attention away from Diana as transcendental signifier and towards the textual mediation of popular interest in Diana, in the forms of narratives ('stories') and images, as produced for example by paparazzi. These forms are in turn seen to have been politicized in relation to the programmes of second-wave feminism, by their status on the borders of distinctions between private and public, and the personal and the political. In placing an interest in Diana beyond the simple desire for an inspirational heroine, Sofoulis rightly positions her cultural significance at the intersection of politicized understandings of identity with 'mainstream' popular culture.

This relationship is more complex than a simple matter of degrees of explicitness, whereby feminist or other critics can bring to the surface the political implications of the desires and projections involved in the consumption of mass culture. Rather, representations of Diana in popular media are already themselves sites of contestation over gender issues and other identity debates. The iconicity developed around Diana after 1991 drew heavily upon a pre-existing history of the appropriation, dissemination and co-option of elements of identity politics in mass culture. It is not simply that Diana herself articulated an understanding of her own position in a vocabulary drawn from popularized versions of feminist ideas, as in the references to 'harassment' and to a feminized ethic of care in the 1995 *Panorama* interview. This was only one example of how the trajectory of Diana's coming to self-presence was defined against her containment in male-centred ideological structures that came to be seen negatively in popular media. In addition, both her own complaints and the manner of Diana's death drew attention to the importance of gender difference in structuring dominant relations of looking and being looked at, albeit that this was often compensated for by a sense of Diana as developing the ability to communicate through image alone.

This fundamentally mixed and conflicted iconicity complicates any reading of Diana's self-realization in terms of a trajectory of emergent femininity. Diana's activities on behalf of AIDS charities, her participation in the campaign to ban land-mines during the last year of her life and the reaction to her death have been identified with the fulfilment of specifically feminized values in the public and political sphere. In ways discussed in detail in Chapter 5 below, Diana became a potent symbol of a future Britain and new global relations, of projects of national and international transformation undertaken often consciously in the name of the feminine. Yet others have stressed how 'Diana' replayed much more ambivalent or conservative nineteenth- and early twentieth-century iconographies of white femininity.[18] While in some respects Diana's iconicity was powerfully inflected by feminist notions of gender and power, in other ways it perpetuated long-standing mythic structures of exemplarity moulded by conservative notions of royalty and femininity. Both conservative and potentially progressive discourses tended to take for granted Diana's status as exemplary woman. In doing so, both negated the importance of other forms of identity, such as codes of race, sexuality and generation, in determining the apparent universality of the particular kinds of femaleness signified by Diana.

Therefore, in order to see what might be innovative about the identity constructions associated with Diana, it is necessary to decode two sets of discourses. On the one hand, progressive readings must make clear how, in the various constructions of Diana's emblematic femininity, a range of identity formations are subsumed behind the gender binary. On the other hand, we are faced with the persistence of discourses of exemplarity that are either directly royalist, are derived from monarchical structures, or occupy the place of royalty in playing out the symbolic life of the nation. The familial structure and performative nature of monarchy enable it to act as a container for debates over national identity just as much as offering the nation's direct and unquestioned embodiment. Even in revisionist form, such symbolic constructions of Diana's femininity contain gender-based representations within overarching structures of ethnic, national and even humanist identity.

The discursive structures of exemplary femininity and royalty combine to produce the meaning of Diana via myth, that is by the slippage from one level of signification to another, and by the use of certain formations of identity to authenticate and to naturalize others. Of these, notions of emblematic or exemplary femininity are the most explicit, and perhaps the most ambivalent.

The exemplary feminine

Mass media representations have constructed 'Diana' as an exemplary woman in two registers. At one level she epitomized femininity; at another the femininity she epitomized symbolized something else. In the first instance, Diana is understood directly as a model of femaleness. As signifiers, images of Diana and writings about her call up signifieds of female identity. This process of signification can be analysed in terms of synchrony (at any given moment), and diachrony (over time). In its synchronic dimension, the forms of femininity associated with Diana are constituted by the systematic use of other codes of identity such as 'race', sexuality, ethnicity and age. Most of the time these are invoked silently and are only made explicit by analysis. Diachronically, the overlapping succession of archetypes in a historical trajectory from 'Shy Di' to the 'people's princess' is formed by a mixture of pre-feminist, feminist and post-feminist ideas about gender.

From 'English rose' in 1980 to 'England's rose' in 1997, from fashion princess of the early 1980s to ambassadorial queen of hearts in 1996–97, the assumption that Diana embodied essential or ideal femininity was the basis for a series of second-order mythic constructions, such as of national identity, of royalty, of humanitarianism. This placing of Diana's femininity within overarching symbolic structures was initially a direct result of her relation with royalty, and has remained a constant of her cultural meaning ever since she came to prominence as the potential bride of the heir to the throne. Diana's maternity, for example, was always already contained within the royal family's symbolic performance of national identity. Never just a mother, Diana was, as Diana Simmonds put it back in 1984, the 'national mother'.[19] Later elaborations of Diana's significance in terms of a transformative 'feminization' also draw much of their power from the naturalized assumption of her quintessential femininity.[20] What is often forgotten here, or rather, what is strategically elided, is the continued imbrication of femininity with codes of 'race', ethnicity, sexuality, class, generation and others. Even when these begin to come into focus, as for example in celebratory readings of Diana's liaison with Dodi Fayed, Diana's personal affective relations are often themselves being read in political or symbolic terms. Her status as exemplifying a postcolonial whiteness is constructed through a symbolic reading of her affective relations which owes much to highly conservative notions of royalty and femininity.

The multivalent forms of female identity associated with Diana create a certain tension between these symbolic levels and a degree of cultural work is always necessary to make them cohere. The tensions are most acute and the project of coherence most visible during historical moments when Diana's significance in mainstream culture is destabilized. Diana's failure to maintain a poised public persona in the early 1990s created just such a moment, though it was her death that led to the most heightened sense of the gap between a real person and representation. In particular, the mourning events suggested to many that her symbolic significances were proliferating out of control.[21] Several commentators and public figures sought to limit what must have appeared as the excessiveness of signification which developed around the recently deceased Diana. But attempts to stabilize Diana's iconicity by asserting her personal affectivity only proliferated and intensified her significance.

This is most obvious in the common biographical trope of locating Diana's essential identity in her status as 'above all, a devoted mother'.[22] Shortly after her death, public figures as diverse as Earl Spencer and Hillary Rodham Clinton sought to recuperate the excessiveness of Diana's symbolic significance by insisting on the pre-eminence of her status as a mother. Diana's motherhood was construed in three registers that mutually reinforced one another. It defined her more profoundly than any other identity; it was the role she felt most deeply; and it also constituted Diana at her most ordinary. Hence it was as a mother that Diana was seen most powerfully as combining the ideal with the typical. Thus Hillary Clinton contrasted Diana as 'fashion plate, an icon or even a princess' with her status as 'a person who, like many of us, worked to raise her children ...' Spencer's funeral address asserted Diana's human status against her sanctification, climaxed with the importance of her children and closed by invoking her relation as sister.[23] (During the enforced absence of their mother after parental divorce, Diana is said to have comforted her younger brother.) As much as these formulations insisted upon Diana the person at her most private and spontaneous, they could not help but recall the public and national aspects of Diana's motherhood. The same is true of even the most intensely affective and moving statement of Diana's maternity. At the memorial service, Diana was defined most powerfully by one word,

'Mummy', the single inscription on the flowers atop her coffin. This was emphasized by television commentators, and presented in close-up on television and in press photographs. But just as it promised to ground Diana's personhood in a family relationship, it made explicit the national importance of her project of mothering. For Diana, bearing and bringing up her children never had been purely private and personal activities, but were crucial to the reproduction of the monarchy and hence to British identity and political continuity.

As well as being subject to this symbolic discourse, Diana's status as mother was defined in conflicting ways. In the speech quoted above, Hillary Clinton used the initial reference to motherhood to authenticate a list of dynamic and less gender-bound personal characteristics. Her description of the raising of children as an active, non-gendered project contrasted markedly with Queen Elizabeth's more naturalistic and affective definition in her tribute to Diana. Authenticating herself 'as your Queen and as a grandmother', she expressed admiration 'especially for [Diana's] devotion to her two boys'.[24]

These various assertions of Diana's maternity are directly animated by competing notions of desirable gender identity. But something more is going on. In each case, the appeal to motherhood as a naturalized and personal relation is overdetermined by the wish to arrest the proliferation of Diana significations, or in other words, to assert her status as a human being over and against her being turned into a text. The appeals to motherhood on the parts of Earl Spencer, Queen Elizabeth and Hillary Clinton are thus attempts to arbitrate discursive tensions between multivalent constructions of Diana as, among others, saint, icon, mother, princess, sister, humanitarian, national heroine and ideal white female. What is at stake here, therefore, is both gender politics directly and the mutually constitutive nature of gender and representation. Hence the issue of Diana's maternity calls up the familiar double-bind of progressive gender politics: the need to contest ideologies of gender while acknowledging the effects of sexual difference produced by biology and culture. In seeking to deconstruct this mutual containment of gender and sexual difference, Teresa de Lauretis has pointed out how the historical production of gender as discourse works on both sides of the distinction between representation and the real:

... gender, like the real, is not only the effect of representation but also its excess, what remains outside discourse as a potential trauma which can rupture or destabilize, if not contained, any representation.[25]

De Lauretis's comment highlights the double significance of the contests over Diana's essential nature described above. The anxieties about the knowability of Diana evidenced by commentators as diverse as Gerrard, Spencer and the Queen, and the counter-claims of Diana's maternity, transcendence or enigmatic unknowability, are simultaneously attempts to resolve the conflicts over Diana's significance produced by its construction through plural and often antithetical discourses, and assertions of the gendered real.

De Lauretis's formulation helps us to understand the ways that the invocation of motherhood works in these examples as a way of resolving the structural problematic of representation. Maternity, it could be argued, is offered as a means of grounding female identity in reality, in order to contain the feminine (the non-male in androcentric language) as the real, or excess of representation. There is a circularity here. When Diana's felt and lived condition of motherhood is invoked by Spencer, Elizabeth and Clinton as a supplement to ground their discursive statements, the very sense of gendered embodiment that is necessary for this guarantee positions Diana outside discourse, as, in de Lauretis's terms, the gendered real. What de Lauretis highlights is the inherent instability of such linguistic forms, and thereby the possibility of destabilizing androcentric constructions of gender difference by turning this logic inside out.

Attention to the work of de Lauretis and other feminists who have developed poststructuralist and psychoanalytical critical practices suggests readings of Diana in relation to the gendering of textuality and representation. Such a project can be seen in work by Rosi Braidotti, Jean Duruz and Carol Johnson, and others.[26] For our purposes, de Lauretis's work suggests a crucially important critical perspective on the double exemplarity discernible in the posthumous tributes quoted above. In these and many other descriptions, the figure of Diana functions to make present both femininity as a lived identity on the one hand, and transcendent notions of humanity, self-realization and nationhood 'in the feminine' on the other. Such constructions tend to polarize critical responses around two extremes, positive celebrations of Diana as figuring social and cultural feminization, and negative critique of 'Diana' as an effect of representation. De Lauretis's sense of gender as both the effect and the excess of representation offers the possibility of going beyond this polar opposition. What emerges is a double critical project which both historicizes and deconstructs. In this book, such a project is undertaken by first offering a detailed account of how representations of Diana have operated as sites of conflict over notions of identity. This descriptive and analytical project is supplemented by deconstructing the effect of the real in Diana representations, registering difference while continually interrogating Diana's status as embodying the universal feminine.

The fact that gender is one among many codes of identity operative in Diana representations underlines the importance of this latter strategy. The complex and multilayered nature of Diana representations demand critical projects of semiotic analysis or myth criticism, in order to bring to light the slippages between levels of signification and the structures that naturalize them. To make explicit, for example, the importance of codes associated with middle-class identity and whiteness in blurring the distinctions between 'Diana' as an ideal and Diana-the-typical. The rest of this chapter is devoted to uncovering these relationships in more detail. The next section offers a brief history of Diana representations which focuses on the symbolic and emblematic construction of femininity. This is followed by a description of another major ideological context which has so far been touched upon very briefly: the particular mythic structures through which the British royal family is perceived as embodying national identity. With this in mind, later sections consider some questions of methodology before revisiting the historical development of Diana representations.

A brief history of Diana as a sign (take one)

The layering of symbolic significance on top of biographical narratives suggest the usefulness of seeing 'Diana' as a multivalent sign. At an initial level of signification, Diana appears as exemplary woman, incarnating gendered identity for popular discussion, aspiration and emulation. At a second, drawing upon the naturalizing effects of the first, femininity is deployed in the service of symbolic formations of various kinds, such as the family, the role of the individual in society, royalty and national identity. For different producers and consumers and at different times, the figure of Diana was regarded as alternately marking and crossing the boundaries between private and public, between personal and political. At the starting point of Diana's trajectory, dominant representations constructed her femininity as a means by which social affectivity, or what Sofoulis called in the passage quoted earlier, 'the familial, sexual and emotional dimensions of life', was contained within the sphere of individuated domestic relations. It was the symbolic power of the family, defined in middle-class and strictly heterosexual terms, which underwrote the ability of royalty to play out these dimensions via mass culture. Against this, even during Diana's engagement the naturalization of her position in a familial royal romance was challenged by feminists, as for example in a campaign taken on by the feminist magazine *Spare Rib*, which sold badges with the motto 'Don't Do It, Di'. She was also the first British royal bride not to promise to 'obey', a potential precedent not followed by the more overtly independent women who married Charles's brothers, Sarah Ferguson, Duchess of York, and Sophie Rhys-Jones, Countess of Wessex.

By the end of Diana's life, as Sofoulis and others have argued, this position can be seen to have been reversed.[27] Where Diana's femininity was initially invoked in dominant culture as a means of policing the binaries of public/private and personal/political, it became a mode of transgressing or shifting them. What has remained constant is that Diana herself continues to be read emblematically both within and alongside notions of gendered identity. Such figurative significances are produced in a variety of terms ranging from the continuation of traditionally monarchical (as, for example, in the majority of popular souvenir books and serials) and overtly feminist and post-feminist discourses of survival and empowerment (for example, Campbell and Burchill). Subsequent chapters will examine in detail specific moments in this history, beginning by positioning Diana with respect to the formation of royal femininity that pre-dated her first coming to public attention, and ending with a consideration of Diana as standing for a rethinking of British national identity. First, though, it is important to sketch this historical trajectory against the semiotic structures that have given it meaning.

Despite the wide newspaper coverage accorded *Spare Rib*'s 'Don't Do It, Di' campaign, initially, in the early 1980s, Diana Spencer was portrayed almost everywhere in the mainstream British media as an ideal incarnation of white womanhood, according to notions of heterosexual romance, marriage, glamour and (potential) maternity that pre-dated second-wave feminism. Albeit with a few false moves, all of them recuperable through the discourse of innocence, the ideal white virgin with the transparent dress was transformed, Cinderella-like, into the glamorous blonde who was also an active and devoted mother.

The first real complications to this mode of representation within mainstream media occurred from the mid-1980s on, when instead of being read in terms of ideal embodiment, Diana began to be presented in various ways as dysfunctional or excessive. The popular press described her as unhappy, neurotic and given to spending large amounts of money on clothes and other fripperies. Such negative images of Diana were contingently useful for attacks on the royal family in conservative-supporting tabloids inspired by the proprietor Rupert Murdoch's republicanism, and also in the exercise of Thatcherite anti-establishment feeling. Anti-Diana pieces allowed Thatcherism to be presented as forward-looking, democratic, fiscally sound and entrepreneurial, as against backward-looking, privileged, spendthrift and empty-headed royalty.[28] Implicit comparison with Margaret Thatcher herself complicated Diana's status as ideal female by reference to class, work and professionalism. Mrs Thatcher had a job; Diana 'just' seemed to be a clothes-horse, wife and mother. Yet, though only the critic Joan Smith and a few others acknowledged it at the time, hostile coverage in the popular press enabled the beginning of a feminist interest in Diana representations. The shift from celebration to criticism could be read as unmasking patriarchal codes of femininity through showing the impossibility of living up to them.[29]

At this point Diana began to be understood in relation to exemplifying femininity both positively and negatively. Images and narratives of Diana continued to circulate as representations of ideal femininity, especially in picture books celebrating the 'princess of fashion'. At the same time, as Smith argued, the changing tone of press coverage could be read critically as demonstrating the fantastic nature of the ideal previously celebrated in the same publications. Paradoxically, it was the very success of the early representations in producing Diana as effortlessly embodying the ideal female that ended up highlighting the limitations of notions of femininity employed by the popular press. If even someone who had invested so heavily in these fantastical gender relations, and who had been universally read as fulfilling such roles so successfully, could not sustain them, what hope was there for ordinary women? Thus Diana came to be understood in two antithetical ways: as the embodiment of ideal forms of femininity, and as exemplifying what might be (subject to correction by those with direct experience) the most commonly shared aspect of real-life femininity; the dissonance between such forms and lived experience.

In a crucial, highly influential move, these antithetical understandings of Diana were synthesized in 1992 in Andrew Morton's biography *Diana: Her True Story*. Morton managed to sustain both readings of Diana, as ideal and abject. He did so by reworking the relationship between Diana and the Windsors, such that it was she who embodied the most desirable royal characteristics, while proving unable to submit to forms of royal discipline. Morton represented Diana as the embodiment of a specifically female 'warmth'. This warmth was defined in contradistinction to the coldness associated with her royal husband and his family, whose repressive regime set standards of behaviour she was unable to match, and failed to support her when she encountered difficulties. The bulimia and suicide attempts recounted by Morton confirmed Diana's status as exemplifying both the negative effects of male power on women and women-centred traditions of resistance. On the one hand, they registered the degree to which she had been victimized and isolated within the royal family in terms that linked Diana to patterns of self-harm which historically have affected women disproportionately. On the other hand, it was through them that Diana was connected to the feminized and feminist traditions of confession, self-help and consciousness-raising.

Diana: Her True Story also introduced two further elements into Diana narratives: recovery and empowerment. Drawing upon both pre-feminist notions of female qualities and feminist ideas about gender and power, some of them mediated through Diana's own use of therapies which themselves drew upon feminist ideas, Morton produced Diana as an inspirational figure. This was a crucial development. From this point on, it was possible for those interested in progressive notions of gender to make some kind of an investment in Diana as well as simply to see her representation as evidence of antifeminism and the exercise of patriarchal power.

The fourth and final moment in this trajectory is also perhaps the most important. It can be summed up as the notion that Diana somehow brought feminized and humanitarian values into the public and then the political sphere. This has been signified in a variety of ways. The discontinuities between Diana's apparent identity and patriarchal notions of femininity allowed commentators with a range of views to use Diana as an occasion to raise issues to do with femininity as private and public identity. More significantly, from the end of 1994 it was possible to discern a shift in Diana's activities, often regarded as a professionalization of her involvement with charities. This intensified in the last year of Diana's life, with her visits to Angola and Bosnia on behalf of the campaign to ban land-mines in January and August 1997, and between them the Dress Sale to raise money for AIDS and other charities in June. The reaction to her death substantiated this development, and was elaborated, again in a variety of ways, in terms of feminizing national identity. This final moment in Diana's trajectory demonstrates most clearly how her cultural meaning pivoted between exemplary and symbolic femininity. A sense of her biography in terms of the victimization, recovery and empowerment specific to the condition of being female fitted exactly with the narrative of female values coming to the fore in the public and political spheres. It is no coincidence then that Diana's ascendancy was sometimes read in contradistinction to Margaret Thatcher's infamous comment that 'there is no such thing as society'. As Heather Nunn has pointed out, Diana's emergence provided a neat symbolic expression for the death of Thatcherism. A few years after the supplanting of the professional woman who embodied phallic power at its most excessive, here was the apogee of the family woman who performed feminine values on the world stage.[30] But as Nunn implies, this is *too* neat.

Such positive representations of Diana as the public fulfilment of 'feminine values' remain politically ambivalent. Diana's emblematic femininity remains indebted to monarchical and other conservative formations which construct it largely in terms of embodiment and affect, negating any connection with labour or ideological commitment. Because of this the alignment of Diana with 'feminine values' perpetuates a gender binary that can still be activated to marginalize them, reinstating the androcentric definition of politics as being distinct from the personal and the humanitarian. The association of Diana with affectivity, the body and emotional contact confers upon her the symbolic power of living out social transformation in ways that no politician could – or should – emulate, but renders it always susceptible to marginalization as the 'other' of real politics.[31]

The mixed and often contradictory significances set up by Diana's trajectory are demonstrated by her explicit denial that the campaign against land-mines was 'political', made during her visit to Angola in January 1997. The appeal in the name of a caring femininity, explicitly 'as a mother', allowed a blurring of distinctions which authenticated Diana as figuring yet transcending specific identities: this was a quasi-official event, in which Diana represented at various levels Englishness, Britishness, whiteness, the first world and a generalized appeal to humanitarianism. Yet it also set up an apparently unresolvable paradox: was this the transformation of politics by the deployment of 'feminized' values, or did it take the land-mines issue out of the realm of politics altogether, putting it instead into a feminized sphere of humanitarianism? In other words, were the traditionally gendered distinctions between politics and humanitarianism being redefined, or was this an exceptional moment of feminized intervention, demanding recognition for humanitarian issues within the political status quo rather than launching a challenge to it? And did the deployment of female identity transform or reinvigorate existing racial and national power relations? The conflicting modes and uses of femininity in Diana's iconicity ensure that these questions can only be answered historically and in detail.

Any historical summary of Diana representations must emphasize their instability. The trajectory just outlined should not be regarded as a sequential progression of autonomous meanings. 'Diana' is continually overdetermined and resignified by its producers, its readers and the sign systems which give it meaning: discourses of royalty and aristocracy, of Britishness and Englishness, of the ordinary and the extraordinary, of whiteness and of femininity, of style and fashion, of health and disease, of politics and national identity, and ultimately of humanity (and even its opposite monstrousness) conceived of as transcending all of these categories. The relative importance of these codes also varies over time and in different contexts.

'Diana' is both determined by and plays a part in changing these discourses. What makes 'Diana' interesting in the widest sense is the way that the trajectory of coming to self-presence is elaborated as an historical shift between times when 'Diana' worked in terms of deferential femininity and Englishness to reinvigorate notions of royalty (and to shore up the authority of the monarchy), and more recent times when the significances associated with Diana worked to produce alternative notions of femininity and national identity. 'Diananess' could thus be seen as moving from being overdetermined by notions of royalty, to being reconstructed in terms that appropriated elements of monarchical legitimation actually to displace the royal family. Yet this remains a possibility rather than being fully realized.

Already by the early 1990s, the instability of 'Diana' in relation to notions of gendered and royal identity had made the Princess a controversial figure, eliciting a wide range of identifications and readings, some of which were irreconcilable. Some of these were listed in the 1993 passage by Anthony Holden quoted in the Introduction above. But acknowledging the proliferation of Dianas does not necessitate the throwing up of one's hands and the abandonment of any attempt at definition. Nor is it enough to claim definitive knowledge of Diana through personal contact, as Holden went on to do and as so many others have done before and since. The very proliferation of these insider accounts of Diana has worked against the sense that any one of them could be definitive. Their truth claims are finally unresolvable because what is really at stake are investments in definitions of identity.

The royal family, Britishness and myth

What are clearer and more identifiable are the structures and practices through which the British royal family and the iconicity of Diana herself are associated with the embodiment and performance of national identity. In the mid-1990s notions of Englishness and Britishness began to attract explicit discussion, first within the Conservative Party and later widening out to include novelists, academics and cultural commentators such as Jeremy Paxman, Julian Barnes and Anthony Easthope.[32] John Major's failed attempt to cohere the Conservative Party around an understanding of an autonomous Britain within Europe was part of a wider political and cultural debate intensified by the successful New Labour challenge to the traditional association of the Conservatives with national identity.[33] Clearly, the resort to the specific articulation of an English/British identity, whether it is the old maids on bicycles (first raised strategically enough by George Orwell), warm beer and cricket cited by John Major in 1996, or the 1999 William Hague version supplemented by the Notting Hill carnival, is itself a sign of weakness. Major, and the Conservatives, were in a much more powerful position while national identity could be left unspecified and the naturalizing pull of Englishness operated strongly on behalf of Conservatism. The explicit political debate over national identity in the mid-1990s created a gap for the performance of English/Britishness that Diana came to fulfil. Where politicians debated or at best visualized, Diana embodied.

The discursive structures which enabled Diana to be represented in these terms are strongly linked with the cultural construction of the British royal family. In stressing the reciprocal relations between royalty and nation, monarchical apologists and members of the royal family alike correctly identify a major element of its cultural function.[34] The British royal family as we now know it is tied only very loosely to a specific notion of historically generated identity, and concomitant ideological programmes of naturalization. Instead, with its invented traditions, its German ethnic and national roots, and its significance for Commonwealth as well as nation, the British monarchy repeatedly synthesizes identity around a series of performances.

A sense of the importance of practices and structures associated with the royal family in mediating the significance of Diana's trajectory has significant implications. Most obviously, it directs attention away from the mourning events which occupy centre stage in the vast majority of academic and critical accounts. The mourning events are clearly of major interest from the perspective of an understanding of the relationships between the media, publics, individuals, and social and cultural change. But such goals have predisposed commentators to seek a definitive understanding of the 'Diana events' as symptomatic of some singular or compacted social or cultural formation. Critics on the political left and right attacked the celebration of affective feeling as dangerous and, because mass-mediated, fake, both of which were taken to diagnose their cultural and/or political moment. This moment was variously defined as the *reductio ad absurdum* of identity politics, or the triumph of authoritarian populism and conservative modernity, or alternatively celebrated according to a positive view of postmodernity.[35]

A focus on historical representations produces 'Diana' as something continually written and overwritten, read and re-read, rather than as the epiphenomenon of historical and material forces. The cost of this is to remain largely within the sphere of signification, but this is counterweighed by explicitly relating the multiple and conflicting readings of and investments in narratives and images of Diana to debates over identity. Within this framework, the mourning events are significant as part of a series of developing readings of Diana. As such, an understanding of them in terms of the fulfilment of a trajectory of feminization must be balanced by a sense of the ways that posthumous Diana representations reconfigured an objectifying discourse of iconic expressivity that had been disrupted by the events of Diana's last year.

What critical tools are appropriate to accomplish this sort of analysis? Clearly, the work of Roland Barthes on 'myth' as a *'second-order semiological system'* is important for understanding the multiple significances of femininity associated with Diana, but it is by itself inadequate.[36] Symptomatically, Barthes's early work on myth was cited highly ambivalently in several essays published shortly after Diana's death. While Elizabeth Wilson used Barthes's myth criticism to demystify Diana-as-caring-feminine, for Mica Nava, the name of Barthes denoted the position of the academic 'cynic' who lacked the ability or the inclination to engage with the affective dimensions of the Diana phenomena.[37] Part of what is at stake here are the shifts in cultural representations brought about by the rise of the politics of identity since Barthes's death. His sense of myth as 'hollowing out' the meaning of the linguistic sign has been a useful mode of critique but has ultimately been seen to be inadequate to intervene strongly in the process of signification.[38] The composition of Diana's iconicity through the conflicted femininities described above suggests the importance of revising the programme of myth criticism. How this might be done can be seen by reference to the initial representations of Diana Spencer when she first came to public consciousness in the early 1980s.

Diana and myth criticism

Early images and descriptions signified Diana as 'English rose'. In the first instance, such representations are readable in parallel terms to those famously used by Barthes to analyse a photograph on the cover of the magazine *Paris-Match* showing a Black soldier in French uniform giving a salute.[39] Hence 'Diana' can be seen to be a sign composed of the signified, which we could call for the sake of clarity 'Diana as English rose', and signifiers drawn from discourses of, among others, gardening, 'race', botany, social class, Englishness and perhaps chiefly, as suggested above, the visual discourse of white femininity described by Richard Dyer. The effect of the welding together of the sign in this way is immediately to naturalize a particular kind of femininity, defined in terms of deference to a male husband-to-be. Just as the French tricolour was absent from the *Paris-Match* cover image but strongly implied as the focus of the soldier's salute, so, whenever Diana was photographed without Charles, his presence was also strongly implied. And just as the Black soldier in Barthes's example had 'made present' French Imperiality, in this particular sign Diana's image made present the patriarchal power of the Prince of Wales, and by extension the British monarchy and British state as androcentric institutions.

In fact, as the botanical metaphor of the rose implies, there is at least one further level of semiotic displacement in 'Diana as English rose' than Barthes elaborated in the example of the photograph of the Black soldier. In 'Myth Today' Barthes defined the appropriation by myth of this image of Blackness as a process of alienation. As a signifier of blackness, the saluting soldier is deprived of history, in the form of what Barthes calls 'the biography of the Negro'.[40] A few pages later, it becomes clear that this is not the personal, racialized history of the man himself. Rather, what has been taken over by myth is termed 'a primary language, a factual discourse which was telling me about the salute of a Negro in uniform.'[41] Thus Barthes tends to collapse the distinction between the actual man in the photograph and his representation. The effect of this is to reinscribe uncritically a naturalizing discourse of photographic representation as taking place outside of the power relations of 'race'.

In one sense this elision of race is symptomatic of Barthes's methodology. It reflects a crucial distinction, according to which Barthes's project is constructed in terms of the refutation of the naturalizing strategies of myth, rather than as the direct contestation of mythic versions of history. When a few pages later Barthes asserts that in using myth 'I rob the Negro who is saluting', this term is glossed not as a person or a racialized identity, but a photograph, an expression in one of the 'primary languages [that are] a prey for myth'.[42] This critique of myth, then, is only in the second instance an anti-Imperialist strategy (and ultimately only through the identification of myth with bourgeois culture), since it originates in a rejection of the mythic process of signification, the 'transforming [of] a meaning into a form'. According to this framework, the project of colonial mythic discourse is problematic not because it naturalizes Blackness as deference, but because it calls upon Blackness to 'naturalise ... the Empire'.[43]

This last point suggests that the flaws in Barthes's analysis can be regarded other than as being fatal. Rather, the semiotic method has not been applied rigorously enough. It is as if Barthes has failed to register a level of signification at which Blackness is associated with deference. The image of the black soldier saluting is itself taken for granted. This now seems remarkable, given the violent break-up of the French Empire taking place at the time. No doubt the *Paris-Match* image initially surprised some of its viewers by conflicting with images of anti-colonial liberation struggles. One by-product of such struggles has been the acknowledgement of identity/difference as crucial components within representation, in ways that Barthes did not anticipate in the 1950s.

By 1981 the cultural production of deferential femininity in British culture had already been contested by second-wave feminism. Even during Diana's engagement, the lifestyle choice of defining oneself primarily in terms of wife and mother was challenged by those badges advising 'Don't Do It, Di'. Images of Diana with children, looking up shyly through her fringe, embarrassed and soft-voiced, glossed explicitly by reference to 'Shy Di' or the 'English rose', were involved in a primary and active process of naturalizing deferential femininity. It was only once this identification of Diana with deferential femininity had been secured that it could be used to naturalize patriarchal power and to legitimate the monarchy. This comparison highlights the potentially endless chain of signification involved in the production of myth, something Barthes registers but leaves unexplored in 'Myth Today', and which is taken up at length by Derrida and poststructuralism.

What makes all this crucial for understanding the history of 'Diana' are the fraught relations between discourses of gender, the royal and national identity. In *Monuments and Maidens* Marina Warner has called attention to the ways in which femininity has been persistently utilized as allegorical form in Western and Christian cultures.[44] Warner pointed out how in figurative and monumental representations of femininity, women are presented as signs and symbols for something beyond themselves, such as justice, purity or national identity. In the process the historical gendered and sexed specificity of womanhood is evacuated. The significance of Diana's trajectory, as described above, lies in its promise to reverse this process. The historical development of 'Diana' can thus be seen as beginning with the symbolic appropriation of a certain kind of femininity in the service of royal legitimation and national identity. This was arrested by suggestions of marital discord and Diana's unhappiness, and displaced by the emergence of femininity for itself predicated on her self-fashioning. However, this reversal is not complete. The terms in which Diana's self-fashioning were made, understood, contested and celebrated were rarely grounded in specific historical positions with respect to class, gender, 'race', sexuality, ethnicity or other power relations. Instead, as in the Demarchelier photograph on the cover of *Diana: Her True Story* and in many elaborations of Diana as mother, they were emblematic, symbolic and transcendental. To read this historical development as one of straightforward unmasking and demystification is to fail to recognize the ways in which 'Diana' has always been constructed by reference to myths of femininity involved in processes of erasure and displacement, and in relation with other mythic discourses. Diana's status as 'icon' has proved a powerful means of eliding these relationships, through the structure of the iconic sign, in which signifier and signified are understood as homogeneous.

As has been seen, early representations of Diana performed the cultural work of naturalizing certain 'feminine' attributes while at the same time these definitions of femininity worked to naturalize royal and patriarchal power. By the same token, post-divorce representations of Diana as emblematic female, whatever their relation to gender politics, continue to engage in complex practices of encoding and recoding. For example, the latter-day construction of Diana as charity ambassador and campaigner against land-mines deployed further notions of femininity both in terms of self-realization and to produce symbols of postcolonial whiteness. Even attempts to produce realist discourses of Diana in terms of personal and historical specificity, as in her portrayal as businesslike charity professional intermittently from 1995 on, remain embedded within material and discursive circuits of representation founded upon mythic structures of emblem, symbol, and other forms of making 'present'.

The persistence of mythic structures in apparently progressive representations of Diana necessitates the continued importance of the Barthesian project of denouncing 'the illusion of the natural', a project summarized by Seán Burke as challenging the ethos of representation through which a society transforms culture into nature.[45] But the multiple political valencies that have accrued to phrases such as 'woman', 'family', 'working mother' and even 'feminist' since then have complicated the project of critically reading 'Diana'. The multivalent and conflicted nature of these mythologies necessitate a critical response that is more complex than a simple matter of decoding, whose limitations Barthes himself came to register.[46]

'Myth Today' seeks to contest the power of bourgeois myth in arresting the slippage of signification, the lateral shifting which transforms the 'purely linguistic' into the 'mythic', and which ultimately engenders the provisionality of both terms. The above examples show how analysis of the significance of Diana must concern itself with both structural displacements of this sort and their shifting relation over time. Put another way, 'Diana' is overdetermined by a range of interlocking discourses, whose relations are historically unstable. Popular and academic writing has registered these complications and employed a range of structures to try to contain them, ranging from the staging of Diana discussion as formal and informal debate to the invocation of notions such as the 'enigmatic female' or even the floating signifier. Such structures are themselves invoked in the service of particular positions and in any case have never been adequate to successfully contain the dynamics of Diana meanings.[47]

In sum, then, the multiple and shifting significances of 'Diana' are produced by overlapping and sometimes conflicted historical processes of mythologization, demythologization and remythologization. While a variety of discourses are called upon in these processes, the crucial relationships are between femininity, monarchy and national identity.

It is by reference to these that we can make clear how the historical trajectory of the Diana sign outlined earlier is related to identity debates.

A brief history of Diana as a sign (take two)

The 1980–1 'Diana' has already been described. Diana was represented at this stage in terms of mythic discourses of Englishness and femininity largely constructed iconically, as for example in the well-known September 1980 press photograph of Diana with sunlight silhouetting her legs through her skirt. 'Diana' functioned here iconically and mythically to stabilize conservative notions of Englishness (as white, aristocratic, with family mansion in the country and bachelor flat in South Kensington) and of femininity (virginal, oriented around marriage and childcare). Lady Diana, Lady Di and the Princess of Wales became objects of emulation and fantasy, especially for women. Simultaneously, these identifications also played a crucial part in rejuvenating the royal family. At a direct level, Diana's youth, her ability to perform both naturally and with a developing aura of stardom, and her connections with popular culture via the populist tastes attributed to her, were used to present her in a median position between the royals and non-royals. Proximity by marriage to Diana and her ancestral Englishness normalized and reinvigorated the Windsors, while preserving both their pre-eminence and their unique status as performers of national identity.

Diana's motherhood and maturation during the 1980s did little to shift the terms of these mythic structures. As was suggested above, certain misogynistic and democratic impulses in the tabloid press did re-read Diana's erstwhile populist credentials in terms of irresponsibility and self-indulgence. However, dominant assumptions about desirable femininity remained the same; for the popular press it was just that Diana was lacking. Revelations of marital tensions, substantiated in Andrew Morton's *Diana: Her True Story*, did produce a major change. In Barthes's terms Morton effectively reversed the lateral shift of signification from femininity to the royal. Contained within the deep structure of heterosexuality, Diana's deferential femininity had worked to naturalize the royal. In place of this, at one level Morton elaborated royalty and femininity as opposites (Diana vs. Charles), while at another he presented Diana as carrying out royal functions better than the Windsors did. It was also possible to read Morton's text as liberating femininity from its containment within the mythic discourse of the royal altogether, so that Diana's biography could be interpreted as the emergence of femininity 'for itself'. The (at one level) antithetical relationship between Diana and the royal family popularized by Morton elicited and continues to elicit a range of responses. Very many of them seek to contain this conflict by various means, avoiding a negative identification with or against Diana and royalty and maintaining their position within an unacknowledged discourse of whiteness. With some exceptions, positive representations of Diana have perpetuated his production of femininity as an ostensibly universal gender category, despite its being heavily dependent on unacknowledged assumptions about whiteness, heterosexuality and middle-class identity.

Diana's reinvention of her public image in the last year of her life as a professional charity and quasi-political campaigner, in particular by reference to the campaign to ban anti-personnel land-mines, effected a further shift in these mythic structures. Whether self-consciously or not, Diana performed on an international stage what was perceived as potentially a new kind of white and/or British official identity, 'in the feminine', and also as an empowered woman. Such ambassadorial projects pivoted between Imperialist and postcolonial modes. At the same time, her attempts to assert a distinction between her private affective life and her public activities were continually frustrated. The instability of Diana representations in the last year of her life is now almost forgotten, but can be exemplified by the marked change in popular press treatment of Diana's relationship with Dodi Fayed immediately after their deaths.

It would seem that Diana's death and its aftermath have not added to this trajectory so much as fostered the proliferation of variations on already existing narratives, images and mythic structures within different contexts. Two developments can be discerned, however. As with many cases of celebrities who die relatively young, it did provoke a sense of Diana as a person whose identity was dynamic, and in turn as a cultural icon whose meaning was perpetually in progress. So much so that commentators as conceptually distant as Julie Burchill and Rosi Braidotti have both been led to wonder at the implications of Diana as perpetually failing to realise femininity. In another, potentially crucial development, the objectifying discourses of Diana as cynosure have been somewhat moderated by an increasing sense of her relational status, allowing the specificity of identities associated with Diana to become more explicit.

This trajectory finally positions Diana's cultural meaning at the centre of a series of tensions, some of which are apparent in the dichotomizing of feminist responses into the deconstructive reading of

Diana's femininities as a precursor for reinvigorating a feminist politics (Rosi Braidotti) on the one hand, and views of Diana as inspirational feminist heroine, as elaborated by Suzanne Moore and to a lesser extent Beatrix Campbell, on the other. Could or should the lateral displacements of myth, perhaps crucial to forging popular feminist understandings of Diana, be arrested in the name of historical accuracy, lived experience or first-order language? Diana's own position is also problematically double. She is at once a real person, in semiotic terms merely the (always neglected) referent component of the sign, while also arguably one of the key producers of myth.

Diana textualized, but not a text

In closing this chapter I would like to position the use of textual and semiotic analysis with respect to some complementary and alternative approaches. A useful general framework for understanding the performance of national identity in mass media is provided by David Chaney's work on 'public drama' in *Fictions of Collective Life*. Chaney develops an expanded sense of performance in order to suggest an understanding of the function of public drama in cohering modern societies. He characterizes modernity in terms of this social function of spectacle. In a plangent phrase, 'the abstract crowds of mass politics have become simultaneously the audiences of popular entertainment.'[48] Chaney is mainly concerned with the performative structures of mass media rather than the factors influencing the reproduction of specific identities. Nevertheless, he points to the powerful effects generated by the interaction of the self-reflexive procedures of dramatized fictions with naturalizing myths of national identity. For Chaney, this combination ensures the dissemination of nation, race and ethnicity as dominant fictions that sustain both individual and collective identity in modernity.

What is particularly significant about Chaney's work is the scope with which it operates, in particular through its aim to offer general structures which bridge between the individually meaningful and the sociologically functional. In particular, *Fictions of Collective Life* suggests an overarching framework within which can be placed sociological and semiotic readings of events such as major royal spectacles. Thus, for example, Daniel Dayan and Elihu Katz's essay on the semiotics of the wedding of Charles and Diana could be taken as exemplifying exactly the process outlined in general terms by Chaney.[49] The ways in which the wedding event overtly solicited the participation of spectators both directly and via mass communication networks are identified by Dayan and Katz as crucial elements in its claims to cohere sociality. Chaney's rethinking of participation in terms of performance, as facilitating both individual self-reflexivity and the transmission of cultural forms, enables the forms identified by Dayan and Katz to be understood also with respect to the function of monarchy in reproducing national identity.[50]

However, in concentrating on such exceptional, if memorable events, there is an inevitable tendency to emphasize both the volitional and multivalent nature of participation in them, and their success in effecting social cohesion. Nick Couldry's insistence that the Diana funeral events offered images of social integration rather than perfecting sociality itself is all the more applicable to royal ceremonial in general.[51] The danger here lies in viewing such public spectacles as self-contained mechanisms for the reproduction of social life. Couldry thus questions the direct applicability of Durkheimian concepts of the social and the sacred to such events and suggests their revision. His argument throws into relief a certain functionalist tendency present in much celebratory writing about the Diana events. As Couldry shows, lived and mediated royal events stage sociality in ways that are necessarily exclusive. Royal spectacle thus formally marks both social difference and sameness, diversity and collectivity, but can never, by definition be completely inclusive.

The historical accident whereby the British monarchy has only a slim claim to English, Scottish, Welsh or Northern Irish or other Commonwealth ethnicities, however such might be defined, has ensured that the royal incarnation of national identity is understood in terms of performance rather than as the direct embodiment of some simple ethnic or racial essence. This means that the shift from one discursive level to another, in terms of myth from one order of signification to another, is guaranteed by the performance of these individuals. It is thus always having to be reconstituted. The popularity of Diana was due in large part to her success at maintaining this popular belief more successfully than other members of the royal family. This had as much to do with the reinvigoration of the royal feminine as with the historical emergence of femininity for itself from behind its strategic deployment for royalist legitimation.[52]

Hence the continued importance of an emphasis on textual encoding and decoding, despite the tendency, noted by Chaney following the cultural anthropologist Clifford Geertz, of textual metaphors to abstract themselves from the sensuous affects of sociality. One is loath to pass up an emphasis on affectivity, especially since the events following Diana's death are so apt to be construed in terms that exceed critical analysis or explanation.[53] Yet the celebration of Diana as affect was itself highly problematic. Affectivity did figure as a productive outside to normative media representation in the immediate aftermath of Diana's death and funeral, such that the aura of sufficiency surrounding media representation began to crack. However, this was quickly reconstituted, largely by repositioning journalistic practices as being themselves informed by 'feeling', in contradistinction to the royal family's inexpressivity. Hence the focus during the funeral week on the movements of the royal family and the protocols of flying the Union Flag at half-mast from Buckingham Palace. This repositioning was subsequently cemented in contrast to academic analysis, stigmatized by some journalists as 'Dianababble', 'Dianaology' and 'academic gobbledegook'.[54] Such later commentaries repeated the word 'sign' as if it were a hilarious joke. Nevertheless, a terminology of sign, myth and textuality remains crucial to understanding the cultural significance of Diana, all the more when she is positioned in terms of transcending the social by virtue of her femininity, her status as unofficial ambassador, as royalty, or simply the emotional reaction produced by her death. Part of the project of this book is to demonstrate that such readings of Diana as transcending the social, the national and the human are themselves mediations, dependent upon strategies of displacement between discursive and semiotic registers.

This emphasis on the textual production of notions of transcendence constitutes an approach to Diana representations which is cognate with Nick Couldry's discussion of the mourning events. However diverse and inclusive the mourners for Diana appeared to be, they presented the image of an integrated society rather than actualizing one. To read them as such was a misrecognition, however creative and useful. Hence Couldry considers the Diana 'affect' as throwing into relief the relations between producers and consumers of media representations, rather than permanently transforming such relations. It might be added that all unitary constructions of identity are exclusionary, including those of gender and nation, since they fail to acknowledge their construction through constitutive others. There are no pure models of social unity, any more than there are meta-social discourses. All such claims are made in the name of something or other, whether it is a transcendent femininity, a multicultural nation or a nationally-based internationalism, and can therefore be understood in terms of language and myth. Having said this, clearly as the work of

Judith Butler demonstrates, mythic speech just like any other gains its authority by performance in that it is materialized by repetition and open to displacement by citation.[55] This allows us to see the trajectory of 'Diana' meanings outlined above as a series of textual performances, whose variation produces a series of sedimentations rather than a linear history.

A more fundamental objection to the emphasis on textuality is raised by materialist critics and sometimes from positions within sociology. For critics such as Jim McGuigan and Don Slater, an 'excessive textualism' diverts attention away from the material circulation of objects and the social relations that underpin cultural meanings.[56] McGuigan in particular persuasively and often acerbically points out the excesses and indulgences of certain kinds of cultural populism. There is insufficient space here to engage these positions fully, with which I am in some agreement. Instead, I would, therefore, offer three reflections in addition to the points made above.

First, and least originally, the cross-cutting of multiple economic and social relations seems currently to pre-empt an *a priori* grounding of cultural discussion by reference to social power relations. In the absence of such a material structure within which discourses could be embedded, my focus is perforce limited in scope to textual readings and the consideration of the relations between textual producers and consumers. Second, the long-term cultural fall-out from the liberation struggles of non-whites, women, gay men and lesbians continues to problematize distinctions between dominant ideology, declining and emergent forms (to use the influential terminology of Raymond Williams). The taking up of discourses of identity politics in mass media forms such as situation comedy and soap opera, their appropriation by economically disadvantaged white males, and the recent development of self-reflexivity concerning whiteness (and, for that matter, Englishness) from a variety of political positions, all demonstrate the complexity of relations of cultural value and political power. These developments must vitally inform an understanding of the unstable and overlapping codes of meaning through which 'Diana' was constructed.

Finally, there is a need to demystify the ways that the affective power of the Diana phenomenon in general has camouflaged its relation to discursive structures. As mentioned above, some journalistic material took this as far as to discredit in principle the discursive analysis of Diana as 'meaning'. In doing so, it tapped into a powerful sense that the significance of Diana is in some important ways beyond analysis. In seeking to come to terms with this, academic critics have been led quite rightly to question their own theoretical and analytical apparatuses, and many have done so in the light of the Diana events.[57] However, the necessity to rethink the utility of one's methodological tools must not be inflated into an injunction to destroy them. Populist material that parades a resistance to analysis on the grounds of immediacy remains structured by the unconscious and unexplained assumptions of its editors and compilers. Attempts to describe Diana's significance as universal often employ, unselfconsciously, specifically Christian images and assumptions, as for example in much memorial poetry, including that of the then British poet laureate Ted Hughes.[58] Moreover, the framing of 'Diana' in terms of the unmediated and the directly personal negates its significance in relation to culture as dynamic and interpersonal. A focus on the representation of Diana offers the means to navigate the multiple, contradictory and overlapping significances and investments made in her. I hope also that it enables us to recover with precision a sense of 'Diana' as potentially suggesting a break in certain structures of gender, monarchy and national identity, a break that is at time of writing already being re-sutured by the projects of 'modernizing' politics and royalty.

2
Diana, Royalty and Femininity

> Those who are married live happily ever after the wedding day
> if they persevere in the real adventure which is the royal task
> of creating each other and creating a more loving world.
>
> Robert Runcie, Archbishop of Canterbury,
> address at the wedding of Charles, Prince of
> Wales and Lady Diana Spencer, 29 July 1981[1]

The people's princess?

In the mass media and in academic writing, the emblematic figure of
Diana as popular heroine and agent for transformation has been sustained by defining her against the monarchy. During the week of
Diana's funeral, the popular and broadsheet press placed the reaction
to her death in opposition to the 'Establishment' and 'tradition' made
visible in the royal family's failure to make an adequate public
response. This opposition was subsequently elaborated in Beatrix
Campbell's influential book on Diana. As her subtitle, 'How Sexual
Politics Shook the Monarchy', implies, for Campbell, as for more populist writers such as Julie Burchill and Suzanne Moore, Diana's trajectory from victim to survivor to strong woman was defined in
contradistinction to royalty. The 'uniquely patriarchal' royal family,
whose 'economic and political power' is said to 'cast an authoritarian
shadow over our society', is the prime focus of Campbell's critical
attack, even more than the intrusive tabloid press and the pornographic iconography of News International.[2] In turn, the opposition
between Diana and the Windsors sustained a symbolic reading of her
trajectory as the emergence 'for itself' of feminized identity from
behind its strategic use to legitimate the monarchy and male power in

general. The relation between monarchy and gender is crucial in shaping Diana's significance. However, attention to the longer history of royal representations shows that this relationship is much more complex than a direct opposition.

If the monarchy is a bastion of patriarchy, it performs this cultural work in complex ways that are much less visible and do not allow for the authoritarian power sometimes credited to it. Until very recently, for example, the rules of gendered primogeniture were actually less biased towards men for the British royal family than in the aristocratic class from which Diana came. More importantly, the fact that three of the most successful British monarchs have been female suggests a synergy of sorts between female identities and royalty. As the examples of Elizabeth I, Victoria and Elizabeth II demonstrate, dominant notions of femininity played a crucial role in figuring national identity long before Diana entered the family.[3] Moreover, for at least the last century and a half, women and girls have been the primary consumers of material about the royal family.

The familiarity of the phrase 'the people's princess' has diminished its power as a paradox. The continued dissolution of the tension between its two terms obscures the relation of Diana's cultural meaning to notions of royalty. It remains a moot point whether the royal has been displaced or whether it continues to inflect the ways in which Diana is understood. To what extent are feminist, democratic and post-Imperialist versions of the Diana myth compromised by the continuing presence of royal structures of feeling? How far does the cultural importance afforded Diana displace or rework royal traditions of thought, and in the name of what kinds of femininity and social organization might such displacement or reworking take place?

As a first step towards answering such questions, it is necessary to consider the relationships between gender identity and the cultural meaning of the British monarchy from the 1930s childhood of Elizabeth II up to and including the construction of Diana as princess in the period 1981–92. As I hope to show, certain notions of femininity were already crucial to the ways in which the post-war British monarchy performed national identity well before Diana entered the family. The emergence of the 'people's princess' must therefore be understood in relation to the pre-existing, albeit problematical importance of royal femininity.

What is ultimately at stake here is the status of Diana as a 'positive image' of female identity, and in turn the political valency of the 'feminization' associated with her example. Popular memorializations of

Diana as a special example of those 'royal ladies, who represent the feminine, caring side of monarchy',[4] as one glossy magazine described her, demonstrate the importance of critically interrogating the continued strength of notions of the royal in constructions of Diana. With comparatively little effort, such formulations as this one, from the part-work *Diana: An Extraordinary Life*, recuperate the various ways that the femininities associated with Diana could be read as progressive or subversive. Feminist understandings of Diana's significance as diverse as Rosi Braidotti's sense of her trajectory enacting the impossibility of patriarchally defined femininities,[5] or as the bridging of civil society and politics envisaged by Campbell, or in the various other readings of Diana in terms of exemplary and inspirational femininity, are all negated here through the invocation of the gender binary as being contained within the category of monarchy.

The confinement of Diana's affective force in the 'feminine, caring side of monarchy' calls upon a hierarchical binary opposition whose powerful term, masculinity, remains unstated and thereby normative. While in certain respects the understanding of gender being called upon here might be thought of as being prior to the notion of monarchy, in this example the patriarchal gender hierarchy is reinforced by appealing to notions of royalty. Yet a reverse strategy of simply negating the importance of monarchical discourse in constructing popular and feminist Dianas is itself highly problematic. Assertions that Diana 'transcended' the status of the royal are by themselves insufficient to explain her exemplary status. Simply not being royal is not the same as being ordinary. Since the status of the royal has long been bound up with the synthesis of the ordinary and the extraordinary, it is well to wonder to what extent Diana iconography perpetuates monarchical structures of feeling and exaggerates similarities between the historical Diana Spencer and women in general. Rather than a clean break then, the cultural meaning of Diana is generated through a series of overlapping historical developments, in which the relations between discourses of gender and monarchy shift dramatically but remain mutually interdependent.

Female consumption and the gendering of ordinariness

For Tom Nairn, one of the most perceptive critics of the contemporary monarchy, 'what really matters' about the royal family is their function in performing national identity. According to Nairn's *The Enchanted Glass*, which first appeared in 1988, a 'national spirit-

essence' functions as a kind of master-code behind the popular consumption of the royal family, who appear as 'facets of some underlying
Thing'.[6] This enables the royal family to function as 'palpable
exemplifications' of British (or what he calls Ukanian), identity, which
Nairn argues have been 'historically fostered to replace theory and
principle'.[7] Nairn's sense of the monarchy as providing a diversion
from and a substitute for the democratic negotiation of Britain from its
class-bound, ethnic, regional and national components could be
glossed as culture standing in for politics.

Nairn and other critics have emphasized the importance of binaric
combinations of the ordinary and the extraordinary in allowing the
royal family to perform this cultural work.[8] Conversely, many feminist
critics have pointed to the importance of royal women as models of
femininity and discussed the often feminized modes of dissemination
of such material.[9] Yet relatively little has been done to combine these
approaches through analysis of the relationship between gender and
notions of the royal. The typification of royal consumption as feminized, and the symbolic deployment of notions of royal femininity,
figure prominently in the presentation of the monarchy as bridging
ordinary and extraordinary, private and public. At the same time, historical developments have positioned femininity as a dynamic and
prominent term in royal representation. Here, then, I want to sketch
out the function of gender in the post-war construction of the
Windsors as a modern monarchy, before going on to consider Diana in
this context.

The nineteenth-century constitutional journalist Walter Bagehot
articulated a project similar to that uncovered by Nairn when he
argued for the importance of the monarchy as a camouflage for the real
workings of political power. In retrospect, Bagehot's emphasis on what
he called the 'dignified' as opposed to the 'efficient' role of the monarchy has seemed prescient of the emblematic role of the royal family in
securing political stability for almost a century and a half. Also
significant, though almost unremarked upon by Bagehot and most of
his readers, is his sense of the gendering of the royal performance of
family life, 'A *family* on the throne is an interesting idea,' wrote
Bagehot, especially to women, who 'care fifty times more for a marriage than a ministry.'[10] This remark suggests the importance of gender
difference for the function of monarchy to mediate between culture
and politics, especially notable given that, while he was writing at a
time of major debate over the extension of the franchise, this remained
understood exclusively in terms of classes of men. Hence Bagehot

defined feminized interest in the royal family as being within the realm of consumption.

Taking up the notion that 'a *family* on the throne is an interesting idea', historians such as David Cannadine and Ben Pimlott have identified various phases in the history of the British royal family's representation.[11] Cannadine's indispensable essay drew attention to the invention of ceremonial, ritual and other royal traditions in the nineteenth and twentieth centuries. More recently, Pimlott summarized his own detailed narrative in terms of a trajectory 'from 1950s "Shintoism," through 1960s dullness and 1970s accessibility, to the ravening 1980s ...'[12] The re-making of the royal family in the post-war media has also become a staple of a certain kind of investigative publishing.[13] It has become axiomatic in both genres that the increasing media exposure of the Windsors and the relative decrease in the political power of the monarchy have been accompanied by their reinvention in terms of the paradigmatic structure of the nuclear family. Nothing makes this clearer than Sir James Gunn's 1950 family portrait of George VI, Elizabeth Bowes-Lyon and Princesses Elizabeth and Margaret Rose as a nuclear family, taking tea, 'Conversation Piece at the Royal Lodge, Windsor'.[14] The Windsors' status as palpable exemplifications of national identity has come to be predicated less and less on hereditary right and the symbolic link to a specific historical or mythic past, and more on their emblematic position in relation to the contemporary nation and commonwealth.

For Pimlott in particular, who argues that the family unit headed by Queen Elizabeth's parents had taken on paradigmatic 'ordinary' status even before the unexpected accession of her father in 1936, the tabloid journalism of the 1980s and 1990s brought about a kind of dramatic irony for a monarchy that had promoted itself on the basis of private virtue. Such coverage put into crisis notions of the Windsors as a 'normal' family, or in Judith Williamson's phrase, 'ourselves writ large ... the ordinary held up for everyone to see', itself a construction that had superseded the royals as ideal family when that fiction became unsustainable in the 1970s.[15]

In addition to the more theorized and critical work by Williamson, Billig, Nairn and others, a host of other commentators have followed Bagehot in stressing the importance of the royal family as bridging the ordinary and the extraordinary. Comments such as Harold Nicolson's diary entry on the day of Charles's christening, focusing on 'the identification of natural human experience with this strange royal world ... one's own life enlarged into a fairy story' have become in turn the touchstones of popular representations of royal events.[16] These developments could be summed up as an ongoing process of displacement of the performative activity of the royal family from political power to the invented traditions of ritual and ceremony and the incarnation of family life. This historical trajectory has conceptually located the 'ordinary' in royal identity in terms of the feminine, not only through the gendered consumption noted with patriarchal condescension by Bagehot, but also via the conventional links between women and the family as constituted within the domain of the domestic. Although the kinds of femininity at issue here are heavily inflected by androcentric traditions, the coming to prominence of the 'feminine side' of royalty begins to shift gendered power relations.[17] For example, the activity of the present Queen and of Diana as mothers is clearly readable in a double sense as both domestic and public work, while also suggesting symbolic and political registers in which, for example, Elizabeth is construed as mother of the Commonwealth.[18] Yet at the same time, and crucially, gender difference has been put to work in the service of such renegotiations of public and private that are necessary to continue to legitimate the monarchy through popular investment in the royals as archetypal family.

Throughout the twentieth century the consumption of official, semi-official and unauthorized information about the royal family in domestic settings has played a vital part in securing their perceived ability to embody national identity. While critical attention has been focused on the ceremonial and ritual events of royal weddings and coronations and their dissemination via mass media,[19] postcards, photograph albums, books, pamphlets, souvenir programmes, videos and other television events have performed a crucial if neglected function in tandem with official ceremonial. Implicitly and sometimes explicitly directed towards female readers, this material has been constituted as feminized knowledge.

The reproduction of domesticated femininity is a secondary and to some extent incidental aspect of this material. Its primary ideological purpose is the presentation of the royal family for popular consumption as a focus of universal and national identities through the combination of ordinary and extraordinary. Conventional formations of gender and the family are strategically manipulated in order to secure this aim. It is the invocation of the framework of the nuclear family, and the construction of certain kinds of royal femininity largely within these unvalued cultural forms that has to a large extent enabled the bridging of the ordinary/extraordinary distinction so widely noted by commentators. The deployment of gender difference has thus been crucial in facilitating a dynamic relationship between the royal family and the shifting status, ethnic composition and self-images of the British Empire/Commonwealth/Britain/England (and more) from the 1930s to the 1990s.

Domesticated representations of the royal family under the sign of the feminine have contextualized and embedded the royal ceremonial events. As this implies the key function of gender difference is not to enforce but to regulate the distinction between public and domestic life. Royal femininity is a dynamic term which mediates between public and domestic as well as marking their difference. Thus, at one level, masculinity and femininity are used to denote separate spheres of respectively ceremonial and ritual performance, and informality and embodiment. From the 1930s to the 1990s, with the partial exception of Princess Anne's work for Save the Children, the traditional gendered division between public sphere on the one side, and the private and domestic on the other, has been reproduced at the level of consumption in ways that would not have surprised Walter Bagehot. Yet even within this distinction the feminized, domestic side of royalty appears as the historically dynamic term against the sense of stability associated with the masculinized public ceremonial. At another level, it is the female presence of the Queen Mother, Elizabeth II and subsequently Diana that moves between these spheres. Historical accidents of lineage and personality, exemplified by the present Queen Mother and the Queen in comparison with their spouses, and recalling the massive historical prominence of Victoria, have cemented this. Not born into royalty, Elizabeth Bowes-Lyon earned from the *Daily Telegraph* the plaudit of 'the saviour of the British monarchy'.[20] She has long been credited with a personal dynamism that revitalized her husband and the institution of the monarchy after the abdication crisis.

Especially since the Second World War, royal femininity has been at the centre of popular understandings of royal personages as simultaneously discrete individuals and as symbolic figures. Royal femininity has been constructed in ways that fuse the public and the private, while royal masculinity has remained for the most part split by these categories. This strategic manipulation of gender categories has continued alongside the major shifts in gender representation and gender identity of the latter half of the twentieth century. Some of these developments, as for example the representation of royal weddings and the 1969 behind-the-scenes documentary *Royal Family*, will be discussed later in this chapter. First, I want to consider how the trajectory of royal representation can be seen to have been positioned in terms of feminized culture, and thereby installed femininity at the centre of the cultural reproduction of British national identity.

Due to technological advances in colour reproduction and especially television, since 1947 monarchical consumption in general has become increasingly 'feminized', where femininity is defined in terms of the domestic and familial. What had been primarily auratic spectacles of national reproduction where audience and performers shared the same metropolitan public space, became available for reproduction and consumption at home. In the process, the familial and exemplary importance of royal ceremonial has become increasingly prominent, to some extent displacing its official and ritual significance. This should not at all be confused with a process of demystification. In such representations the royal aura is largely preserved by the strategic manipulation of the medium. Dayan and Katz have described the practices used to maintain auratic distance in the television coverage of Diana's wedding;[21] another example is the withholding of access to the anointing from the cameras at Elizabeth's coronation in 1953. Alongside the marking of such hierarchies, television representations of royal weddings have tended to link the human/universal with the splendid/specific by the spectacle of the bride. Even the most ordinary bride is a spectacle, which cannot be said of all bridegrooms. The increasingly populist trajectory of royal representation has intensified this focus on the bride as democratic spectacle. In the case of Diana, the Independent Broadcasting Association's *T.V. Times* went so far as to publish a special supplement which trumpeted the power of television to convey intimacy and literally to 'unveil' Diana herself.[22]

The presentation of the monarchy as a royal family has enabled it to respond to the historical shifts of identity associated with the nation it is held to embody. Individual biographical narratives of maturation and the sense of generational shifts in identity produce personae which bear the marks of historical change, while their participation in the repetition of ceremonial forms supplies a framework of historical continuity. The increasing emphasis on the domestic life of the royal family through this period has come about partly through strategic planning and partly also through historical accident. The accession of a woman to the British throne in 1952 was fortuitous, but the presentation of Elizabeth as mother of the Commonwealth from the 1950s to the 1970s was deliberately contrived by both Conservative and Labour governments.[23] In the 1930s, different roles were self-consciously assigned to the Prince of Wales (later Edward VIII) and the Duke of York. The gregarious Bertie was to attend to Britain's external relations, while his younger brother consolidated the social fabric within Britain. What could not have been anticipated was the subsequent unexpected elevation to kingship of the Duke of York on the abdication of Edward VIII. This historical accident meant that the Yorks were introduced to the British public as an ordinary family before they became 'the' royal family. The Duke of York's most characteristic public works, factory visits and socially integrated summer camps, were already positioned on the 'feminine side' of royalty, through their configuration of domesticity and human contact. The Yorks played out the roles of the domestic and the familial in contradistinction to the cosmopolitan, stylish and sophisticated household of the Prince of Wales. Thus, for example, in 1936, the year of the abdication crisis, the attractively produced children's book *Our Princesses and their Dogs* presented the Duke and Duchess of York and their two daughters as living modestly in London and Windsor Great Park. Seemingly the only extraordinary thing about the family was the intensity of their love for their corgis and labradors. In semi-jocular fashion the Foreword took a dog's perspective to emphasize the good husbandry of the Yorks, speculating that Dookie and Jane (the favourite corgis) share human knowledge 'that in all the world there are no Royalties so unselfconscious as our own, none so considerate of others, so devoid of artificiality, so rich in human qualities'.[24]

Subsequent history has enveloped books like *Our Princesses and Their Dogs* in several ironies. Not the least of these is the reversal whereby the position of the ordinary, occupied by the Yorks in the 1930s in ways that complemented the then Prince of Wales's aristocratic cosmopolitanism, came to be associated from 1980 on with Diana Spencer, in contradistinction to succeeding generations of the same family. Then again, in retrospect, the playful tone with which this material controls any sense of incongruity enacts in seemingly trivial form what have remained powerful ideological structures, through which the royal family has embodied national identities and social hierarchies.[25] *Our Princesses and Their Dogs* performs important ideological work, naturalizing the social and symbolic status of royalty by presenting the princesses as good stewards and housewives. Yet this is done in playful and informal fashion which is embedded in a sense of Elizabeth and Margaret first as children and second as trebly distanced from real monarchical power, by gender, generation and lineage. To this end, the book's text and photography focus repeatedly on

Y Bwthyn Bach, a small house in the grounds of the Royal Lodge in Windsor Great Park which had been a sixth birthday present to Elizabeth from the people of Wales. This 'fairy house that is a real house – "*MY* house" as Princess Elizabeth emphatically calls it', is, we are told, cleaned and cared for by the princesses themselves.[26] Here as elsewhere there is no acknowledgement of an outside to the domestic realm inhabited by the York family and no expectation that either father or daughter will have to bear direct monarchical responsibility. In fact, the Yorks are portrayed as being as fond of fun as of dogs, an informal brand of royalty, almost spare parts, in whom the discourses of mastery and domain can be replayed without the seriousness demanded of the head of state.

Having been established half seriously and in these popular genres, since the coronation of George VI the ordinariness of the royal family in domestic situations has been continually invoked as background to or context for the political and ceremonial functions of the monarchy. The primary site for reproducing this ideological formation has been material intended for domestic consumption by women and children. While these books and magazines maintained a steady interest in the Windsors' domestic life, publications of record cited it in passing as exemplifying their common touch.[27] Thus for example in 1937 the *Daily Telegraph*'s sumptuously produced Coronation supplement concentrated overwhelmingly on the national and Imperial ceremonial, with features on the service itself, royal regalia and tradition, George's 'high ideals of life and duty', Westminster Abbey and the procession's route, and the adjuncts to the ceremony from British aristocracy and dominions overseas. Metaphorically on the margins of this material were a few photographs of George and family in domestic settings, gathered on a single page and headed 'Delightful glimpses of the royal family'.[28] The four glimpses included by now familiar images of the princesses with dogs and horses, and were supplemented by an advertisement for Cow & Gate, 'The food of Royal babies'. Although the royal babies in question were heirs to the thrones of Yugoslavia and Iraq, this sleight of hand enabled deference to the Windsors to be maintained at the same time that readers were offered the possibility of emulating the royals through consumption; a trope of continued importance in advertising which reinforced the negotiation of ordinary and extraordinary made in the main text.

A few pages earlier the *Daily Telegraph*'s summary of influences on George VI had extended to his wife. 'What the King owes to the Queen,' it was asserted, 'every woman knows and perhaps most men can guess.'[29] This elliptical formulation normalized the royal couple via an implicit appeal to gender identity and heterosexuality presumed to transcend distinctions of social and economic class. The points of similarity between royal and ordinary were framed as being both outside the scope of this official and formal discourse, and as being so transparent as not to require explication. Moreover, with its nod towards a specifically feminized knowledge that was somehow unsuitable for the present official and commemorative discourse, the anonymous author reiterated the gendered distinction between public and private.

Since the 1930s differences of genre and implied readership have continued to facilitate this distinction and to naturalize the perception of the royals as combining the ordinary and the extraordinary. Published by the Girl Guides Association, *Royal Guides* (1948) reversed the emphases of the Coronation Supplement and filled in the background of royal domesticity. This book, clearly directed at a young female readership, began with the remembrance of Princesses Elizabeth and Margaret at the coronation and foregrounded the issue of how 'real Guiding', could be brought to the heir to the throne. The tension is swiftly resolved, and the book as a whole is dedicated to demonstrating the truth of governess Marion Crawford's assertion, quoted on the first page, that 'You will find them just like any ordinary little girls.'[30] Working in tandem with more upmarket publications, books for women and children like these were crucial in securing the understanding of the Windsors' domestic life in terms of the ordinary, and in mediating their consumption as ordinary by reference to the domestic. The much better known examples of the reported conduct of King and Queen during wartime, summed up by the Queen's often quoted assertion that, after Buckingham Palace sustained bomb damage, 'now we can look the East End in the face', developed out of this already existing tradition while serving to reinvigorate it.

Marion Crawford's *The Little Princesses* (1950) is regarded as representing an epochal moment in the relation between the royals and the media.[31] The unauthorized revelations of Crawford, who had been governess to Elizabeth and Margaret for seventeen years, were serialized in *Woman's Own* in advance of their phenomenally successful book publication. According to John Pearson in *The Ultimate Family*, they improved its circulation by half a million.[32] Quite apart from the coincidental femininity of the royal children, the biographical and autobiographical content of Crawford's book addressed it to what were quite specifically gendered adult interests. Predictably, child-rearing looms large in 'the story of two happy girls growing up to womanhood', but still more indicative is Crawford's emphasis on her own education and role as governess, on the steadying presence of Queen Mary, seen most prominently in her insistence on taking seriously the education of the princesses, and her choice of the birth of Elizabeth's first child as the book's conclusion.[33]

In bringing into the public domain various childhood images and stories of the princesses, 'Crawfie's' book was fairly similar in tone to *Our Princesses and Their Dogs, Royal Guides* and other semi-official publications, but its more sustained and intimate portrait of the princesses reputedly earned the wrath of the monarchy. Clearly, what was at issue in the royal family's heated and long-lasting antagonism towards Crawford was not by itself public access to information about the royals as a domestic family, but control over the dissemination of such information. The Windsors' intense antipathy towards Marion Crawford, reputedly lasting even after her death, can be explained not simply in terms of the betrayal of their confidence in an employee, but also, and more significantly, in the sense that she had wrested control of the distinction between their public and private representation from them. Yet such tensions were invisible in the material produced by and associated with Crawford. If the loss of this control over specific representations of themselves was an epochal development, it was not until the quite differently motivated tabloid press representations of the 1980s that it could be seen as damaging to monarchical legitimation and prestige. For thirty years in fact, the reverse was more often true. A major reason for this was the intensified deployment of notions of femininity to position insider information within the realm of the personal and domestic. Thus *The Little Princesses*, its sequel *Princess Margaret* (1953) and their many successors could still be understood as working in tandem with public royal ceremonial, in presenting personal and intimate information about the royals as specifically feminized knowledge. The dissemination of the royal family's domestic life in mass media forms was contained within a circuit of female characters, 'female interests', female producers and female readership.

This process is exemplified by the coverage of the 1953 coronation in women's magazines. *Woman's Own* recruited Marion Crawford to write captions for its pictorial 'Coronation Gallery', which ran in the three issues published closest to the event. Images and commentary explicitly articulated together Elizabeth's status as monarch and as mother, which worked in turn to authenticate the Windsors as paradigmatic nuclear family. One pair of photographs, reproduced side by side in the coronation week issue, demonstrated this emphasis and the muting of dynastic authority.[34] The image on the left shows the future Edward VII and George V standing behind a seated Queen Victoria, who holds an infant Duke of Windsor. In the right-hand photograph Queen Elizabeth holds the infant Charles. She is flanked by Queen Mary, while George VI stands behind. Formally composed, at first these seem to be analogous dynastic portraits. However, the caption beneath draws attention to their difference, in terms of the 'years of change' that lie between them. Compositionally, what has changed is that the child's mother, absent from the earlier image, occupies the centre of the more recent one. While both are in some sense dynastic, the nineteenth-century image presents the royal family in terms of generational succession by the male line with Victoria as matriarch, while the more recent photograph adopts the emergent popular imagery of the nuclear family.

This shift in models of the family is amplified in the centre pages of the same issue of *Woman's Own*, which featured a large black and white photograph of Elizabeth and Philip posed with their two infant children against the backdrop of a lawn, flanked by much smaller colour images of various British military in full ceremonial dress.[35] A caption reiterates the visual message, announcing, 'Royal Heritage: Against the backcloth of pageantry that is her Royal inheritance the Queen has created a warm and tender family life as wife and mother'. This centre spread gives visual form to the emergent mode of the royals as emblematic nuclear family, constituting this as specifically feminized knowledge that exists behind the public spectacle. While the page layout tends to marginalize the ceremonial, the magazine bridges private and public, offering itself as both souvenir of and supplement to the coronation as a spectacular event. The small colour photographs at top and bottom are cropped with rounded corners that give them a resemblance to television images. Another caption makes explicit that these images of pageantry are both memorial and guide. 'When you watch the Coronation,' readers are advised, 'keep this page beside you so that you can identify many of the ceremonial figures you will see in the Procession.'

Woman's Own registered the emergence of television as a domestically viewed and thereby feminized medium both explicitly as here and implicitly, by comparison of the 1953 coronation with the 1893 wedding of George V and Queen Mary. A double-page spread on George and Mary is dominated by a photograph of the largely male crowds outside St Paul's on their wedding day.[36] An accompanying caption stressed the changes in fifty years, citing advances in popular consumption of clothes and leisure, including seaside holidays and weekends. The magazine's framing of the television spectacle of the coronation to its female readership is significant in proposing links between the royal and femininity which are not solely through the consumption of images of domesticity. Instead, television mediates between public spectacle and domestic consumption.

Like this magazine coverage, the genre of royal books exemplified by Crawford and overlapping with official souvenirs and specialist periodicals such as the 1950s *Vogue*-like illustrated magazine *The Queen* and the later *Majesty* is largely consumed by and addressed to female readers. As I have suggested, the importance assigned to femininity in this material, in terms of role modelling, cross-class identification and the embodiment of national identity, is inflected by patriarchal power. However, both this gendered consumption and the construction of insider royal knowledge as feminized knowledge links this material to the construction of a 'women's world' of, among much else, aspiration, fantasy and, more arguably, as described by Janice Winship and others, possibilities of empowerment, liberation and the envisaging of transformation.[37] The meanings put into circulation by such material are further complexified by the privileged and exemplary social and cultural status of the royal girls. For example, the portrayal of Princesses Elizabeth and Margaret as home-makers and girl guides in the books discussed above operates almost exclusively in a female world in which the absence of males is hardly felt. Not only the pre-adolescent age of the girls, but also their social status and the direction of their 'feminine' stewardship towards a nation, negates for them the paramount importance of training for maternity and deferential status as wives.

The coming to prominence of the domestic nuclear family as a major focus of royal performance has generally echoed wider developments in notions of gender difference. In making visible a historical trajectory from Victoria to Elizabeth, magazines such as *Woman's Own* offered a revision of royal femininity from the reproduction of dynastic continuity to motherhood as an active project. In a more general sense, gendered identification with female royals might produce more empowered models of femininity. Yet femininity is never offered directly for itself in these discourses, but instead is formed within the category of the royal. To the extent that the royal has remained a patriarchal institution (it still retains *male* primogeniture), royal femininity remains defined in terms of the supplementary, even where that supplement is what guarantees the validity of the whole structure. It is in this limited sense that, as Beatrix Campbell has stated, the maternal figure of the reigning Queen obscures the patriarchal and phallogocentric power crystallized in the British monarchy.[38] Given all this, it is not hard to see why the trajectory of Diana, Princess of Wales is so often read, as by Campbell, in terms of the explosion of these patriarchal structures by femininity's self-realization. Hence the widely understood significance of the 'Diana events' for a remaking of British national identity in the name of the feminine, which was itself defined in a variety of ways from the deployment in the public sphere of the domestic virtues of caring, emotional sympathy and nurturing, to the reinvigoration of the feminine as a political project. While there is no disputing the significance and the popularity of these understandings of Diana, the material reviewed above should serve at least to suggest caution in viewing Diana's popularity as ranged uniformly against royal, patriarchal and phallic power. As the example of *Woman's Own* showed, the gendered division of public and private realms into the masculine and the feminine has for some time had only a limited effectiveness in this material. Rather than being confined to one side of this binary, femininity tends to be used to transcend it. In this sense, the transcendental qualities attributed to Diana can be seen to be largely indebted to pre-existing forms of royal identity, which were themselves related to patriarchal power in ambiguous ways. This is not to deny that these structures were decisively reformulated in respect of Diana, but it is to suggest that a focus on the historical continuities representing royal femininity is overdue. I want to start to do this now by considering in more detail how femininity is deployed as a mode of negotiation between the private and the public in popular representations of royal weddings.

Royal weddings and the transcendence of public/private

In line with the populist trajectory of royal representation from 1947 to 1997, royal weddings have invited spectatorial investment mainly via the structures of heterosexual romance and the pleasures of scopophilia and decreasingly in terms of deference or even very explicitly a normative English-Britishness.[39] The 1947 wedding of Princess Elizabeth and Prince Philip, of which several films were made for popular circulation, was described widely in terms of the relationship between the two major protagonists and the transcendent status of the conventional ceremony itself, predicated on the supposed universality of heterosexual monogamy. The issue of *Picture Post* which previewed the wedding presented Elizabeth and Philip as above all an ordinary couple. There were baby pictures of Elizabeth, informal photographs of 'the happy couple' and of their bridesmaids and best man, and in the centre pages colour photos in *trompe l'oeil* frames labelled 'Bridegroom' and 'Bride'.[40] More expensive memorializations aped family wedding albums, with their thick embossed covers and entwined initials, a form that would be revived for subsequent royal weddings.[41] At least one popular souvenir gave pride of place among its black and white photographs of the spectacle to a passage from the Address by the Archbishop of York, who stressed that:

> Notwithstanding the splendour and national significance of the service in this Abbey, it is in all essentials the same as it would be for any cottager who might be married this afternoon in some small country church in a remote village in the dales.[42]

Quite unlike the discourses surrounding Elizabeth's coronation six years later, which announced the dawning of a new Elizabethan age, the wedding was not invested with nation-boosting symbolic significance. Instead, according to Ben Pimlott, it went down in popular memory as a comparatively straightforward moment of escape from the stresses and anxieties of immediately post-war Britain, linked symbolically to consolidation of the national economy and of imperial and commonwealth ties.[43]

The popular souvenir of the event published by specialists Pitkin reproduced both the populist normative discourse of the wedding and the more traditional, and highbrow understanding of the royal family as providing a link with the past. While the Archbishop of York's words rehearsed the former, it was left to the poet laureate, John Masefield, to deal with the latter in the only other extended piece of writing in the booklet. 'What is the crown …?' begins Masefield's poem, before going on to answer first that it is a symbol of national unification and rallying-point for national defence. Registering the ongoing transition from Empire to Commonwealth, he went on to invoke 'those young lands, the countries of our kin', alongside wartime allies, before going on to explicitly address commonwealth nations:

To those dear lands, still calling Britain 'Home'
The Crown is still the link with Britain's past,
The consecrated thing that must outlast
Folly and hate and other human foam.[44]

It is not just post-war austerity, registered elsewhere in the cardboard binding of the booklet on to which was fixed a photographic image of Elizabeth and Philip leaving Westminster Abbey as newlyweds, that lends an anxious edge to Masefield's formulations here. The use of 'must' signals a sense of contingency about the future even as it asserts the continuity of the Crown. The problem here is the pre-eminence of the sense of monarchy as 'the link with Britain's past'. The poem hints at the danger that the monarchy will remain too much associated with an age now irretrievably lost to global conflict and Imperial decline. Masefield's concluding stanzas offer public participation in the wedding through prayer and the metonymic ringing of bells as the means of resolving this doubt. The royal marriage then becomes an occasion for national self-renewal. In a way, Masefield's poem makes clear that the power of the royal family to embody national identity derives from popular interest in their performance of rituals, rather than from their legal and religious legitimation or 'consecration'. In this context, the Archbishop of York's explication of the universality of the wedding service was offered as a guarantee of the place of the monarchy in a modernizing Britain, even as he invoked a backward-looking vision of Britain as rural life.

Subsequently, mass-marketed souvenir programmes for British royal weddings invoked similar frameworks, often in more populist discourses than those adopted by the poet laureate and Archbishop. Thus the equivalent Pitkin publication memorializing 'Princess Margaret's Wedding Day' described it as 'a Royal occasion and an utterly democratic one'. The same company commemorated the wedding of Charles and Diana with the explanation that 'As marriage services go, it was like all others magnified a hundred times'.[45] In the 'official', charity-sponsoring programme for the wedding of Princess Anne it was maintained that 'a royal wedding is a reminder that the happiness of the individual is linked with that of the nation of which we are all part.'[46] Expanding upon the latter point, Sir Arthur Bryant offered a gloss on the cultural significance of the royal family which neatly delineated public, formal and political on the one hand from private, personal and domestic on the other hand. Royal princes and princesses, he claimed

are seen as the symbols and embodiment, not only of the political cement which unites us as a nation, but of those family virtues, affections and obligations which bind every family in the land.[47]

In all these formulations the wedding as heterosexual union was put at the service of formulating British identity as a synthesis of a series of binary oppositions. This ideological structure reached a kind of apotheosis in 1981 with the wedding of Charles and Diana, which was made to stand as the foundational synthesis of a wide range of pairings. According to one hardback souvenir book, Kathryn Spink's *Invitation to a Royal Wedding*, the wedding effected a synthesis of 'historical and contemporary, commercial and spiritual, public and personal'. Even this list was outdone by the Dean of St Paul's Cathedral in the foreword to the same book.[48] There the Very Reverend Alan Webster staged four complementary sets of oppositions: St Paul's was royal yet also 'the People's Cathedral'; it was also both holy and challenging. The words of the service were ancient and modern. (It was in fact an amalgam of the Church of England Series I marriage service and prayers from the new Alternative Service Book; most remarked upon was the dropping of the bride's promise to 'obey' from the service laid out in the 1662 Prayer Book, a break from the tradition which had been upheld by the Queen, Princess Margaret, and Princess Anne.)[49] Webster went on to stress the ecumenicalism of the service itself, which was historic yet also enacted a 'new unity'. Representatives of Anglicanism, the Free Church and Roman Catholicism attended, and the leading of a prayer by a Roman Catholic, the Archbishop of Westminster Cardinal Hume, was widely touted elsewhere as evidence of a deliberate and innovative inclusiveness.[50] Finally, and as the guarantee of all the rest, Webster revisited and extended still further the traditional sense of the universal marriage service. The 'place, service and music' of the wedding are 'special', while its purpose 'is the same as that in every wedding, religious or civil, in every culture and country'. In what had become typical fashion for the British royal family, the heterosexual bonding of Charles and Diana was made to support a vast range of official, religious and public syntheses.

Despite the scope of Webster's concluding apotheosis, these binaric syntheses were not represented in material produced after the wedding as producing a totally united nation. Instead, they worked to cohere national and communal norms outside which non-royalists and others were situated. Thus the presentation of the wedding as unifying Christian affiliations of various kinds had the effect of marginalizing non-Christians. More explicitly, most extended souvenir publications gave some attention to those unable or unwilling to accept the synthetic pull of the royal event. Councillors in Porthmadog, Clay Cross in Derbyshire and members of the Greater London Council were all mentioned in several publications as exhibiting what was called 'bad grace'. The ruling Labour group on North East Derbyshire District

Council was reported as having decided to fly the red flag from the council's flagpole on 29 July 'as a matter of principle'. Welsh nationalists were blamed for blocking the offer of a local solicitor to provide 300 celebratory crown pieces for local schoolchildren. The GLC, Trevor Hall explained in *Royal Wedding Album*, voted to decline their invitations to the wedding. Ken Livingstone, then newly ensconced as its leader, was recorded as deriding the prospect of attendance as 'self-inflicted torture'. Elsewhere, Spink quoted an unnamed GLC spokesperson as saying that '[n]o-one elected us to go to weddings. They elected us to try to get the buses running on time.' Clay Cross planned anti-monarchist plays, though allegedly the event caused local controversy and supposedly 'was virtually called off'. Still, one councillor's voice was reported in Spink's book, declaring that when Diana rides into St Paul's she will also be 'riding on the backs of the working class and not realising what a mess the country is in'.[51]

Most accounts, mindful of their intended audience above all else, reported such dissenters with muted disdain. More exceptional was a children's book of the wedding published under the name of television presenter John Craven. Here, it was asserted that anti-royalists must have 'had their televisions and radios switched off all day'. Some had tried to escape to republican France, though the joke was on them because President Mitterrand had gone to the wedding.[52] Less tendentiously, before the wedding, the *Sunday Times* magazine signalled the presence of other dissidents in relation to a series of badges ranging from the surprisingly ubiquitous 'Don't Do It Di', to the unimaginative 'Stuff the Wedding', to the scurrilous 'The King an' Di', which featured an image of Charles which exaggerated his baldness and the size of his ears.[53]

In the discourses surrounding the 1981 wedding, 'Diana' played a specific and highly gendered role in securing the syntheses described above.[54] Diana and Charles were presented in terms of a double binary: as two halves of a couple, and as individuals split by conflicting but resolvable pressures. These internal binaries were produced in significantly different ways in which gender difference was articulated to monarchical hierarchy. Thus the primary issue for Charles lay in harmonizing the demands of 'head and heart', while Diana simply embodied – and by embodying, synthesized – binary oppositions. After describing her in a series of paired attributes divided under 'old-fashioned virtues and modern vivacity', a children's book *HRH The Princess of Wales* concluded that she was 'in fact, the girl next door to the Royal Family'.[55] Spink provides a further typical example of this discourse, where she describes Diana as a 'fresh, unblemished "English rose" who will be given the distinctive Royal grooming'.[56] The binary syntheses through which Diana was presented, combinations of real-life and fairy-tale, of everywoman and Princess, facilitated her own notional integration into the royal family, while also revitalizing it through demonstrating its ability to admit the 'ethnically', as opposed to symbolically, English into its midst.

What amounted to the revivification of the royal family's claims to embody English-British identity was thereby predicated on Diana's being understood to embody a particular kind of femininity conceived of not only as domestic, caring, deferential and defined in relation to a more powerful male, but all these things as naturally as a rose blooms. In these constructions conventional notions of deferential femininity and heterosexual bonding were knotted together with notions of national signification. Hence the presentation of Diana as darling not only of Charles but of the nation in 1981, when the *Daily Express* headlined its wedding-day front-page 'Happy Britain greets our new Princess'.[57] Hence also the deployment of the Cinderella story with Diana at its centre as the pretext for a narrative of national regeneration in which Diana fulfilled a supplementary function.[58]

The importance of Diana's aristocratic status, and of the class- and race-boundedness of the English rose as a national ethnicity, were all the more powerful here for not being particularly marked. Even without reference to royalty, representations of the socially privileged white woman continue to retain considerable status as signifiers of national identity. As recently as January 1997 when *Vogue* devoted 50 pages to celebrate 'the Englishwoman', the language of flowers was again used to create a taxonomy of the English and to naturalize whiteness. Billed as 'a look at every type of Englishwoman', including aristocrats, models, designers, television stars, writers and other celebrities, the only non-white woman pictured was Naomi Campbell.[59]

Mass media representations of the royal wedding portrayed Diana as an ideal model of English femininity, while also appropriating her femininity for symbolic elaboration. It would clearly be wrong to neglect how at the first of these levels representations of Diana served initially as models of femininity, naturalizing patriarchal notions of gender. The importance of Diana as an icon of empowered femininity after 1992 is underlined by the apparently inauspicious, at least for feminists, beginnings of her trajectory as role model for young women. Still, an understanding of this trajectory needs to take seriously both the mixed notions of femininity that continue to figure in Diana representations, and the ways in which, for some, Diana's gendered identity remains subject to overarching symbolic frameworks of royal and national identity.

Diana and royal femininity

The invented tradition of the royals as domestic family in the lens of national spectatorship does not necessarily abolish the distinction between public and private, but it does position that distinction as the subject of continual renegotiation. I will now focus more closely on the ways in which the femininities associated with Diana have been deployed to facilitate this. While the separation of the male royal body into public 'performance' and private 'self' has largely been maintained, such distinctions have proved much more permeable for royal females. This is due in part no doubt to Mountbatten and Windsor family traditions whereby males are expected to serve in the armed forces. Their public selves are thus almost always clearly distinguished from the private and the personal because they are uniformed in one way or another.[60] This helps to keep separate their extraordinary, unique status on one hand, and their likeness to 'ourselves' on the other. In some contrast, without recognizable 'jobs' to do outside royal ceremonial and reproduction, the principal female royals are represented in ways that continually confuse public and private. In the cases of Queen Elizabeth the Queen Mother, Elizabeth II and Diana Princess of Wales, the slippage between public and private female selves plays a crucial role in sustaining the monarchical project of national embodiment.

This is most obvious in respect of Diana, and can be seen as far back as 1980, when a variety of media representations (television news, and press coverage including the famous 'transparent dress' photograph discussed in Chapter 4 below) blurred her shy demeanour with her deferential status as youthful bride-to-be of the heir to the throne. However, the management of a strategic slippage between personal and public via the deployment of femininity is also very apparent, if somewhat differently articulated, in representations of Elizabeth the Queen Mother and Elizabeth II. There are significant continuities between the discourses used to represent Diana and Elizabeth Bowes-Lyon, who prefigured her trajectory as the aristocrat with the common touch marrying into the Windsors. In many accounts, the Queen Mother is described in terms of fairy-tale and class transcendence, able to bridge the public/private distinction effortlessly and playing a crucial role in enabling her husband, George VI, to do the same. The major counterpart here is of course Edward VIII, as the man whose inability to distinguish between personal (happiness) and public (duty) necessitated his abdication and the accession of the present branch of the family. In a 1998 television programme devoted to Elizabeth Bowes-Lyon, the historian Elizabeth Longford stigmatized Edward VIII's abdication speech as being made in the language 'of women's magazines'.[61] Edward was caught on one side of the dichotomy that his sister-in-law negotiated brilliantly.

Diana representations are also comparable with the dissemination of Elizabeth II as mother of nation and Commonwealth in a variety of registers, and in some ways dating back before her accession. Ben Pimlott's biography *The Queen* contains a wealth of examples, from the importance of Elizabeth's own domestic situation as young mother in authenticating a speech against 'materialism' in 1949, to the highly (if temporarily) successful reinvention of the royals as model family by Richard Crawston's 1969 documentary *Royal Family* and subsequent Christmas broadcasts, to the affective impact of Elizabeth's status as the mature mother of the Commonwealth.[62]

The construction of the Queen in this way worked to stabilize the potentially disruptive effects of the media exposure of the royals as domestic family from the late 1960s on. Consider, for example, the following discussion by 'royal expert' Hugo Vickers of the television film *Royal Family* as revelatory of the royals in private:

> The Royal Family film lifted the curtain on life behind the Palace walls as never before. Suddenly viewers learned that the figures they were accustomed to seeing on public occasions had private opinions and senses of humour of their own. They sprang to life on the screen and from then on the Queen, Prince Philip and others were slightly different people. Although the majority of those who saw the film would never meet their Sovereign, those that did found her very much as portrayed in it ...[63]

Vickers opens with a conventional sense of a binary opposition between public and private, where the private, usually hidden but made visible by this film is privileged as the site of one's 'own' identity. In order to sustain this distinction, Vickers succeeds in sidelining issues of the impact of the film's intrusion into royal domestic space, the effects of its control and planning, and the staging of the domestic entailed by the cameras. But he runs into difficulties when trying to specify the location of the private self to which he has alluded, since (of course) it is only visible on screen in terms of some kind of performance, the articulation of opinions or humorous behaviour. The distinction between public-performed self and private-authentic self further dissolves in the next sentence, where it is the screen that enables the authentic self to spring to life and to become 'different'. The final sentence of the passage quoted attempts retrospectively to clarify matters, placing the visible royal selves firmly in the sight of the film's viewers, and finally grounding itself in the person of the Queen, who attains self-presence by virtue of resembling her televisual representation. The only way of sustaining this rather recondite logic seems to be via the authenticity of queenly self-performance across distinctions between public and private.

Vickers raises in this passage some long-standing issues concerning the nature of monarchical embodiment, performance and spectacle. This is provoked, it might be suggested, by a sense of the danger that television exposure of the royals in private might demystify the monarchical performance of sovereignty and national identity. Walter Bagehot had warned in *The English Constitution* against letting in 'daylight upon magic', a comment widely quoted in commentaries on the royal family and the media in the latter part of the twentieth century.[64] In fact, the immediate context for Bagehot's use of this particular phrase was the political discussion of the monarch's constitutional and political role. Elsewhere, and more relevantly, Bagehot recommended that royal performances of a political and constitutional nature be kept rigidly separate from the personal and familial realms.[65] As Margaret Homans has shown, such a distinction is logically unsupportable and is achieved in Bagehot's work only by the deployment of gender difference, notably in his celebration of Victoria's absent presence.[66] Notions of femininity are crucial in maintaining Bagehot's positioning of the monarchy in terms of the 'dignified', as opposed to the 'efficient' functions of the Constitution. By accident or design, Vickers similarly accounted for the success of *Royal Family* in terms of the magical properties of royal femininity to bridge public and private.

Vickers's account also highlights the importance of royal femininity in securing the status of images as being expressive and revelatory of royal identity. In ways that update and revise Bagehot's celebration of Victoria's absent presence, he confidently proclaims the success of the film by reference to the doubled selfhood of the Queen herself. Vickers's focus shifts from the royal family *in toto*, through 'the Queen, Prince Philip and others', to rest finally upon the sovereign alone.

What enables the resolution of the Queen's public and private performances of self are androcentric assumptions about female embodiment
as being proximate to the natural, while at the same time being
defined in terms of difference from an implied male norm.
Despite the reservations of monarchists such as David Attenborough
and Milton Shulman,[67] Vickers's celebratory assessment of *Royal
Family* was matched by its popularity with critics and the public.
Sixty-eight per cent of the population watched one or other of its first
showings in June 1969, according to BBC audience research, and it
was repeated a further four times in the next 18 months, garnering 40
million viewers in total.[68] Historians and commentators from Kitty
Kelley to Sarah Bradford to Ben Pimlott have considered the subsequent relationship between the monarchy and the mass media as
bearing out the truth of the warnings given by Bagehot and
Shulman.[69] Clearly, there is a kind of dramatic irony in the way that
the deployment of 'private' representations of the ideal family generated two sets of expectations, of further intimate revelations and the
maintenance of private virtue, which were ultimately unsustainable.
In some ways the revelatory mode of the post-Morton Diana fits well
within this historical trajectory, though the importance of gender
symbolism in producing both the royal family and Diana's own narrative complicates this relationship.

In general the distinction between the corporeal body of the royal
male and the mystique of royalty, in Ernst Kantorowicz's term 'the
King's two bodies', has largely been maintained, while the body of the
mother queen or princess is thought of much more in terms of multiple performances.[70] In Diana's case this distinction was intensified by a
series of contingent circumstances. The technological and cultural
developments of celebrity journalism effectively made public her every
move outside domestic space during the engagement, yet her youth
and lack of biographical history meant that even with this blanket sur-
veillance, very little in the way of information was found and circulated.[71] This helped to create a situation whereby Diana's status as
young mother could be presented in mythic and universalist terms,
marginalizing personal history and social status. As early as 1983 the
'national mother' with the common touch had already largely displaced the Queen in transcending public and private through royal
femininity. In that year the picture book *Queen Elizabeth II and Diana
Princess of Wales* separated its account of the former into sections entitled 'The Public Face' and 'The Private Face'. In some contrast, the photographs of Diana's public performances as wife and mother were

framed by the much less distinct titles 'In the Public Eye' and 'Ambassadress for Britain'.[72] Mass media representations of Charles before his marriage sometimes enforced and sometimes blurred the public/private distinction. This unstable iconicity was maintained within a provisional framework for distinguishing between Charles's private identity and his public persona. Key here was the relation between on the one hand the notion of Charles maintaining a personal intellectual life, hinted at in interviews and by publicized friendships with mentor figures such as Laurens van der Post, and on the other hand Charles as keen participant in physical pursuits. By the late 1970s an official version of Charles's biography had emerged, whereby his five years in the Navy enabled the shy intellectual to mature into a confident and thoughtful man of action. While this distinction provided a provisional framework for the separation of private and public, it was only in relation and in contrast to Diana that this was fully stabilized. Uncertainties over his transformation were channelled into and, arguably, discharged by, the performance of certain dominant masculinities. Hence the ubiquity in the 1970s of semi-official, semi-public occasions featuring Charles surrounded by excited women while on the beach or playing polo, Charles making a parachute jump, Charles flying a helicopter, Charles in uniform. These adjuncts testify to the structural impossibility of fully realizing phallic masculinity, as noted by Mark Simpson in *Male Impersonators*.[73] In Charles's case, this disjunction was framed – and eased – by the nickname widely used of him in such contexts: 'Action Man'.[74] Some of these associations were replayed in the sections on Charles's biography in wedding souvenir programmes, where he was described in terms of 'adventure unlimited', and as often risking 'life and limb'.[75] In the latter contexts though, the 'action man' epithet was no longer necessary and was not used, since Charles's masculinity could be much more effectively stabilized in relation to his deferent bride-to-be, whose much shorter biography complemented his own.

While for the women involved, and especially Diana, this state of affairs has led to intensely stressful invasions of privacy, the deployment of femininity as mediating between public and private in this way has done much to sustain the symbolic power of monarchy. By contrast, throughout the post-1981 period, representations of Charles from all positions have taken for granted the separation of his public and private selves. Tellingly, when the so-called 'war of the Waleses' was at its height, Charles sought to refashion his public image by reasserting this distinction. One of the principal strategic moves here was his extended television interview with Jonathan Dimbleby, shown on 29 June 1994 and entitled 'Charles: The Private Man, The Public Role'. The phrase was echoed by Penny Junor in her paean to Charles that accompanied the *Mail on Sunday*'s pre-publication serialization of her book *Charles: Victim or Villain?*.[76] So far at least, the attempt has largely failed, in large part no doubt because Charles's style of masculinity was generally judged incompatible with the confessional elements of the Dimbleby interview. Without a persuasive means of mediating between public and private, the admission of adultery simply branded Charles an adulterer without engaging audiences in the reciprocal form of confessional television.

I hope to have demonstrated the usefulness for the modes of royalist legitimation under discussion of having a female monarch. Still, this should be understood in terms of historical contingency rather than structural necessity, and the deployment of 'royal femininity' to bridge public and private as strategic and intermittent rather than a constant theme. For example, representations of Anne, the other 'caring princess', conventionally follow the rigid separation of public and private associated with male family members. According to Paul James in a 1987 biography of Anne:

> With a private life at Gatcombe Park and a public life at Buckingham Palace she has been able to draw a clear distinction between the two. A sensible approach enables her to be wife and mother in Gloucestershire and a princess elsewhere.[77]

As James's title, *Anne: The Working Princess*, implies, he presents princess-hood in terms of a professional occupation carried out in the public sphere, which can be strictly differentiated from the domestic responsibilities and affective ties which occupy rural privacy. The rigid, or 'sensible', policing of this distinction frames Anne in popular culture in ways which are similar to her brothers and her father. Indeed, Anne is widely assumed to have inherited the Duke of Edinburgh's businesslike and utilitarian understanding of the royal. Any sense of performance or iconic significance is severely attenuated here. Anne's double selfhood is structured in ways that are conventional and widely applicable.

Conversely, before his marriage Charles was sometimes represented as bridging public and private through performance in terms similar to those employed by Vickers to describe the Queen.[78] Alongside

Charles's engagement and subsequent marriage, however, this gender distinction was recrystallized, so that Charles was understood as, at any given moment, being either 'on duty' or in private. By contrast for Diana this distinction was constantly blurred as her embodiment was continually reproduced and read.

If the 'magic' of royalty, in Bagehot's term, is seen to lie in its female members, what happens when that magic ceases to be deployed from deferential positions? From 'Shy Di' to saint, representations of Diana have put little distance between Diana's personal and private self and her public image.[79] In the coverage of the 1981 wedding, the sense of proximity and slippage between the two functioned largely to consolidate the symbolic function of Diana as deferential female in the service of monarchical legitimation. During and after the marital separation, these same properties continued to align Diana with notions of the royal, and could thus be understood as enabling the displacement of the Windsors in the name of a more vital royal femininity.

The deferential femininity embodied by Diana in the early 1980s was coextensive with, if not determined by, the needs of the royal family for legitimation. When the heterosexual container of this gender construction broke apart, the Windsors' apparent inability to internalize Diana's natural femininity rebounded. Images of Diana as wronged wife and good mother took on the ordinary/extraordinary paradigmatic significance previously evoked by the royal family as a group. This was in one respect a profoundly anti-monarchist development, making the royal term superfluous and incidentally bringing to light the strategic use of the family paradigm to legitimate the status of the monarchy. Yet in displacing representations of the members of the Windsor family, the proliferation of Diana's image may have done more to reinvigorate logics of royalist legitimization than to refute them. At the same time, the fetishizing of images of her intensified still further. As one posthumous souvenir book has pointed out, albeit with hindsight, informal images of Diana leaving hospital with the newborn Prince Harry rendered the formally posed official family pictures obsolete, if not artificial, if not demeaning to the Princess.[80] In the picture-book *Diana: Her Life in Photographs*, published in 1995 during the marital separation, the vast majority of its 200 images show Diana alone or with undifferentiated others. Pictures of Diana with one or both of her children make up roughly one tenth of the total. Other members of the Windsor family are almost totally absent. Her estranged husband appears only once in the entire volume, and then as an image of an image. Charles is visible in a photograph displayed on top of a piano in the background of a picture of Diana and the boys.[81]

The continuing importance of negotiating public and private in celebratory versions of Diana's iconicity suggests that they remain indebted to notions of femininity developed strategically for the legitimation of the monarchy as a domestic family. In this sense, the crux of Diana's wider significance can be seen to be the ambivalence of the 'people's princess', as the perfection or supersession of monarchical ideology. Diana was simply better at being royal than were the Windsors. One 'lesson' of this interpretation has been well learned, in the Windsors' adoption of some of Diana's practices after her death, aided by the advice of the Labour government. However, the history of Diana representations, as a trajectory reflecting negatively upon the royal family, can also suggest a more progressive 'outside' to royalty. In order to register fully this potential however, it is necessary to dispense with a simple opposition between Diana and the monarchy, and to treat with caution triumphalist readings of Diana images. As a way of exemplifying this, we can look at a widely reproduced family portrait of the Windsors from October 1991.

As early as that date it was quite possible to read Diana as having perfected or transcended the category of royalty. October 1991 saw the publication of a photograph of the Waleses by Lord Snowdon, ostensibly to mark their tenth wedding anniversary. It shows Charles, Diana and their two children in formal picnicking pose, complete with expensive accoutrements, clothing and horse. The family group is assembled before an oak tree, with an English landscape, identified officially as Windsor Great Park, in the background. The image and its mediation in the British popular press have been discussed by John Hartley, who has called attention to the multiple ways in which the press mediated Snowdon's photograph, as news, fashion, middle-page colour spread, pin-up and subject of serious commentary.[82] Building on his work, I want to consider the image as marking a particular moment in the discursive relations of Diana, royalty and the family. In particular, as the press commentaries show, the photograph was eminently readable as contrasting Diana with the Windsors such that she appears undifferentiated in terms of social class, and open to emulation through consumption, while they are strongly identified with aristocratic privilege. Yet at the same time that Diana could be seen as displacing the Windsors in performing national identity, she is also objectified.

The Snowdon photograph was presented by Buckingham Palace as contextualizing the Waleses by reference to family life. Since it was released as part of the publicity surrounding the Waleses' tour of Canada, at some levels it reiterated by now familiar connections between the family, Englishness and national identity. However, of the publications Hartley surveys, only the *Sun, Vogue, Today* and the *London Evening Standard* produced unequivocally positive readings of the image, stressing Diana's glamour (the *Sun* and *Vogue*) or the way in which the photograph compositionally articulated the 'happy family' theme. More critical mediations of the image appeared in the *Daily Mirror* and *The Independent*. Both newspapers produced readings of the image that accused it of fakery, and sought to unmask what their writers perceived as the illegitimate use of the picnic format to legitimate the Waleses as 'ordinary family'. As Hartley points out, the *Mirror* article distinguishes 'the *false* royal picnic from *authentic* ones', contrasting the studied calm of the royal representation with the generational tensions and unappetising proletarian food of picnics enjoyed by 'the rest of us'.[83] *The Independent* focuses almost completely on Charles, arguing that the overtly materialistic strain of the image (compared to advertising images here as also in *Today*) belies the Prince's avowed concern with spiritual life. Charles appears here as a hypocritical yuppie, who 'although he has said "I am not in favour of an elite if it is solely based on birth and wealth", he shows no sign of relinquishing his own membership'.[84]

It was possible to read the fashionable gear paraded here in terms of democratizing the monarchy, as did *Today*, which pointed out that the photograph presented the possibility for readers to emulate the royals by copying their acts of consumption. However, in different ways the *Daily Mirror, Daily Star* ('Nice Picnic. Shame about the price ...') and the *Independent* all found fault with the image's presentation of the Waleses as both ordinary and extraordinary. The notion that one could emulate Diana's taste in jodhpurs is clearly divisive in terms of economic class, and it is no coincidence that *Today* celebrated the possibility for its aspirational readers, while the more left-wing *Mirror* deplored it. More to the point, however, was the dangerousness of the notion that royalty could be emulated by consumption at all. In fact, probably the most ingenious coverage was in *Today*, which offered a double reading of the photograph, contextualizing it firstly by reference to Gainsborough's 1748 portrait of Mr and Mrs Andrews in the park of their house, which the paper reproduced in colour, and then via the discourse of advertising to the notion of emulation by consumption.

The first of these contexts is authenticated by Mark McDonnell, a fine art expert at Christie's, who as Hartley points out draws heavily upon John Berger's celebrated 1972 book *Ways of Seeing*. Arguing against the patrician aestheticism of Kenneth Clark and Lawrence Gowing, Berger had insisted on the importance of landownership in the portrait's meaning. Mr and Mrs Andrews, Berger argued, 'are landowners and their proprietary attitude towards what surrounds them is visible in their stance and their expressions'.[85] Much of what Berger articulated controversially in the early 1970s is presented by McDonnell in terms of the received wisdom of the art world. What *Today*'s makeover of the image for the Thatcherite 1980s ignores is Berger's further argument that the landownership enjoyed by the Andrews was protected by draconian laws against theft. Instead, *Today* paraphrases the Christie's experts as finding similarities not only with Gainsborough, but also with the advertising styles of houses such as Ralph Lauren and Mulberry. John Hartley's reading of the *Today* article tends to emphasize its ideological closure, which mirrors and reinforces the intended message of the image. What *Today* finds in the photo is a convincing synthetic rearticulation of royalty, combining the traditional formal portrait of the aristocratic family surrounded by land which they own, with advertising images suitable for brands which offer high-class identity for sale as part of the semiotic value of clothes.

It seems to me that the analysis of the photograph in *Today*, and Hartley's reading of it, is substantially convincing, at least for the intended meanings of the piece if not the interpretations actually put into circulation. The photograph clearly borrows liberally from Gainsborough and from upmarket clothes advertising, in order to carry out two sets of displacements. In one, the Waleses are reconfigured as English aristocrats, whose identity and authority is presented as deriving from the land which they own, here concretized as an oak tree. In the other, their clothes signify the Waleses as middle-class consumers, whose emulation is fostered by press identifications of labels and prices. Yet there are limits to the persuasiveness of this configuration, which are perhaps more visible after the apparent decline of Thatcherism. Such images of aristocracy can never fully naturalize social privilege, since the act of representing landownership pivots between antithetical understandings of ownership itself: the aristocratic self-image of husbandry and hereditary right, and bourgeois notions of commercial acquisitiveness. In what could be considered a master-stoke, this image triumphantly reworks these meanings, separating the aristocratic assumption of hereditary ownership from bourgeois materialism by channelling one into the landscape context, an oak tree in private grounds, and the other into the family's clothing. Thus to the sympathetic reader of *Today*, the photograph's representation of the royals as aristocrats and as star consumers served to reinvigorate their status as both ordinary and extraordinary.

However, where *Today* read displacement as synthesis, others constructed the identifications of royalty with aristocracy and with consumption in antithetical terms. The former could be considered to invert the proper relationship between royalty and national identity, drawing upon notions of landscape-as-Englishness to construct royal identity, instead of presenting the Windsors as a focal point of Britishness. This is problematic less because of the slippage between Britishness and Englishness, a habitual trait in dominant constructions of Britain and largely perpetuated by the Windsors, than because of its implication that national identity is already defined, by landscape, hereditary landownership, and so on, in comparison to which the Windsors appear as supernumerary johnnies-come-lately, appropriating signifiers of Englishness in order to shore up their own identity. In this sense what the photograph reveals is that the royal family's status is dependent on a sense of the provisionality of British national identity, of Britishness as a problem to which they represent the solution. This particular image is antithetical to such a structure, since it implies that Britishness (as Englishness) is self-evident while it is the identity of the Windsors that needs grounding.

The other side of the displacement is equally problematic. Conspicuous consumption as a marker of the 'ordinary' side of royal identity might be read as an innovative way of modernizing the monarchy. Yet it goes against one of the crucial rationalizations of royal wealth, whereby it is considered to be not really 'theirs' at all, but in their stewardship for the nation. The reworking of royal wealth in terms of private consumption thus appears as the antithesis of 'true' royalty.

In the accounts of the photograph in the *Independent* these antinomies were focused on Charles as a fake. Little mention was made of Diana's image and representation, despite her wearing the instantly identifiable clothing of the country set. What I want to suggest here is that the glamour incarnated by Diana in this photograph, and registered in most of the press discussions, worked to exempt her from the fierce critique of fakery, partly by invoking plainly objectifying notions of femininity, and partly also by silently calling upon naturalizing notions of Englishness based on whiteness and aristocratic status. For some viewers then, Diana occupied in this photograph the position of royalty, but was readable as something else. This something else was defined partly by the jodhpurs worn by Diana in the photograph, and partly also by the long history of connections between titled families and advertising in women's magazines. Those with long memories might recall that Queen Elizabeth's coronation had stimulated several such images in the commemorative editions of *Woman's Own*, *Vogue* and *The Queen*. The picnic photograph presents Diana's media image at an impasse. Tensions between Diana herself and the Windsors make it difficult to read her as one of the royals. Her iconicity is strong enough to pre-empt her being overtly associated with aristocratic status, but only at the cost of either scopophilic fetishization or identifying her as a consumer.

3
The Ambivalent Femininities of Diana Narratives

It also makes for a literally enchanting transformation when you are the one plucked out of millions to dance at the ball. The glass slipper was missing, but the youngest sister from a broken home did get the gown, the glass coach, and, of course, the charming prince. The wand was waved by us because we want her to carry and keep alive our hopes and dreams and fantasies.

Robert Lacey, *Princess* (1982)[1]

Narratives and mourning practices

For most people, the significance of Diana is dominated by the reaction to her death, the mourning or so-called Diana events. This is so because of their relation to notions of the social. The mourning for Diana was not only felt to affirm basic human bonds through shared affective response, but also, largely through the unexpected presence of certain groups, staged the integration of difference into social unity. What has remained more debatable is the nature and the extent of any change in the terms in which social unity is imagined. This combination is apparent in the description of mourning Diana by Adrian Kear and Deborah Lynn Steinberg as holding out possibilities of 'inclusive intersubjectivity' and 'counter-hegemonic utterance', and is reflected in Kear and Steinberg's concern with theorizing Diana's significance in terms of 'the narrational remarking of the boundaries between the culturally central and the socially marginal'.[2] It is precisely the coupling of these possibilities with the multiple dispossessions and foreclosures also effected by the mourning for Diana, that have made the Diana events worthy of the detailed analysis made by the contributors to Kear and Steinberg's *Mourning Diana*, Tony Walter's *The Mourning for Diana*, Re: Public's *Planet Diana*, and in the special issues of the journals *theory & event* and *New Formations*.[3]

This chapter is concerned with the centring and marginalization of identity in the narrativization of Diana from 1991 to early 1997, some eight months before Diana's death. In part, it is important to do this because a critical focus on the mourning events is too easily misread as assuming a unitary, stable iconicity up to August 1997, which is ruptured by a posthumous explosion of competing mourning practices. As the *Mourning Diana* collection demonstrates, a privileged focus on the Diana events does not necessarily negate the complexity of pre-1997 Diana representations.[4] However, in bringing into sharp focus the problems and possibilities of social integration associated with the mourning, the longer history of contestation over Diana's cultural meaning tends to be flattened into the background.

The period 1991–7 was itself significant in terms of the production and dissemination of narratives about Diana. As has been seen, it was in 1992 that the phrase 'the People's – and Pop's – princess' was coined by Julie Burchill to position Diana as a site of social integration defined in explicit opposition to the traditional monarchy. Largely as a result of the breakdown of her marriage and the publication of Andrew Morton's *Diana: Her True Story*, this period saw the destabilization of representations of Diana within mainstream discourses, and the dissemination of a series of contesting Diana narratives. Mainstream media responded to this proliferation with strategies of containment, some of which would be reactivated after Diana's death in order to co-opt or resist counter-hegemonic possibilities. This already conflicted and debated status of Diana before her death negates a sense of the mourning events as exploding a previously stable and conservative ideological formation. Rather, Diana's death intensified a series of contests over her cultural significance which were already taking place. Conservative formations of social integration under the sign of royal femininity would remain important after Diana's death, both in structuring her as a symbol of unity and transcendence, and in authenticating a putative hierarchy within which she was or was demanded to be located. Diana's posthumous status as fusing antithetical forms, suggestively elaborated by Kear and Steinberg in terms of combining 'ahistorical myth and historically grounded mythologies', may have been achieved therefore less by conjoining 'the "elevated" status of royal protagonist' with 'ubiquitous "ordinariness"', as they suggest, than through revising the function of royal femininity in mediating between public and private, epitome and exemplum.[5] Hence, instead of seeing the history of Diana representations as a trajectory from the extraordinary/royal/patriarchal towards the ordinary/popular/feminine, it is perhaps more accurate to regard it as a repeated iteration of contrasting syntheses of ordinary and extraordinary, predicated on conflicting formations of femininity and exemplarity. Such conflicts and resolutions are clearly visible in the narratives of 1991-7.

This is not at all to deny the importance of notions of *property*, to use the term employed symptomatically by Joe Kelleher in his contribution to *Mourning Diana*.[6] Clearly, the Diana events were characterized by shifts in both material and symbolic economies of representation. Groups hitherto lacking in cultural capital (for example gay men, 'non-white' Britons and the ladies of middle England) were newly, if temporarily, accorded status in authenticating Diana's significance. The transparency of mass media representation was made opaque, albeit temporarily, and television momentarily gestured towards its inability to make Diana present. Authorship matters politically, and because it does so Kear and Steinberg are right to configure 'performativity of grief and loss' as crucial to 'the (re)construction of cultural identities and political hegemony'.[7] Alongside this project, what I want to do here is to look at the ideological formation of 'Diana', ownership of which was being competed for in the various mourning practices. Hence, I propose to supplement their evident concern with the performative cultural politics of grieving with analysis of the representational politics of making 'Diana' meaningful as an explicit focus of identification and social integration.

The Diana myth as narrative of female transformation

One effect of first coming into public knowledge as a possible royal bride was that Diana was understood from the beginning in terms of potential, in this case the unfolding of a romance with symbolic national implications. Her early death seemed to come at the beginning of yet another 'new life', this time, one that most affectingly promised a synthesis of fulfilling public role and personal happiness. Between these moments Diana's story has continually been structured around patterns of transformation. Narratives of the blooming of the English rose from 'Shy Di' to Princess of Wales have been supplanted by tales of the emergence of the 'real' Diana from inauthentic official versions, of a powerful Diana from weakness, of a liberated Diana from oppression, an arch manipulator from a media innocent, and many others. The diverse forms of such transformation narratives have been presented in genres varying from myth to realism to sensationalism to folk tale, and have worked in the service of various world-views. Debate continues to rage over personal biographical facts such as whether Charles or Diana was first to commit adultery,[8] the cultural meaning of Diana's biography and its appropriate register.

The fairy-tale of Cinderella remains a powerful structure for grounding these narratives long after its initial enchantment was broken. Its continued importance testifies to a felt need to view Diana as empowered, rather than simply as a victim, and to codify positively the sense of her life as a series of transformations whose fulfilment was arrested by early death. The Cinderella narrative has proved flexible enough to accommodate a Muslim of Egyptian heritage as Diana's last prince, yet it continues to construct empowerment in individualistic terms within a patriarchal, heteronormative and royalist symbolic economy. While the form of the Cinderella story may have been decisively rejected by later commentators (William J. Spurlin, for example, wisely argues for the progressive valency of imagining Diana as staying single),[9] the combination of its embeddedness in conventional forms and the scope it has afforded for revision and reworking makes it a potent sign for the ambivalence of 'Diana'.

The passage by Robert Lacey quoted at the head of this chapter is symptomatic of early 1980s Diana narratives in mainstream culture. It conferred mythic and exemplary status upon Diana as playing out in real life specifically female desires and fantasies of transformation. One might have expected the applicability of the Cinderella myth to have been negated by stories of the marital difficulties experienced by Diana and Charles, which came to public knowledge in the 1990s. The popularity of the 1990 film *Pretty Woman*, which reworked the Cinderella narrative via capitalist feminism, suggested a new cultural currency for the fairy-tale. Still, in large part its continued importance for popular investments in Diana was made possible by the ideological work carried out by one man, Andrew Morton.

In his series of biographies, starting with *Diana: Her True Story* in 1992, Morton decisively reworked the Cinderella narratives previously employed to frame Diana's life, opening up the possibility of seeing her as an inspirational figure through suffering, recovery and empowerment. In the first instance, this was a deliberate and ideologically loaded counter to anti-feminist representations of Diana in the popular and broadsheet press, and television media. Diana's health and happiness, and the state of her marriage, had been the subject of rumour and speculation since the mid-1980s. From 1985 to 1991 popular media produced material that denied or stigmatized the process of maturation through which the deferential 'Shy Di' persona was outgrown. Difficulties in Diana's personal life and problems with her public role were understood in terms of Diana's own failings. After the publication of *Diana: Her True Story*, often the contradictions surrounding Diana's position were deflected on to the traditional figure of the enigmatic female, or dismissed as the products of an alternately neurotic and masterful manipulator of the media. Narratives of Diana's transformation and empowerment can be seen to work to refute these attitudes. Yet such narratives often maintain an investment in the authority and status of the royal, while at the same time celebrating an exceptionalist and privatized liberation from patriarchal power.

These ideological ambivalences can be traced by reference to the Morton biographies, their cultural and material contexts, and subsequent re-presentations of Diana's life. Therefore what follows is a detailed discussion of the biographies with respect to press coverage and competitor volumes. Then Diana's more direct attempt to wrest control of public understandings of her own story in the *Panorama* interview of 1995 is considered. Attention is subsequently turned to the ways in which representations of Diana narratives developed in the wake of the Morton and *Panorama* texts, as commentators sought to frame an antithesis that had previously barely been thinkable in mainstream culture: Diana vs. Charles. Finally, the focus shifts to narratives of Diana's life which have explicitly constituted themselves against the Morton myth of Diana's transformation.

Appropriating feminism in *Diana: Her True Story*

Andrew Morton's biographies are by far the most popular and influential narratives of Diana's life, and their mythic construction of Diana remains the closest to a definitive version. It is largely to Morton that we owe the elaboration of Diana's iconicity in terms of an empowered femininity defined in contradistinction to a masculinized monarchical establishment. The series began with *Diana: Her True Story*, which appeared in a storm of publicity precipitated by the serialization of extracts from the book in the *Sunday Times* in June 1992. Two million hardback copies were sold before the paperback edition appeared the following year, featuring a further chapter and new photographs (referred to subsequently as *HTS 1993*). In 1993 combined sales reached over four and a half million.[10] A second volume, *Diana:*

Her New Life (subsequently *HNL*), followed in 1994. Shortly after Diana's death, Morton published a further edition under the title *Diana: Her True Story – In Her Own Words* (henceforward *HTS 1997*), which consolidated and revised material from both books. The publication of this volume was accompanied by the revelation that *HTS* had been partly based on tape-recorded interviews with Diana herself made in 1991–2, and the new edition contained selected transcripts of her responses to Morton's initial questions. Although only on sale for the last few months of the year, it became the bestselling hardback of 1997. As with the 1992 edition, pre-publication extracts ran in the *Sunday Times*, and a paperback edition followed less than a year later with a further chapter. The 'Morton myth' as first articulated in the 1992 *Diana: Her True Story* and subsequently elaborated was innovative in two major ways. First, it broke with the conventions of royal biography by clearly affiliating itself with one member against the rest of the family. Drawing attention to its substantiation from Diana's family and friends, *Diana: Her True Story* maintained that to sympathize with Diana was to be against Charles and the Windsors. Hence it deployed 'insider knowledge' deliberately and strategically in order to damage the royal establishment. Second, Morton cast the tensions in the Waleses' marriage in the form of an ideological opposition structured along gender lines. In order to provide ideological support for the affiliation with Diana, Morton drew upon and appropriated material from two main sources: the historical conventions for representing royal femininity and elements of second wave feminism.

    Diana: Her True Story was by no means the first revelatory biography of the Princess of Wales. Its most (in)famous claims, of Charles's long-standing relationship with Camilla Parker-Bowles, and of Diana's unhappiness, suicide attempts and eating disorders, had all been anticipated in the popular press and in two biographies that immediately pre-dated it, *Diana* by Nicholas Davies, and Lady Colin Campbell's *Diana in Private: The Princess Nobody Knows* (both 1992). What immediately distinguished *Diana: Her True Story*, as its acknowledgements reflected and its jacket blurb proclaimed, was the manner in which Morton's narrative was substantiated. *HTS* marked itself out from its many predecessors by claiming factual insider knowledge provided by family and friends, rather than what was referred to on the inside jacket as 'gossip, the tittle-tattle of disaffected servants, and conjecture'. This in no small part won the book sufficient credibility as *exposé* to ensure its serialization not in the popular press but in the *Sunday Times*. Although the serialization was itself part of a process in which the erstwhile newspaper of record was seen to be moving downmarket under the influence of its owner Rupert Murdoch, it in turn conferred further status upon Morton's revelations. More substantiation came from the extensive use of hitherto publicly unseen photographs from the Spencer family album. These, as was pointed out on the book's inside cover, contrasted with the formal, public and paparazzi photography employed by competitor volumes. Diana's direct involvement was denied and emerged only posthumously, but her well-publicized visit to Carolyn Bartholomew, one of the friends quoted extensively in the text, in the immediate aftermath of publication, was widely understood as signalling her approval.

In all this Morton utilized familiar and conventional structures of revelation, while claiming more prestigious sources than his predecessors. More innovative and subsequently more influential were the book's status as personal testimony (discussed below), and the ideological apparatus used by Morton to construct Diana's story in terms of an emblematic and mythologized femininity, defined largely in contradistinction to the royal family itself. Until Morton, the ideological frameworks of revelation used by tabloid journalists and biographers had failed to distinguish between Diana and other members of the royal family. In reconstructing Diana as struggling against what he portrayed as the monarchical establishment, Morton presented her gender identity as transcending both aristocratic and royal status. To this end the Diana myth produced by Morton drew upon a variety of genres and various elements of second-wave feminism. It would in turn form the basis for many later feminist, quasi-feminist and other woman-centred readings of Diana.

Morton's books are generic hybrids of romantic novel, testamentary (auto)biography, *bildungsroman*, critical moral commentary on aristocratic and royal institutions and behaviour, and sensational revelation of the personal difficulties behind the public image of the monarchy. What held together these realist, romantic and mythic registers was the appropriation of the feminist genre of testamentary (auto)biography. Like the Oprah Winfrey talk show, which repeatedly tried to book Diana to appear, Morton's work plays out many of the elements of second-wave feminism in what Jennifer Wicke has called the 'celebrity zone'.[11] Wicke has pointed to the multivalent and sometimes unpredictable meanings which arise from the interaction of the cultural spheres of feminism and celebrity in such contexts, and the Diana myth embodied in Morton's narratives is no different. In keeping with this and their hybrid generic status, Morton's books offer a narrative of Diana's life which draws upon a basic antithesis between femininity and monarchy, the one warm, tactile and caring, the other cold, withdrawn and insular. This fundamental ideological structure is strongly influenced by second-wave feminism, but is capable of being inflected in a variety of ways, as it is in both Morton's texts and in the voluminous material influenced by them. A major complicating factor, in addition to the notions of celebrity described by Wicke, is the relationship between Diana, femininity and royalty that Morton portrays. Morton's texts are addressed implicitly to heterosexual-identified female readers sympathetic to Diana but unwilling to give up an emotional investment in the 'wedding of the century'. To this end, they invoke the feminine principle embodied by Diana as the antithesis of the royal family. But this can never be allowed fully to negate the monarchy, since Diana's status still largely depends on it as an institution. Thus if the ideological opposition between Diana and monarchy invoked by Morton's terminology of warmth and coldness associates Diana with republicanism, the *Her True Story* books largely resist this implication.

Morton's biographies use three related narrative tropes derived from the culture of second-wave feminism to tell Diana's story: the inspirational story of victimization, recovery and empowerment; personal (auto)biography as exemplary testimony; and the narrative of the emergence of femininity from private and domestic life into the public sphere. In Morton, these feminist tropes are elucidated by an ideological opposition between femininity and monarchy, yet he also utilizes codes of royal femininity as a means of negotiating public and private. The mythic Diana of *Her True Story*, whose feminine identity transcends class difference, is thus both ideologically powerful and unstable. On the one hand Morton's portrayal of the Diana narrative has been read as throwing into relief the ways that male power works through the structure of the model family, enabling feminist critique of patriarchal power at various levels. Yet on the other hand, the liberatory potential of these narratives in terms of feminist realism, persuasively argued for in their original context by Maria Lauret, is severely compromised by the conditions of their articulation in Morton.[12]

The three major versions of Morton's biography (*HTS, HNL* and *HTS 1997*) present themselves as offering the same narrative structure of female victimization, recovery and empowerment. On the inside of its dust-jacket, the first edition of *Her True Story* outlines the story of one individual's unsteady development from girl to princess to a 'woman who found herself through adversity'. Echoing its predecessor, *Her New Life* is announced inside its front cover as revealing 'how Diana, who became a princess before she had reached maturity, is at last learning to become a woman in her own right rather than a puppet of the palace'. The equivalent 'blurb' in the 1997 edition reiterates the story in self-congratulatory manner. Here Diana is described as feeling 'trapped and powerless within the royal family', knowing that 'the truth about her life was submerged under a mountain of royal propaganda'. She is rescued from this situation by her 'collaboration' with Morton, the effect of which 'was to shake the royal family to its foundations and, eventually, allow Diana to seek a new life'.

These prominent summaries signal the harnessing of a narrative of female maturation and empowerment to the antagonistic pairing of femininity and monarchy. While occasionally the sources of negative pressure on Diana are widened to include not only 'her husband [and] the royal system' but also 'the public's expectations towards their fairytale princess' (*HTS 1993*: 106), the major emphasis throughout the books is on the first and second of these. Even where, starting in the Postscript added to the paperback edition of *HTS* in 1993 and continuing in subsequent volumes, media coverage and public opinion are brought into the narrative, they are contextualized by the basic antagonism between femininity and monarchy. Thus Morton typified negative media representations of Diana around and subsequent to the initial publication of *HTS* as 'black propaganda' organized by supporters of Charles and the Windsors both within and outside the official royal organization (*HTS 1993*: 168; *HNL*: 79–86).

Despite its prominence on their covers, the empowerment narrative remains severely attenuated inside the Morton biographies. Even the posthumous triumphalism of the 1997 *HTS* is undermined by its emphasis on the fragility of Diana's personality, her public persona and what the cover text itself calls her 'new, and briefly happy, life'. In the 1992–4 texts, the quantity of material which stresses Diana's victimization at the hands of the royal family, and to a much lesser extent the media, and her ongoing struggles with bulimia and low self-esteem, many times outweighs the evidence of regeneration. Morton's summary comments within the books themselves undercut the cover blurbs. For example, in the opening chapter of the 1992 *Her True Story*, Morton first outlined the negatives of Charles's ongoing relationship with Camilla Parker-Bowles, Diana's loneliness and her eating disorder, before going on:

> Yet the heartening aspect of her story was the way Diana had come to terms with her life and how, with the help of friends and counsellors, she was finding her true nature. The story of her transformation from victim to victor, a process that continues to this day, is the subject of this book. (*HTS 1992*: 3)

The initial delimiter 'the heartening aspect', the use of past imperfect tense and the explicit reference to the ongoing status of Diana's transformation all suggest its incompleteness and instability. The empowerment narrative is further undermined by the emphasis throughout on Diana's victimization. As early as the 1992 *HTS* Morton asserted that Diana had largely emotionally recovered the damage done by her husband's relationship with Camilla Parker-Bowles (*HTS 1992*: 128–9). But such material is undercut by further evidence of obsessive behaviour in the same volume and further reiterated in the 1997 book (*HTS 1997*: 234). Even when in the 1997 volume the above passage is revised and strengthened by dropping the New Age-tinged 'finding her true nature' in favour of the more portentous and more overtly feminist 'in control of her own destiny', and constructing the transformation as '*one* of the heartening aspects' [emphasis added], Morton still stressed its ongoing and hence incomplete status, as 'a process the Princess continued until the very end' (*HTS 1997*: 18).

The closing pages of the 1992 *HTS* and even the 1994 *HNL* had done still more to circumscribe the empowerment narrative. In 1992 Morton stressed the 'impossible balancing act' of Diana's life, her proneness to 'pessimism and despair', her 'self-imposed martyrdom', as 'she drifts inexorably into depression' (*HTS 1992*: 152), all of which severely undercut the somewhat limited assertion that 'Her achievement has been to find her true self in the face of overwhelming odds' (*HTS 1992*: 153). The more upbeat 1994 book still concluded that 'Her challenge is to face the demons within as she embarks on a new life' (*HNL*: 160–1). While the narrative framework of both books remains the same, along with the temporal shift from 1981–91 to 1991–4 the terms of Diana's transformation shifted also. For a variety of reasons, including no doubt the relative willingness of practitioners to be publicly quoted, in *HTS 1992* a variety of 'New Age' therapies and knowledges loom large in working the transformation. Morton quotes Diana's adviser on acupuncture and meditation Oonagh Toffolo, astrologers Penny

Thornton, Felix Lyle and Debbie Frank, massage therapist Stephen Twigg and aromatherapist Sue Beechey (*HTS 1992*: 4, 5, 9, 87, 94, 96, 103–7, 121, 130, 135, 149). Morton is careful to distance Diana from full belief in such material, stressing that while once a 'lifeline', they have become 'tools and guides', interest in which was a 'stepping stone on her road to self-knowledge' (*HTS 1992*: 104). He takes advantage of a well-worn strategy later in the book in stigmatizing Sarah Ferguson as a true believer 'in thrall' to New Age prophecies that Diana uses more selectively, and only for guidance (*HTS 1992*: 139–40). Yet Morton is much more vague on the precise influence of Diana's contemporary 'friends and counsellors' and on defining explicitly the 'true nature' that has allegedly been found by the Princess. The emphasis laid on maternity in *HNL* and on the combination of maternity and Diana's new-found public role in the 1997 *HTS* goes some way to fill in this gap retrospectively, but the popularity of the earlier texts implies that few readers seem to have noticed it in the first place.

Why did the vast majority of readers perceive this elliptical structure as unproblematic? This can be explained by reference to the expectations created by the marking of the Morton texts as belonging to the genre of the popular romance, albeit one without a conventional happy ending. In her influential work on a group of middle-class American romance readers, Janice Radway argued that such readers constitute an 'interpretive community' with its own assumptions about textuality.[13] While Radway's overall positioning has subsequently been debated, some of the interpretive strategies she ascribes to romance readers can be seen to be inscribed in the Morton biographies. In particular, Radway highlighted an important difference in attitudes to characterization between the reading practices employed by fans of the Harlequin romance (the British counterpart is Mills and Boon) and the expectations of readers in highbrow or critical mode. The latter seek to produce what Radway called a 'unified characterization' which takes into account both description and narrative action.[14] Typical romances disappoint these expectations since they assert the intelligence, independence and strength of their central character, before going on to place her in narrative positions of weakness and passivity. Readers used to the conventions of romance fiction do not require such unified characterization, and consequently do not experience the lack of it as a discontinuity. Instead, they read the assertions of strength and independence as accurate descriptions of character and attribute any failure to demonstrate these in the narrative to 'unforeseen circumstances'.[15] The apparent problem of the elliptical structure of the 1992–4 Morton texts, then, is potentially resolved if readers apply the conventions used in reading romance fiction.

However, Morton's rendering of the Diana narrative lacks a crucial element of the romance form, and this lack makes it dysfunctional in the terms outlined by Radway. Though Radway does not identify it as such, she describes romance readers as seeking narrative confirmation of the descriptive attribution of characteristics to the strong, intelligent heroine. In the romances most favoured by the group studied by Radway, the initial assertions regarding the heroine are eventually confirmed by her influence on the male hero, who is taught 'how to care for her and to appreciate her as she wishes to be appreciated'.[16] What really counts for such readers is less the narrated interaction between heroine and hero than the transformation of the hero into a sensitive and supportive partner offering a permanent commitment. It is this transformation which, when attributed to the influence of the heroine, can be read as affirming her power and validating a certain type of femininity.[17]

For Radway these conventions are crucial in determining the ambivalent ideological effects of romance-reading. On the one hand, she argues, romances offered the middle-class female readers she studied feelings of validation and empowerment. On the other hand, what is being valued, and at the same time confirmed, is the patriarchal gender distinction between a masculinized public sphere of competition and paid work, and a feminized domestic sphere of nurturance and attentive care. Although this distinction retains some force, the combined effects of historical change, feminism, class difference and the exigencies of capitalist production weaken it considerably outside the immediate context of the women studied by Radway. The Morton myth can be seen to rearticulate this gender distinction for a contemporary female readership from more diverse class situations, who need to work outside the home, whose responsibility for childcare remains disproportionate and undersupported, and whose access to cultural capital is channelled into magazines and fictions of comparatively low status. Radway's careful distinction between the reading practices associated with different interpretive communities suggests an explanation for the apparent aporia in the 1992–4 Morton texts, which assert that Diana is a strong woman, but articulate narratives dominated by suffering and passivity. What might appear to a critical reader as a contradiction between the claims made for Diana's identity and her narrative is simply in line with the generic conventions of the romance form. However, conspicuously missing from these texts is the narrative of male transformation that constitutes what Radway calls the 'triumph of female values' in the romance.[18]

Read according to the conventions of the romance form, Charles's failure to change marks him out as a villain. This negates some of the satisfactions of romance reading indicated by Radway and offers alternatives, in doing so putting at stake the validation of nurturing femininity. Several readerly positions can be identified. For some, the narrative outlined by Morton and subsequently elaborated by Diana herself in the *Panorama* interview confirmed an ideological critique of deferential nurturing femininity made by feminists who had worn 'Don't do it Di' badges before the wedding.[19] For others, perhaps, the biographies are read in terms of melodrama as Ien Ang has understood it, playing out the limits of (female) subjectivity in fictive and fantasy forms.[20] This would seem to be an ultimately masochistic investment, unless the boundaries between real life and fantastic investment are marked, as for example they might be for some readers by class difference. Reading Morton to a greater or lesser extent against the grain, Diana's elevated class status enables one to disinvest from her struggle. Yet the Morton biographies also offer compensations for readers sympathetic to Diana and seeking the combination of myth and novel described by Radway as characteristic of the romance. In place of offering male transformation as evidence of female power, the Morton texts employ two quite different strategies to achieve a similar result: the assertion (and in the 1997 version the demonstration) of female empowerment, combined with the invocation of a kind of mythic femininity which mediates between public and private spheres.

Instead of looking for Charles to change, readerly interest can be engaged by the thematic binary employed throughout the book to place Diana in contradistinction to Charles and the Windsors. Morton piles up metaphorical and metonymic oppositions between, on the one side, Diana as femininity, defined in terms of warmth, tactility, motherhood (emphasized especially in *HNL*), emotion, spontaneity and expressivity, and on the other side, Charles and the royal system, defined in terms of coldness, remoteness, lack of emotion, formality and inexpressivity.[21] This opposition configures family life in contrasting ways: for Diana, in terms of maternal feeling, emotion and care; for Charles, in terms of the construction of identity and responsibility through heredity. As the personification of the Windsors, Charles stands for masculinity as repression; as someone cold-shouldered by the same, Diana is an emblem of femininity as personal affectivity.

Although femininity is the privileged term in this gender binary, its articulation can hardly be described as feminist. This is because this thematic binary stands in for, and camouflages the lack of, the explicitly feminist content that might be expected in the narratives of empowerment, autobiographical testimony and emergence into the public sphere. In Morton's elliptical narrative structure the realization of femininity 'for itself', that is, over and against the monarchy, is not the result of communal politics, organization or education. As shown above, Morton represents New Age therapies as contributing to Diana's regeneration, while clearly not being directly responsible for it. In fact, Morton offers no definitive explanation of the empowerment of Diana. It is instead simply presented as the realization of the 'feminine qualities' with which his subject began. Diana's empowerment is achieved, then, through the performance of warmth and nurturing in symbolic and familial contexts, that is through reinvigorating discourses of Diana as 'national mother' according to a revisionist but still recognizable discourse of royal femininity.

Romance, realism and myth in Diana biography, 1991–2

The range and scope of Morton's shaping of the Diana narrative can be seen more precisely by comparing it with the pro- and anti-monarchist discourses employed in newspapers and in books about the royal family immediately before the publication of *Diana: Her True Story*. Diana's primary motive for collaborating with Morton, and a determinant influence on the form of his output, was to respond to the negative media representations which appeared in the late 1980s and early 1990s. In *Diana: Her True Story* Morton referred to such negative coverage of the 'royal shopoholic', and quoted gossip columnist Nigel Dempster's description of Diana as 'a fiend and a monster' (*HTS 1992*: 82). Such descriptions had retained the associations of Diana with youth, informality and lack of educational attainment which had been used to characterize her from the beginning, but reversed their meaning so that what had once fitted her as a perfect bride for Charles could now be nothing but an irritation to him. At the time, Joan Smith had argued persuasively that such representations directly resulted from patriarchal structures of feeling which had invested heavily in the two-dimensional 'Shy Di' figure portrayed in the early 1980s. Hence the hostile response when Diana's own maturation rendered this image insupportable. From a feminist position, Smith pointed out that, 'Diana was coming under attack for aspects of her personality which *hadn't* changed'.[22] For Smith, as a feminist and refusing recourse to the royal feminine as a means of negotiating the public/private distinction, what was at stake therefore was not the content of Diana's personality but her ability to have one at all.

While anti-feminist misogyny featured heavily in the popular press's representation of trouble in the royal marriage with Diana principally responsible, gender was not necessarily the determinant structure operative here. The coverage was led by the Rupert Murdoch-owned press, where it was framed by Thatcherite discourses which celebrated macho values of independence and exhibited hostility to certain kinds of inherited privilege, sharpened by the identification of Charles with 'soft', 'wet', decadent liberalism. The dominant parties involved regarded their position as anti-royal, and construed Diana as part of the royal establishment. Their misogyny is undeniable, but it must be understood as being motivated strategically as a useful means of royal-bashing.

The pro-monarchist response to these attacks was undertaken in various texts and images issued during 1991 to commemorate the tenth wedding anniversary of Charles and Diana. The official family photograph by Snowdon discussed in the previous chapter is one example. As has been seen, this attempt to combine backward-looking discourses of rural Englishness with modernist codes of fashion, style and advertising was only partially successful in securing positive press coverage. In advance of this, unofficial material such as Penny Junor's joint biography, *Charles and Diana: Portrait of a Marriage*, and Rachel Mark Clifford's, *Charles & Diana: A 10th Anniversary Celebration* (both 1991) poured scorn on tabloid stories of marital tension, Diana's 'anorexia' and her alleged over-ambition.[23] While Clifford's celebration brooked no suggestion of marital conflict, Junor employed a more investigative approach which allowed that there had been some internal and external problems with the Waleses' marriage during the 1985–7 period but that they had been resolved by the time of writing. In varying degrees, both Junor and Clifford employed the normalizing strategies tried and tested by the Windsors since the late 1960s and to a large extent formalized by Robert Lacey's 1977 biography of the Queen, *Majesty*. The keynote of all of these representations was an understanding of the royal family as essentially ordinary people doing extraordinary jobs. Ben Pimlott has described *Majesty* as an innovative book which subsequently became paradigmatic through its synthesis of tabloid-style 'revelation' and sober analysis, to which we might add fascination and sympathy with the royal.[24] This combination proved hugely popular with readers and served to rejuvenate royal popularity. Junor's book exemplifies the fracturing of that synthesis in the face of splits within the monarchy, ever more intrusive tabloid journalism, and shifting notions of gender and political conservatism.

Robert Lacey's own book *Princess*, from which the 'Cinderella' passage quoted at the head of this chapter comes, is an early example of the difficulty of sustaining the synthesis achieved in *Majesty*. In *Princess* Lacey eschewed the investigative style to produce what he referred to as 'the shortest book I have ever written', whose 127 photo-graph-heavy pages contain only 37 pages of text.[25] Joan Smith referred to it as 'a royal scrapbook for the simple-minded'.[26] While there is some truth in criticisms of evasiveness, it is equally clear that Lacey's trademark style was simply not adequate to deal with the romantic and mythic registers that Diana's marriage activated in royalist discourses. Late in the book, Lacey struggled to make sense of Diana in relation to politics. In so doing, he anticipated what Elizabeth Wilson would call in 1997 'the unbearable lightness of Diana'; what might be understood as the political power derived from defining the 'feminine' as the antithesis of politics. Lacey referred to unnamed 'cynics', who viewed Diana's popularity as being akin to that of 'the other great success story of 1981, the Social Democratic Party'. Since, for these cynics, the popu-larity of the SDP derived from its 'extraordinary ability to avoid speci-fying exactly what it would do', Diana's success might seem open to the same criticism. 'But,' as Lacey quickly added, 'royalty is not poli-tics.'[27] Presumably her success at fulfilling the 'dignified' function of the monarchy, in Bagehot's terms, outweighed her apparent failure at the 'efficient' one. Lacey professed to believe, as did Bagehot, that the special function of royalty is unaffected by a vacancy at its centre; indeed, that royalty works best as camouflage for power exercised from elsewhere. But, as Margaret Homans has pointed out, Bagehot's distinc-tion between dignified and efficient is logically unsustainable, and can be maintained only by the manipulation of 'separate spheres' ideolo-gies of gender.[28] Diana's popularity upset this delicate balance. The powerful mythic and romantic registers to which 'Diana' played appeared to Lacey as an excess of the dignified character of monarchy. To the combination of investigative and pro-monarchist journalism practised by Lacey, the figure of Diana could not help but seem an excess of appearance over content, an anachronistic resurgence of royal mystique. In response, Lacey dropped any pretence at investigative journalism and employed the discourse of mystery, magic and fairy-tale. Opposite the passage just quoted from *Princess* there appears a small photograph of a thin-looking Diana, dressed casually and apparently shouting angrily at someone or something out of shot. None of this expressivity is registered in the simple caption 'Princess in blue jeans. Shopping in Balmoral, August 1981'.[29]

Junor's journalistic credentials are highlighted on the inside back cover of *Charles and Diana*, which lists work for a variety of newspapers, the satirical magazine *Private Eye* and television consumer programming. A *Guardian* review of an earlier biography of Charles is quoted as saying that Junor is 'one of the best, least gushy royal writers'. The jacket blurbs frame the book's aim to address popular emotional investment in 'the wedding of the century' (the title of its first chapter) by the assimilation of evidence and analysis into a 'portrait of a marriage' (the title of its last). Despite the announcement of this project on the opening page in terms of 'evidence' and 'conclusions', the synthesis of *Majesty* is not emulated. Junor's tone throughout is businesslike, and realist discourses dominate the book, but both are encompassed by a straightforward development of the myth as found in Lacey's *Princess*. Here was Cinderella grown up, a homemaker with children of her own. Where in *Majesty* Lacey had combined revelation and analysis, Junor employed 'insider' knowledge to substantiate a representation of Diana as mature Cinderella. In the face of the revelations of bulimia that were shortly to be substantiated by Morton, Junor asserted that 'nothing has caused Diana more amusement' than myths of an eating disorder. Later in the same chapter, entitled 'Diana's appetite', Junor went on to don the pose of the investigative reporter, explaining that rumours of anorexia nervosa were started by misunderstandings of royal eating habits.[30] The point here is not simply that Junor's treatment of the eating disorder issue was either misinformed or economical with the truth, but that the synthesis of revelation, analysis and affiliation associated with the *Majesty* style of royal writing had already degraded into cliché. The posture of investigative but sympathetic journalist has dissolved into disinformation, accompanied by an overblown discourse of insiderism. At the same time, whereas Elizabeth II's status as Queen had installed the question of her agency at the centre of the royalist discourse of *Majesty*, Diana's status and position were naturalized – ineffectually – by a reactionary appeal to essentialist gender identity.

In a manner by now standard, Junor framed and explained Diana's charity work by reference to her maternity. One chapter, entitled 'The Charitable Princess', opens with a fairly neutral description of Diana's involvement with the Birthright charity, but the text is dominated by a full-page photograph opposite of Diana, standing next to Charles, holding up the newly-born Harry. A later chapter, 'The Growing Children', is mainly concerned with Diana's active involvement with the British Deaf Association and contains as much about Charles's experiments in organic farming as it does about the children, William and Harry.[31] Throughout the book Charles's public role is presented in terms of a long-term, serious and intellectual project. 'Parenthood,' according to Junor, 'affected Charles dramatically.' The first and most symptomatic of these dramatic effects was a series of attempts to intervene in intellectual debates, initially over medicine and architecture, and then the environment.[32] In some contrast, Diana's involvement with 'caring' charities is presented as a natural and limited extension of her own maternity. Subsequently, it was exactly this slippage between public and private self that privileged Diana as icon. It is striking that in Junor's book it works in the service of reinforcing the patriarchal power of Charles and domesticating Diana. Thus on the final page of *Diana and Charles*, the following definition of the secret of Diana's success is offered:

> What she has created for Charles is a secure base, a warm, comfortable, happy home that he can come and go from, as his work, his sports and his whims take him, without having to explain or justify himself. Diana, meanwhile, gets on with her life, her work, her friends, the children, and with all her various hobbies and sports.[33]

Romance readers like those studied by Janice Radway would surely have been disappointed with this conclusion. Junor seems to go out of her way to stress the hero's autonomy and his absolute resistance to the sensitive and caring influence of the heroine. In fact, the appeal of *Charles and Diana* is to a fragmented set of readerships. Its emphasis on a notion of maturity (defined implicitly as a state where personal affective relations are neutralized by maternal and spousal responsibility) and its businesslike tone may imply a more accurate picture of aristocratic and royal marriages than that suggested by Morton. However, its realist posture negates from the first an investment in the royal romance as a love story. The notion that Diana had indeed made such an investment (misguidedly enough) has been a crucial factor in allowing her story to be read in terms of working-class and middle-class understandings of marriage as combining emotional and economic ties. At the same time, while Junor never explicitly privileges the masculinized public sphere over the feminized domestic sphere, their separation here clearly works in the service of patriarchal power.

In the 1997 *HTS*, Morton described the 1991 books and articles that celebrated the Waleses' tenth wedding anniversary as welding 'new bars to [Diana's] jail' (*HTS 1997*: 12). The publication of such material, including by implication the Clifford and Junor books, is portrayed as playing a large part in Diana's decision to participate in the project that became *Her True Story*. But Morton's was by no means the first revelatory biography of Diana to appear in 1992 and his mythologization of Diana need not have come to dominate her cultural meaning. As noted above, both Nicholas Davies and Lady Colin Campbell anticipated many of Morton's revelations. But, in addition to its claims for unique insider information from sources among Diana's family and friends, Morton's book was stylistically very different from these immediate predecessors. Where Davies and Campbell sought to demystify royalty, Morton was more interested in reworking the public/private slippage associated with royal femininity (used earlier by Junor to reiterate Diana's domesticated and secondary status) to assert a counter-myth in which Diana was at the centre of the national symbolic. For Morton, revelations of Diana's victimization at the hands of the Windsors were strategic elements in the displacement of the royal family by a new figure of national integration.

Davies and Campbell had spiced up the demystifying approach pioneered by Robert Lacey without breaking from its fundamental emphasis on the royals as real people. Campbell breezily discussed a rounded Diana with faults as well as virtues, who had never fully submitted to the formal rigours demanded by royal status, whose preoccupation with her media image was understandable if, also in Campbell's view, inflected by a competitive flirtatiousness, and whose adult life was characterized by an empowerment narrative of sorts, a 'transition from deflated Princess of Wales to Diana the Good'.[34] Similarly, Davies presented himself in the revelatory mode, as explicitly demystifying Diana's personality and unmasking what he called media 'hype' and 'nonsense' concerning her aristocratic status.[35] Both Campbell and Davies rejected the Cinderella myth in the name of realism, and their biographies work according to the logic of disclosure. But by 1992 and in the context of Charles and Diana, this had a very different cultural meaning from Lacey's reasonable investigation of the Queen in the 1970s. In all major respects, Lacey's position as responsible investigator was made possible by a balancing long-standing respect for the institution and function of royalty. Once this had been eroded, chiefly in the sphere of the popular press in the mid- and late 1980s, revelation of the royals as 'real people' became much more corrosive of royal prestige.

Femininity and empowerment in *Diana: Her True Story*

Like Davies and Campbell, Morton utilized disclosure. Unlike them, he combined it with mythic discourse. Like them, Morton began with the exhaustion of the Cinderella narrative, but he retained an investment in it even as he redirected that investment towards different figurations of female transformation. Morton's narratives offered Diana as an icon of femininity set in opposition to an implicitly patriarchal and impersonal royal family. This femininity is defined in terms of warmth, of feeling, as itself an emblem of the personal. By extension, the act of publicizing its story was to rescue femininity-as-personal-feeling from its imprisonment in the Palace. Thus what were presented in the realist discourse of Campbell's biography as failings on Diana's part to submit to the formal rigours demanded by royal status, became in Morton's story indices of her transcendent personality, which found it hard to brook what he portrays as the empty protocol of a discredited crown. At another level, Diana's unhappiness constituted evidence of her victimization by the same.

If, as Joan Smith had argued, the anti-Diana tabloid commentaries of the late 1980s had simply reversed the polarity of her qualities of youth, populist appeal and glamour, Morton's strategy turned the tables once again. Here Diana was offered as, on the one hand, an object of sympathy and, to some extent, of inspirational significance, and on the other hand, as mythic embodiment of human affectivity in the feminine. This double appeal was held together by reinvigorating the Cinderella myth rather than unmasking the patriarchal power structures behind it. *HTS* maintained emotional investment in the romance by stressing Diana's belief in it. What was wrong was that Charles had betrayed her and popular emotional investment in it by failing to give up his attachment to Camilla Parker-Bowles. Both sides of this appeal were sustained by an essentially pre-feminist paradigm of the wronged woman. The crux here is that the Diana of *HTS 1992–3* and *HNL* is disallowed active sexual desire. In comparison with contemporary royal biographies, this was already outdated. Before the publication of *HTS*, Lady Colin Campbell's more realist *Diana in Private* had already dispensed with the spotless and chaste Diana-image. In 1994 Anna Pasternak's *Princess in Love* anticipated *HNL* by offering the potentially explosive details of Diana's affair with James Hewitt in the form of a full-blown romance. Campbell's breezy style described Diana as an ordinary person with ordinary sexual desires, faults as well as virtues, and a much cared-for confidant in Hewitt. Unlike Campbell, who used the word 'confidant(e)' clearly and directly as code for lover, throughout his books Morton used this and a variety of similar terms with a vagueness that obfuscates sexuality.[36] For Campbell, adultery was 'the royal antidote' to the specific tensions attendant upon royal and aristocratic unions. Both her overtly class-centred approach and the investigative mode employed by Davies presented Diana's seeking friendly, romantic and sexual satisfaction outside marriage as perfectly normal and understandable given the nature of her marriage.[37] Morton strategically eschewed this and set the standard for dominant pro-Diana representations. All in all, the attenuated narrative of female empowerment in the 1992–4 Morton biographies is consonant with the threatened female figures of nineteenth-century novels rather than with feminist iconicity. It was not just that Morton strategically reinvigorated Diana's reputation as a sexual innocent; he based her appeal on her sublimation of personal sexual desire into maternity and generalized 'warmth'.

As the contrast with Campbell's *Diana in Private* makes clear, the sublimation of Diana's sexuality in the Morton biographies works strategically to obfuscate social and economic class and to offer Diana as a transcendently female figure. The issue of sexuality is thus crucial to the ideological project of *HTS*, in which femininity-as-human-affectivity is positioned in opposition to and as a replacement of the monarchical establishment. At best, then, the critique of monarchy and patriarchy enabled by Morton's biographies is compromised by the elision of class difference in the figuration of Diana. At worst, the question of gender difference itself is displaced behind its symbolic deployment in a contest over rival definitions of monarchy. Different versions of the biographies handle these tensions in different ways. The initial hardback publication of *HTS* ended with a discussion of Diana's current state of mind and future hopes. The paperback edition that followed it contained a Postscript in which the focus shifted to a critical meditation on the historical implication of the monarchy's inability to deal equitably with the Princess. There the Princess's story became an exemplum of the Crown in need of revision, and the book ended with the warning that 'The jury is still out and it is by no means certain that the verdict will be favourable to the monarchy' (*HTS 1993*: 170). Only the supplemental status of the Postscript allows the femininity narrative to remain centre-stage in the 1993 *HTS* as it had been in the initial 1992 version.

Against these senses of the strategic deployment of femininity-as-human affectivity there needs to be placed an understanding of *HTS* in terms of 'testimony', the bringing into the public realm of suffering caused by the private exercise of patriarchal and monarchical power behind closed doors. Both Julie Burchill and Beatrix Campbell, in books heavily reliant on the Morton myth, have emphasized the feminist implications of *HTS* in this light. For Burchill, the book was Diana's 'message in a bottle', not only 'cataloguing the wrongs that had been done to her from Day One', but doing so in what was 'unmistakeably' her own voice.[38] Campbell elaborated further, devoting the bulk of her chapter entitled 'Testimony' to the Morton collaboration and quoting from an interview with Morton himself in which he explicitly aligned himself as pro-feminist and 'anti-establishment'.[39] Campbell registered the importance of Morton in mediating Diana's testimony somewhat more than Burchill. She presented him as 'safe hands' rather than as an inert bottle, exempting Morton from her much more critical sense of the ambiguously sexist and democratic activities of the tabloid press in general.[40] While the importance of Morton's books in mobilizing popular sympathy and support for Diana on this basis should not be underestimated, claims for their status as feminist testimony must be treated with caution.

The *Sunday Times* serialization which pre-dated first publication, and to a large extent structured consumption of the book by media and public, was dominated not by the empowerment narrative but by the logic of revelation. The initial extracts were accompanied by a front-page synopsis and commentary under the headline 'Diana driven to five suicide bids by "uncaring" Charles' on 7 June 1992.[41] This material included three 'sensational assertions' as Morton later described them: that Diana suffered from the eating disorder bulimia nervosa, that she had 'attempted suicide' several times, though not necessarily with intent to end her life, and that throughout their married life Charles had continued a close, secret relationship with Camilla Parker-Bowles (*HTS 1997*: 213–14). These revelations doubly compromised any narrative of female empowerment. First, they stressed the most extreme and self-destructive effects of Diana's alleged victimization. Then also, the details of the state to which Diana had been reduced functioned as indices of abusive monarchical and patriarchal power as much as they were biographical details about a person with some control over her media representation.

Even in the 1997 *HTS*, the possibility of fully realizing the empower-ment narrative was compromised by the inclusion of 46 pages of 'Diana's own words' from the 1991–2 interviews. The prominence given to this material in the pre-publication serialization and in the book itself undercut the upward personal trajectory of the biography, drawing attention to Diana at her most weak and objectified. As will be seen later, other commentators were quick to define their own versions of the Diana narrative in contradistinction to what could easily be por-trayed as Morton's emphasis on outdated and demeaning material.

Such problems highlight the generic instability of the biographies and the ambivalence of Andrew Morton as mediator, both of which are obfuscated by the self-presentation of *HTS* as a kind of displaced auto-biography. The trajectory of the cover blurbs implies an increasing sense that truth-telling was a liberating experience in itself, indepen-dent of the impact of the release of information on Diana's public status. Whatever the truth of this notion, it does not sit well with the biographies' mythologized presentation of their central character, their suppression of her own sexual and emotional relationships, and deployment of innuendo concerning Charles and Camilla, which blurred the distinction between a close emotional relationship and a sexual affair. The use of conventions from romance fiction and exem-plary (auto)biography to centre Diana's narrative was itself under-mined by the *Sunday Times* serializations of 1992 and 1997, which positioned *Diana: Her True Story* as royal *exposé*.

Further, the exigencies of disguising Diana's collaboration with the book's production severely deformed its testamentary structure. By necessity, Morton's function as mediator stood in place of the control-ling narrative voice of a recovering or strengthened self. Without such a self, the strongest narrative in the book objectifies Diana and repro-duces her status as acted upon. In place of Diana as narrator the book offers Diana as female emblem, disguising her double lack of agency (biographically and textually, as narrated self) by mythologizing her in terms of the binary of femininity/monarchy. Even with the best of intentions, the more Diana's status as endangered female is empha-sized, the more her spokesperson takes on the mantle of rescuer and the more Diana is objectified.

The issue of sexuality is again key here. Until the posthumous edition of *HTS*, Morton presented Diana's 'warmth' as being directed towards de-sexualized outlets such as maternity, her relationship with the public, and ostensibly platonic relationships with male friends. By suppressing reference to Diana's own romantic and sexual relationships, Morton can be seen as reiteratering the double standard of gendered sexuality. Arguably, at least for Lady Colin Campbell, Diana's class position exempted her from the double standard. Nevertheless, a critical reading of this configuration is rich in feminist and progressive possibilities. As the work of Nancy Armstrong, Kath McPhillips and Lisa Blackman suggests (see chapter 1 above), a sense of the psychological costs of such sublimation enables us to recognize Diana's figuration of specifically female and specifically (post)modern subjectivity. Morton's biographies do indeed allow us to see these costs in terms of a lack in Diana's life, and thus prepare the ground for feminist re-readings. But they are configured in terms of personal tragedy, as the second-best alternative to an emotionally unreciprocated marriage. Hence in Morton, Diana is propelled into a public performance of affectivity by a lack of domestic fulfilment. This class-bound narrative is universalized only by an appeal to a transcendent femininity defined in terms of emotional affectivity.

The posthumous 1997 *HTS* delivered much more fully the empowerment narrative promised in each version of the Morton biography. In doing so, it brought together the trajectory of Diana's personal fulfilment and the mythic narrative of the emergence of femininity 'for itself'. By declassing Diana's experiences, or in effect by reclassing them from the royal and aristocratic codes of marriage for political and familial exigencies to middle-class and working-class codes of marriage for romantic love, Morton enabled her to be claimed by a kind of populist feminism, but he also provided a framework by which femininity could be understood symbolically, taking the issues raised by her life out of the realm of sexual politics altogether. It is to these ambiguous effects, and the complexities of the 1997 *HTS* that I will now turn in detail.

The concluding chapters of the book represent Diana as turning the frustrations and disappointments of her private life into a fulfilling public life. The 'warmth' rejected by her husband is deployed instead for humanitarian work (*HTS 1997*: 235 and Chapters 12 and 13, passim). Diana's separation and subsequent divorce, and above all her successful adoption of a public ambassadorial role in 1996–7, added significant dimensions to earlier editions of the biography. At last, her status as single woman allowed Morton to register a sense of Diana as possessing sexual desire (*HTS 1997*: 261–2), albeit very guardedly and with most emphasis on its frustration. More significantly, Morton elaborated further the femininity/monarchy dichotomy which provided the ideological structure for the previous volumes in order to present Diana explicitly as a type of feminist. Here he took up explicitly some of the arguments made by commentators such as Julie Burchill and Suzanne Moore, who had themselves been strongly influenced by his earlier books.

Back in 1994, on the penultimate page of *HNL* Morton had outlined something of an impasse in Diana's life. 'It is her dearest wish,' he wrote, 'to be accepted and appreciated for the person she is rather than the position she occupies. A woman who is admired for what she does rather than who she is' (*HNL*: 160). These carefully chosen words silently rework conventions about monarchy and gender. They subtly reposition Diana outside the royal, where person and position are yoked together by heredity and thus cannot be in opposition. (Her non-royalness is spelled out more explicitly further down the page.) Yet, Diana is still understood according to the sense that symbolic action constitutes some kind of work, that was pioneered by the Windsors' own sense of themselves as 'the firm'. Another ideological formation associated with the monarchy, the sense of royal persons as being both ordinary and extraordinary, is reworked specifically through Diana's femininity to construct her as sharing the same basic problems as any other woman defined in a patriarchal culture by reference to her relationships with men. Thus Morton conflated royalty with patriarchy, and utilized ideological structures associated with the monarchy to present Diana effectively as superseding it. The brilliance of this manoeuvre should not divert attention from the circularity of Morton's own Diana myth, which had conflated Diana's doing with her being almost as much as overtly royalist material. 'What she does' remains an empty category here, scarcely distinguishable from 'who she is'. 'The person she is' in the first sentence of this passage is placed in opposition to 'who she is' in the second. This is as mystifying as the traditional constructions of royal femininity discussed in the previous chapter. Morton's formulation recalls Hugo Vickers's account of Queen Elizabeth's authentic self being defined through its resemblance to her public image. Both make sense only by invoking exceptionalist notions of symbolic action associated with royal status and especially royal femininity.

In the closing chapters of *HTS 1997*, Morton returned to the transformation from 'being' to 'doing' the frustration of which was the endpoint of *HNL*, and reworked it through Diana's adoption of a public ambassadorial role. He gave this a specifically feminist meaning by reference to an incipient critique of male egotism and aggression as an explanation for global problems, and the championing instead of 'feminine values' and 'feminine qualities of intuition, compassion, compromise and harmony' (*HTS 1997*: 255–7, 283). In passing, Morton also mentioned an interest in 'women's issues' such as partner abuse. Two elements in particular of this construction of Diana as feminist humanitarian continue to make Diana's cultural significance both powerful and contentious. The major innovation of *HTS 1997* over its immediate predecessors is its sense of Diana as deploying femininity in the public sphere, in a putatively politicized way to contest patriarchal power and its effects. Yet this was superimposed over the myth Morton had already outlined, which was prominently recapitulated in the reproduction of Diana's 1991–2 'testimony'. Morton thereby reflected a huge amount of posthumous media coverage which read this public deployment of femininity as the direct uncovering of a private female self, and codified it in terms of the most clichéd stereotypes of gendered identity. Thus, without perceptible irony, Diana is defined on the final page of *HTS 1997* as a feminist icon via 'the way she tapped into a spiritual undercurrent in society ... her intuitive and nurturing nature' (*HTS 1997*: 283). Here, as throughout the Morton biographies, Diana is elevated to mythic status by reference to a diverse and often conflicting combination of ideas about femininity. In this case these include pre-feminist stereotypes of chastity, spirituality and sacrifice, feminist notions of therapeutic recovery, empowerment and inspiration, and more ambiguous images which fused the domestic 'feminine' values of maternal care with symbolic intervention in issues of public health, welfare and even with the land-mines campaign, military and political questions.

With all their complex and often contradictory implications, the overall effect of Morton's biographies was to foreground the gender binary. But they did so in ways that abstracted it from lived experience and class relations and positioned gender in terms of a symbolic economy. As with the dominant constructions of Diana hitherto, her femininity was still presented as transcending her social and economic class, ethnicity or other forms of identity. By making the symbolic feminine/masculine dichotomy the basis for taking Diana's part against the Windsors, in itself perhaps only a strategy to pre-empt the implication of republicanism or to divert attention from the importance of the media or from Diana's own sexuality, Morton made discussions of monarchy and power inseparable from issues of gender and power. This is clearly important for popular understandings of gender, but it also has potentially wider implications. For one thing, the strategic

deployment of femininity to legitimate the royal family had been dis-
abled. At the same time, the function of the monarchy as model family
was also rendered problematic.

In the same year that *Diana: Her True Story* first appeared, Michael
Billig published the definitive sociological study of popular consumption of the monarchy in the 1980s and early 1990s. *Talking of the Royal
Family* is a work of social psychology, based on interviews with 63 families from working-class and middle-class backgrounds. In it, Billig
argued for an understanding of the royals as providing a cultural space
for negotiating relations of power and affectivity within the family.[42]
For our purposes, the great innovation of Billig's book was that it highlighted the importance of irony and cynicism rather than deference in
people's actual discussions of the monarchy. Such language breaks free
of the ideological structures employed by the mass media, dominated
on the one hand by the deferential and fantastic discourses found in
royal souvenir books and the like, and on the other hand by the misogynistic and/or fetishistic news values of the press, that is logics of revelation and scopophilia in the case of the downmarket tabloids, and
logics of revelation, scopophilia and analytical commentary in the rest.
However, like his feminist predecessors Judith Williamson (in
Consuming Passions) and Rosalind Coward (in *Female Desire*), Billig
regarded the *semantic* structures through which the monarchy is disseminated, in particular its status as paradigmatic patriarchal family, as
fundamentally narrowing the horizon of these popular reworkings of
royal meanings. Billig therefore retained a (Gramscian) Marxist sense of
ideology as mystification. Even in non-deferential, postmodern mode,
talking about the royal family was a means of 'ideological settling
down' into the positions assigned by dominant power relations.[43]

For Billig, the construction of an interest in the royal family as part
of a 'woman's realm' worked to police its distinction from the public
and the political spheres and hence to downgrade it. He did acknowledge the possibility that as a focus for the investment of female desire,
typical and emblematic royal events such as romances and weddings
might be construed in such a way as to outflank patriarchal power and
to validate such feminized interests in the royal. However, any such
potential could only be realized momentarily and through fantastic
identification which forgets the 'royalness' of these events and hence
fails to come to terms with the way that their exemplary nature is
encased within structures of family and nation.[44] This ideological structure, Billig's description of which I take to be fundamentally accurate,
is exploded by the foregrounding in Morton's books of gender as

crucial to the project of monarchy. By popularizing the notion that the femininity associated with Diana was antithetical to the royal family, *Diana: Her True Story* positioned gender explicitly at the centre of debates over monarchy, family and nation. The activity of talking about the royal family could now become a process of making these connections rather than forgetting them, of stirring people up rather than settling them down, of remarking the boundaries between margins and centre.

Consideration of the sensationalistic practices of the popular press makes it clear, if any proof were needed, that stirring people up is not necessarily linked to changing power relations. The mixed and contradictory nature of the Morton biographies gave rise to a variety of positions on gender, royalty and the nation. Many journalists, academics and others, including Diana herself, as well as those people with less access to mass media, attempted to elaborate further on the Morton myth. It is to this work that I now turn.

Panorama and other elaborations of the Morton myth

The Diana/Charles antithesis outlined in mythic form by Morton was elaborated further almost immediately by Julie Burchill in the *Modern Review*.[45] In 'Di Hard: The Pop Princess' Burchill largely transposed this opposition from gender to that between high culture and popular culture, via contrasting references to Beethoven, Shakespeare, Racine, Solzhenitsyn, Kafka and Charles, and 'pop', exemplified by Diana's interest in or similarity to the Beatles, Barbara Cartland, Billy Joel, Tom Selleck, Neil Diamond, Madonna, McDonald's, Capital Radio and Joan Collins.

The gendered priorities of the Morton myth were reasserted by Diana's most direct and sustained autobiographical statement, the 1995 television interview with Martin Bashir. The interview, shown in the BBC's current affairs slot *Panorama* on the evening of Monday, 20 November, garnered enormous viewing figures, peaking at 23.2 million, attracted saturation media coverage and caused a power surge equivalent to the boiling of 300,000 kettles for a calming bedtime drink after the programme.[46] It cemented the mythologized femininity articulated by Morton and formalized the definitive iconic status of Diana which was only fully activated after she died. What received most immediate media attention were Diana's admission of adultery with James Hewitt, her comment on Charles's relationship with Camilla ('there were three of us in this marriage, so it was a bit crowded') and the allegation that royal staff had interfered with her mail in order to frustrate attempts to develop a new public role. Overall, the more than 20 million viewers were offered two things: personal substantiation of and further detailing of the revelations in *Diana: Her True Story* and *Her New Life*, and evidence that Diana's trajectory of empowerment had gone beyond that framed in those books.

In the *Panorama* interview Diana intensified the narrative of *Her True Story*. On the one hand she amplified the evidence of her victimization by the royal establishment, and on the other hand she stressed her recovery to claim the status of a 'strong woman', a phrase repeated several times. This emphasis was signalled by the programme's opening sequence, shown in advance of the opening titles, which literally played out the displacement of one transformation narrative by another. The very first images of the show were library pictures of the 1981 wedding, accompanied by Bashir's voiceover identifying the scene and adding 'But the fairytale wasn't to be'. This was followed by a clip from the interview with Diana at her most assertive, stating 'She won't go quietly, that's the problem. I'll fight to the end, because I believe I have a role to fulfil, and I've got two children to bring up.' Only then did the opening titles roll.

The interview proper was structured partly as linear narrative, with intertitles such as '1985 – Press reports of difficulties in the royal marriage began to emerge', and partly as thematic juxtaposition. Out of this emerged testimony of suffering and victimhood, stressing isolation within the royal family, lack of training and support, media intrusion and bulimia, and referring also to post-natal depression, self-harm, marital tensions and partner infidelity, and betrayal by lover Hewitt. This was balanced by assertions of recovery and strength framed by therapeutic discourses, a narrative of maturation and the articulation of a wish for some kind of ambassadorial status. What linked these two areas was the argument that it was only through her own experience of having been a victim that Diana had become able and fitted to relate publicly to others who had also suffered, especially, she suggested during discussion of the Morton book, women. Invited by Bashir to define her role, Diana expressed a wish 'to be an ambassador for this country … to represent this country abroad'. Few commentaries emphasized this and, one suspects, few viewers took it very seriously. Where Diana was depicted as an exemplary figure in the subsequent media coverage, as Lisa Blackman has argued, this was in terms of privatized suffering rather than as an empowered public figure.[47] It was only later, in a process culminating in the land-mine related trip to Angola, that this aim of parlaying empathy into a public and national ambassadorial role, the 'queen of people's hearts', was fully realized.

One thing foregrounded in the *Panorama* interview that had received rather less attention in Morton, Burchill and other coverage, was the role of the media. In the interview Diana's comments often conflated media pressure and intrusiveness with the difficulties caused by a negligent royal system. But at one point at least she drew upon an explicitly feminist and therapeutic understanding of her relationship with the media: 'it's become abusive and it's harassment.'

As with the Morton books, the *Panorama* interview employed a variety of discourses about femininity. While Diana described herself several times as a strong woman, when it came to matters of sexuality she reactivated the discourse of female innocence and victimization found in the earlier Morton biographies. In admitting adultery with James Hewitt, Diana seemed to anticipate criticism by referring to her own strong feelings and a sense of Hewitt's subsequent betrayal; 'Yes, I adored him. Yes, I was in love with him. But I was very let down.'[48] This assertion has been coupled with Diana's explicit refusal to accept Charles's marital infidelity to produce a sense of the *Panorama* interview as a 'refusal of sexual shame' and an 'expose [*sic*] of the sexual politics of elites'.[49] Such a reading can be supported by reference to Diana's emphasis on her desire to develop the ambassadorial role, her accusations of obstruction on the part of Charles's staff, her protests against her being treated as if she were still an immature 19 year old, and her laughing insistence on the importance of a 'fulfilling job' over a relationship with a man. However, this inspirational significance must be held in tension with a sense that the interview elided class privilege in order to present Diana's position as exemplary. The programme's inspirational qualities are also held in check by its privatized presentation of gendered identity and its framing by implicit and explicit notions of gender that pre-dated the public culture of second-wave feminism.

The most significant of these frames was that of the confession. This was iterated not only in the admission of adultery, but also in the posing and answering of questions concerning blame for the marital breakdown, and in Diana's self-presentation and performance more generally. Her appearance was sober; mostly dark even black clothing, heavy black eye-liner, her manner and tone of voice deferential but assured. For most of the time Diana was shown listening and speaking with her head inclined a little forwards, so that in order to make eye contact with Bashir she had to look slightly upward. In this and other ways the presentation of Diana's performance reinforced its identification with the confessional mode, and hardly registered its mass dissemination. She was filmed from the front and slightly to her right, with the camera at head height and at the same distance as Bashir, who occupied a symmetrical position in front of Diana and slightly to the left. This gave the effect of Diana directly addressing viewers as if they were present. All of this belonged to, in the terms Kathleen Dehler has used to discuss realist feminist fiction, the (self)-repressive discourse of the confession, rather than the liberating mode of 'sociological autobiography'.[50] It was only extrinsically that the interview could be seen as a public mode of address. The trajectory proposed by Diana herself in the interview from victim to empowered survivor remained contained within this privatized form. Her claim to be a 'strong woman' was thereby offered in terms of a personal fulfilment that was isolated from social relations of any kind, except possibly those of maternity. It therefore worked against any linking of her empowerment to female friendship or feminism in general.

   This orientation was continued in the single way that Diana's self-presentation breached the distinction between public and private, when she explained her wish for a public ambassadorial role based on her knowledge of suffering and her ability to communicate. In fact, this desire was enunciated twice, in two different registers. First in the form of a straightforward wish for an official occupation for which her personal and public experience would prove useful, and subsequently in terms of the displacement of the royal, as 'queen of people's hearts, in people's hearts'. The privatized and confessional format of the interview itself offered no way of mediating between these discourses, except by grounding the realist discourse of a professional occupation in an overarching mythic construction of femininity as transcending public and private. Thus the *Panorama* interview presented the sign of Diana as national ambassador within the myth of Diana as transcendent feminine. It thereby foreshadowed the final development of the Morton myth during her lifetime, Diana's reinvention of herself – and her media image – as strong woman in the mode of the charity professional and the unofficial national ambassador. In many ways Diana's visit to Angola in January 1997 to publicize mine-clearing and the campaign to ban land-mines would deliver on the desire for an ambassadorial role. In fact, its status as independent, and even anti-governmental, gave it a power that the official national role desired in the interview could not have provided. The *Independent* columnist

Suzanne Moore, who had previously written unsympathetically on Diana, construed the visit in terms of Diana's triumphant assumption of a public and political role and simultaneously control over her representation.[51] The notion that Diana brought a powerful and potentially politicized femininity into the public sphere is one that has exercised many commentators since, and can be traced back to the claim for ambassadorial status voiced in the *Panorama* interview. Rarely for Diana, it was words that were important here. The *Panorama* interview was thus crucial but exceptional in the framing of Diana narratives, putting into words, which at the time were not taken seriously, what she would eventually become best known for enacting.

The empowered Diana initially glimpsed in the 1992 *Diana: Her True Story* and brought into more focus in the *Panorama* interview was subsequently recast in a variety of ways. The theme was taken up in some of the posthumous publications which narrativized Diana's empowerment in terms of the development of an ability to present herself through dress and appearance in a way that communicated personally across mass media.[52] A muted variation on the theme was taken up by Elizabeth Wurtzel, who wrote of Diana as occupying a somewhat uncertain position with regard to tragedy, glamour and power. Although Wurtzel reiterated a positive version of the Morton myth, she described its appeal in terms of a momentary 'breaking free' from patriarchal control and construed its structure in terms of a continued fracturing of public from private.[53]

Conversely, as early as August 1992, Camille Paglia warned against conflating the power of Diana's mythic significances with her personal power. Paglia suggested that the multiplication of mythic roles which Diana performed only served to reproduce her for voyeuristic pleasure, and that they put extreme pressure on Diana to sustain them.[54] This warning highlighted the fraught relationship between Diana, the media and the public that is obscured by the various transformation narratives based on the Cinderella story. Yet alternatives existed: between 1992 and 1996 some realist representations of Diana did circulate in the popular media.

Realist representations of Diana empowered, 1992–6

From 1992 it is clear that Diana herself sought to develop a more dynamic and influential public role, with much success. Even before this date she was known for an interest in causes such as AIDS and drug rehabilitation which were outside the conservative traditions of royal patronage. In his 1992 biography Davies pointed as far back as December 1990 to Diana's speech at the Annual General Meeting of Turning Point (a charity involved in treating addiction) which was widely interpreted as criticizing government policy. 'Those rosy words Care in the Community,' Diana had said, 'do not, I believe, convey the harsh reality faced by the mentally ill when they are released from hospital.' The comments aroused the conventional 'storm of protest from MPs', but she refused to withdraw them.[55] After announcing a year out of public life in December 1993 these interests and activities were increasingly professionalized. In the immediate aftermath of divorce proceedings, in the summer of 1996, Diana dropped her figurehead role for more than 100 charities in order to concentrate in a more businesslike fashion on the six that remained (*HTS 1997*: 252–3).

Such moves were accompanied by newspaper features, often on the inside pages and in supplements directed primarily towards female readers, which portrayed Diana remaking herself as a businesswoman or an independent divorcée. The *Daily Mirror*'s February 1995 feature 'Diana – the business' suggested at the time an identification made later and more approvingly in Burchill's *Diana*: that the power-dressed, professional and ambitious Diana fitted the clichés of powerful femininity associated with the Thatcherite 1980s more than the 'caring' 1990s.[56] Features such as 'Diana – the business' and more extended supplements like the *Mail on Sunday*'s 'Diana: her own woman', which followed it, occupied a transitional position between the full-blown mythic representation of Diana as suffering femininity associated with the 1992–4 Morton volumes, and empowered charity professional and unofficial national ambassador recognised by Moore and the 1997 Morton.

What is significant about these features is that they represented the post-separation Diana in ways that were generally positive and sympathetic, but above all realist. They eschewed myth, either in terms of the royal or femininity, and related Diana to the project of embodying national identity in the lowest of keys, if at all. Diana was constructed here primarily in terms of a professional worker, with her celebrity status a fairly distant second. Even where 'feminine' concerns of fashion, shopping and cosmetics are discussed, she is presented as unexceptional and directly open to emulation. 'Diana – the business' described a network of business advisers and broke down her expenditure via a pie-chart. 'Diana: her own woman' explicitly distanced Diana from her former role as 'fashion icon', emphasized the professionalism of her work for the Red Cross, and poured scorn on the way that Charles and his advisers had allegedly quashed plans for Diana to become a British ambassador-at-large.

In comparison with the mythologies that preceded it and followed it, even in the same newspaper, the importance of the realist mode in 'Diana: her own woman' is striking. The concluding section of the piece does make some of the connections between public and private that were elaborated in mythic terms elsewhere. 'Her identity,' it states, glossed immediately as the love of helping people, 'was always closely bound to her work.' However, these connections are contained within an understanding of national identity predicated on the businesslike diplomacy and the conservative modernism of the Major government. She is linked to a project to restore good relations with Malaysia after the Pergau dam arms-for-aid row (stymied by Charles's advisers), and she meets regularly with Baroness Chalker, Minister for Overseas Development. International commerce is set against and privileged over Colonial history. Diana's foreign visits are short, focused and goal-oriented, to be contrasted with 'prolonged, formal foreign visits' which are 'merely a reminder of an imperial past'. Diana's charisma and iconicity are mentioned, and she is pictured ladling food out of two huge cooking pots surrounded by officials and a couple of African children. But the photograph is clearly posed and Diana wears a sheepish expression. Thus even the image of Diana the caring female draws attention to the formality of her performance. In the accompanying text this sense of formality is elaborated to produce an understanding of Diana's performance in terms of a public role as representing pre-existent national commercial and political interests. In this context Diana's qualities of empathy and the ability to communicate human warmth are presented as potential national assets. Were it not for the outmoded traditionalism of the royal family, she could have been deploying these qualities positively, 'officially pitching for Britain'.[57]

'Diana: her own woman' reworked Diana's cultural meaning in two ways. First it took her out of the context of the monarchy and removed her from the mythic status of performing national identity. The resultant independent and talented individual was then placed in the role of the professional ambassador. This realist representation of Diana has a significance beyond its fleeting appearance. It demonstrated the possibility of relating her activity to national and global interests without invoking mythic notions of the 'Queen in people's hearts' or femininity-as-affectivity. However, outside these contexts Diana was framed as nothing more than a career diplomat, working in the service of nothing more sympathetic than the interests of big business, and possibly the nation.

Diana vs. Charles

As the discontinuities between reportage in the same newspapers immediately before and after Diana's death showed, the orthodoxy of public grief was a late invention. Television and press representations of Diana following the 1992 publication of *Diana: Her True Story* are characterized by their diversity, internal inconsistency and the use of multiple perspectives. Itself utilizing a range of inconsistent discourses, Morton's work split the basic binary between pro- and anti-monarchist positions, which had previously structured media coverage of Diana and the Windsors, into a fourfold ideological opposition. After Morton, it was still possible to be in favour of Diana and the monarchy, or to be against both, with the added positions of being pro-Diana and anti-monarchist, anti-Diana and pro-monarchist. In fact before 1996, mass media coverage rarely offered up one or other of these positions in any definitive way. While individuals might take them up, such as for example Julie Burchill in 'Di Hard', and Nicholas Soames in his denunciation of the *Panorama* interview as a work of paranoia, before 1996 such positions were almost always presented in terms of an ongoing debate, whose resolution was perpetually deferred. Burchill's piece appeared in the self-consciously rebarbative *Modern Review*, while Soames's comments were made as part of a televised panel discussion prompted by the *Panorama* interview. It was only in 1996–7 that popular media began to attempt coherent resolutions of this fourfold ideological structure. This took place under a range of pressures to produce definitive readings, most significantly the intensification of Diana's iconic status independent of her connection with the monarchy apparent in the Dress Sale, the land-mines campaign and finally her death and popular responses to it. Even here, the ambivalent relation between Diana and monarchy, and the dependence of Diana's iconicity on symbolic structures associated with the monarchy continued to undermine coherent resolution of her cultural meaning.

Television documentaries and book-length biographies and discussions of the royal family characteristically employ a 'both ... and' rhetoric of disavowal. Critical and revelatory tendencies to demystify the allure of the monarchy, to present it as failing, or to demonstrate other kinds of royal unworthiness are balanced by the implication that the royal family are important enough to justify such attention. Typically, while James Whitaker's *Diana v. Charles* described its contents as 'the most explosive yet', it also promised to offer 'hope for the future of the British monarchy'. Even the relentlessly demystifying Kitty Kelley ended her 1997 tome *The Royals* with a sense of their continued survival. Beyond disgrace lay 'the need for enchantment' and the 'hope for renewal'.[58] A whole genre of monarchy-in-crisis books, videos and television programmes developed in the early and mid-1990s which combined serious consideration of the monarchy's constitutional function with more or less sensational revelations of royal behaviour.[59] A document entitled 'The Fall of the House of Windsor', with its gloating narration, can only be described as a royal video for royal-haters.

There is more at stake here than the strategic justification of an interest in the personal lives of celebrities that might otherwise be judged prurient. Jacqueline Rose has argued for an understanding of celebrity in general as a mode of licensing curiosity in the lives of others whose roots are to be found in psychoanalytic investigation of subjectivity and sociality.[60] More specifically, Michael Billig has shown how the complex public interest in the royal family as privileged, emblematic, ordinary and extraordinary is structured and ordered by popular activities such as 'double-declaiming' and 'form-filling'.[61] Billig's identification of these reading strategies across a diverse sample of people who aligned themselves with indifference, royalist or anti-monarchist positions strongly implies that the cultural centrality of the royal family outweighs affiliation for or against.

As was suggested earlier, the Diana/Charles antithesis popularized by Morton put at stake the containment of these readerly activities within patriarchal and monarchist ideological structures. In particular, the Diana/Charles split threatened to undermine the layering of national syntheses predicated on the royal marriage. The balancing strategies employed in the discourses of television, press and royal books worked to maintain and to stabilize these structures by containing the potentially explosive tension between the Diana myth and popular investment in the monarchy as exemplary family. It is worth looking at these strategies in more detail, since their success is not confined to the 1992–6 period.

The synthesizing of national identity upon the heterosexual union meant that the problem posed by Diana for mass media was a complicated one. It was rarely a matter of being able to take sides with either Diana or the Windsors. Instead a certain affiliation with both sides was required, hence the containment of different, often contradictory points of view within the format of an ongoing debate or flow of information. Common methods for handling the Diana/Charles antithesis were therefore based on offering readers multiple contradictory understandings of Diana within the same feature. At the same time, the hitherto popular construction of Diana's persona in terms of synthesis, as 'both ... and', was largely replaced by representations of Diana in terms of singularity, constructed explicitly in opposition to rival definitions. Direct claims to describe Diana's personality, significance and meaning were supplemented and complicated by discourses of judgement and argument.

Eventually widely disseminated among the British popular press, a typical example of this strategy was the cover story of the December 1993 edition of *Tatler*. This ten-page feature, headlined 'Diana: monster or martyr?' was composed of two main articles, one hostile to Diana and one supportive, and shorter comments by 50 celebrities, with the results of a survey of '1,000 hand-picked, well-informed people who quite probably have danced with the Princess of Wales or at least with a man who has'.[62] Although this description of the survey criteria implied that personal knowledge of Diana was the key to understanding the 'monster or martyr' question, the proliferation of answers in these three different forms suggested that meaningful content was actually being evacuated from the sign 'Diana' itself and power over meaning instead transferred to its readers. This impression was substantiated by the numerousness and diversity of 'opinion leaders' each of whom contributed a sentence or paragraph defining Diana. The list is a mixture of journalists, pop performers, nightclub owners and interior designers, minor aristocracy and others. It included such luminaries as Ruby Wax, Madonna, Peter York, Julie Burchill, Sir Peregrine Worsthorne, Trevor Nunn, Joan Bakewell, Imogen Stubbs, Count Nikolai Tolstoy, David Sullivan (somewhat euphemistically described here as newspaper proprietor), the Hon. Mrs Rocco Forte, novelist Sue Townsend, Dennis Skinner MP, nightclub-owner Johnny Gold, the UK's Eurovision song contest hope Lisa B, poet Fiona Pitt-Kethley, plastic surgeon Dr Freddie Nicolle, wit Frank Muir and film director Michael Winner. No overarching perspective was offered; nor were *Tatler* readers offered any criteria with which to arbitrate between the often conflicting points of view expressed.

The two leading articles, by the *Daily Express* diarist Ross Benson and Charles's biographer Anthony Holden, offered antithetical ways of making sense of these proliferating meanings. Both arguments hung on the multiplicity of identities readable into Diana's image. Benson sought to resolve any ambiguities via a misogynistic understanding of femininity as performance, such that surface bore no relation to depth. Beneath the 'panstick of illusion', he wrote, lay a manipulative and capricious nature. 'What we have been witnessing,' he continued, 'is the victory of image over evidence and the institution of the monarchy has been sorely damaged as a result.'[63] By contrast, Holden contextualized the multiple meanings of 'Diana' with respect to its production and consumption as a conversation piece. In his article, part of which was quoted in the Introduction above, Holden came close to suggesting that the key to understanding 'Diana' lay in its production from codes of meaning, far from any definable or 'authentic' content. However, as the piece went on, it became clear that this was itself only an opening gambit in order to substantiate the authority of Holden's own reading of Diana. He presented the latter in the by now familiar form of personal insider knowledge of his subject, sharply differentiated from the diverse Dianas produced by the gossip of the ill-informed. Nevertheless, its place in the multi-voiced discussion of Diana-ness presented in the feature as a whole undermined the persuasiveness of this strategy. Although Holden invoked a sense of proliferating understandings of Diana as a term in process only in order to dismiss it, this sense was borne out much more forcefully in the feature as a whole.

The proliferation of contradictory readings of Diana noted in Holden's commentary and enacted in the 'Monster or Martyr' feature intensified during the mid-1990s and received a major boost from the *Panorama* interview. Coverage of the interview in the *Sun* newspaper was symptomatic in the way it contained the fracturing of the binaric syntheses predicated on the romance and familial narratives. On the day of the interview the paper gave over its first five pages to diverse and contradictory Diana coverage. The front page led with the upset caused to Diana's eldest son William. Pages two and three balanced this under the headline 'I won't hurt my boys'. Later in the same edition no less than six alternative viewpoints were articulated. Anne Robinson contributed a populist version of the Morton myth in a column headed 'She has evened the score for every cheated wife and mother'. In fact, Robinson eschewed consideration of the children and instead reiterated the Diana/Charles antithesis in terms of Diana against the 'Establishment'. This was followed by paragraphs from four different commentators placed side by side on the same page to construct the meaning of Diana in terms of a debate, while an editorial took yet another view.[64] Two days later, the paper printed the

Panorama interview in full, along with a four-page extract from Anna Pasternak's book *Princess in Love* detailing Diana's affair with Hewitt, and a further editorial that explicitly rejected the suggestion made on *Panorama* that Charles give up the succession to his elder son, William.[65] Alongside these containing structures the *Sun* and other media ran phone-in polls predicated on either/or questions such as 'Do you think Diana is right to go on *Panorama*?' and later, 'Should Charles be allowed to marry Camilla?'[66] On 22 November the 'thought', a timely motto printed under the *Sun* masthead, underlined the opening out of debate over Diana with a pun. 'Let's have a Di-alogue', it read. The phrase was indicative of the ways that 'popular opinion' was solicited, gathered, articulated and structured by a battery of apparatuses including opinion polls, radio phone-ins and by phonelines sponsored by the tabloid press and on teletext.

In some respects, these developments can properly be seen as having democratizing effects. The multiplication of contradictory 'insider' and 'expert' perspectives on Diana served to devalue the authority of such positions. At the same time, the Diana/Charles antithesis was opened up as a public debate, rather than as the subject of privileged knowledge. Yet for all that control over the meaning of 'Diana' was thereby democratized, the terms within which it was constructed remained largely contained inside existing power structures. At one extreme pro-Diana positions were articulated solely in terms of reforming the monarchy; at the other extreme the Morton myth of empowered femininity was construed as transcending political affiliations and economic and social class. Thus when details of the divorce settlement became public the *Mirror* launched a campaign featuring a car-sticker with an image of Diana's head and the demand, 'Give her HRH back'. Conversely, *Independent* journalist Suzanne Moore celebrated Diana as feminist heroine alongside the Greenham Common women. As I have argued elsewhere, these attempts to stabilize Diana's iconicity by reference to a cultural politics of 'positive images' have a significant role to play, but must be supplemented by engaging more explicitly with the conservative elements of Diana's gender mythology.[67]

The production of conflicting Diana iconicities on mainstream television and in the tabloid press involved the appropriation or co-option of elements of popular feminism. When Diana appeared at a fashion awards show at Lincoln Centre, New York in January 1995 with a radical hairstyle entitled the 'flip', both the ITN *News at Ten* and the *Daily Star* read the move in terms of an epistemology of style.[68] Both newsreader Trevor Macdonald and *Star* journalists compared the look to that of female celebrities regarded as powerful. Madonna was featured heavily in both contexts, and both read the 'flip' look as an empowering move. *News at Ten* launched a mini-biography of Diana through her changing hairstyles, from 'Shy Di' through the 'big hair *Dallas* look', taken as indicative of a more confident persona, towards the present. This implied what was made more explicit in the *Star*, which directly connected the haircut with the break from Charles, reading the new hairstyle as an emblem of independence. While this appeared a little like a kind of mainstream low-brow version of the sub-cultural practices identified by critics such as Dick Hebdige and Angela McRobbie, in both contexts the notion of style as meaning, and as potentially empowering, was firmly contained. Both the *Star* and *News at Ten* set up the 'flip' style as meaningful, offered several comparisons and confessed them-selves unable finally to resolve what its meaning might be. Not far beneath the surface of both treatments was the fear, for British audiences, that Diana's new-found empowerment might result in her leaving the UK and setting up home in New York or elsewhere in the USA. Such anxieties were displaced on to the 'problem' of the meaning of the hairstyle created spontaneously in New York, and thereby rendered trivial. The *Star* used a multitude of bad puns and drew upon a variety of expert opinions, none of which could offer a definitive reading, while the news item was placed in the quixotic 'and finally' slot at the close of the programme. As this example makes clear, representations of a more or less empowered Diana were overdetermined in the popular media by the necessity of containing the Diana/Charles antithesis. It was perfectly possible for the *Star* and *News at Ten* to represent Diana as independent of Charles. What was at stake in this case was to maintain a sense that she was not independent of Britain, and this was achieved by containing the rep-resentation of empowerment through style within a trivializing framework and through the presentation of multiple contradictory readings.

These containment strategies were necessary only because during the period 1992–6 the 'Diana' sign made the transition from a magical syn-thesis of binary oppositions to a focus of argument and debate. In *Diana: Her New Life* Andrew Morton had written that the pre-separa-tion Diana was seen as 'an exquisite enigma … whose elusive personal-ity was a blank canvas on which we were invited to paint our fantasies and dreams' (*HNL*: 9). Morton, like Holden in the *Tatler* piece discussed above, went on to offer his own, definitive insider version of Diana.

But his biographies initiated a proliferation of discourses of Diana from a range of perspectives which were not containable even in forms such as the enigmatic female.

From a structuralist perspective, these developments can be read as splitting the 'Diana' sign, prising signifier away from signified. Holden's account of multiple Dianas as 'reflections of their creators' can thus be reformulated to suggest that the meanings of 'Diana' were produced discursively according to the investments of those reading it, rather than being determined by their object, the referent and real person Diana. The point that needs to be made here is that, *pace* Holden, there never was a natural, direct relation between signifier, signified and referent; such connections are generated by linguistic systems, are thus culturally produced and are in the last analysis arbitrary. What changed during this period was the extent to which the discourses of the popular media could arrest the slide of signification. Previously, access to 'what Diana is really like' was conducted in terms whereby character, personality and biography were merged and subsumed into a discourse of iconicity. This formed part of an ideological structure which effectively naturalized patriarchal power and national identity by reference to Diana as embodying deferential femininity, related to the royal family via narratives of romance and family. Therefore the shift from definitive descriptions to judgement and argument, despite its essentially conservative motivation by a felt need for containment, opened up to a deconstructive reading the processes by which the meaning of 'Diana' had historically been produced.

Contesting the Morton myth

The centrality of the Morton myth to the production of Diana's cultural iconicity is reflected not only in the elaborations discussed above but also in the variety of material that has positioned itself explicitly in opposition to Morton. The combination of different discourses in the Morton texts and in the *Panorama* interview articulated feminist tropes to essentially pre-feminist notions of femininity. This provided a variety of 'Dianas' which could be developed in the service of a range of ideas about gender, monarchy and national identity. Conversely, explicitly anti-Morton positions are also diverse, though they tend to seek to stabilize understandings of Diana.

During the 1992–6 period most attempts to refute Morton recalled the negative pre-1992 representations of Diana which portrayed a general lack of intellect and a particular failure to appreciate high culture, combined with an excessive attachment to shopping. To this they added a somewhat prurient focus on her relations with men such as James Hewitt, Oliver Hoare and Will Carling, and on her supposed mastery over her representation in the media. Where this kind of writing appeared in the tabloid press, it was framed by misogynistic and anti-feminist notions of the enigmatic female, sometimes taken as far as the full-blown *femme fatale*. Shortly before the *Panorama* interview, for example, the *Daily Express* published a collaged illustration of a smiling Diana pulling the strings to animate a puppet-like image of herself. This accompanied an article by Brian Hoey which began by contrasting Diana's lack of academic qualifications with her 'first-class honours degree in media manipulation'.[69] Like Benson in the *Tatler* article and Nicholas Soames in his comments on the *Panorama* interview, Hoey presented Diana as dangerous here not only through the control over the media he ascribed to her, but also through her lack of self-control, which made her a prey to the need for a 'daily "fix" of media attention'. Unlike them, Hoey's tone was almost neutral, and he drew upon misogynistic notions of the *femme fatale* only implicitly. The headline under which his piece appeared, 'Diana is just a shrewd and selfish manipulator', made these connections much more explicit than the text itself. This apparent neutrality enabled Hoey to recycle much of the text for his contribution to the expert panel brought together by the *Sun* to discuss the *Panorama* interview four days later. There a different sub-editor with another agenda framed his description of Diana in antithetical terms to the *Express* headline, as a 'Role model that we can't ignore'.[70]

These shifts underlined the complex ways in which realist and mythic discourses were employed strategically across differently motivated representations of Diana. Benson, Soames and Hoey ostentatiously deployed realist journalistic language to position themselves as unmasking the mythical Diana produced by Morton. The obvious trope here was to distinguish between an actual person and a set of media representations. Yet this realist discourse was often framed, explicitly or implicitly, by negative myths of femininity. These were made visible in the tendencies to exaggeration displayed overtly by Benson and Soames, and used to headline Hoey's *Express* piece. Where Morton had elaborated Diana as transcendent feminine in terms of victimization, empowerment and maternity, these and similar writers invoked the transcendent feminine as at best enigma, at worst *femme fatale*. In neither case was there a sense of the power structures which

underlay the relationship between Diana and the producers and consumers of media representations. Thus for Morton it was simply a
matter of presenting the truth about the real Diana, while for the
others it was a matter of tactical manoeuvring in the struggle against
one or more of Charles, the monarchy and 'the establishment'. The
illustration in the *Express* of Diana 'pulling the strings' enacted this
oversimplification. Readers' attention is drawn first to a large image of
Diana cropped at the waist at top right, and then follows the line of
her arm, down the strings to the smaller full-body image. It thereby
put into visual form the surface/depth metaphor used by Benson in the
Tatler. The relationship between Diana and her media image is thus
presented as one of complete control, with no reference whatsoever to
the ideological and discursive frameworks used to produce such
representations, nor to the relations between their producers and
consumers.

By drawing upon the work of feminist cultural critics such as E. Ann
Kaplan, Marina Warner and Myra Macdonald, it is possible to see constructions of enigmatic femininity such as those made by Benson and
Hoey as fulfilling several functions.[71] At one level, as demonstrated
most directly in *film noir*, they construct female independence in terms
of sexuality and disorder, and move to contain it. As Kaplan has
argued, the cinematic thriller or *noir* genre presents female characters
in prominent roles that are unconstrained by the fixed functions of
wife, mother or prostitute.[72] Through their attempts to contain female
power and sexuality through other means, such films become limit
cases of patriarchal and androcentric ideology. In wider cultural contexts, the evacuation of selfhood associated with enigmatic status shifts
femininity from an historical form of gendered identity into a 'sign, a
symbol for something beyond'.[73] Both these versions of enigmatic femininity can be found in the anti-Morton representations. Benson, Hoey
and Soames all ascribed to Diana both cleverness and a lack of self-
control, the classic attributes of the *femme fatale*. Benson and Hoey
developed this association further. In discussions ostensibly focused on
Diana's relationship with the media and mass audiences, they emphasized her friendships with men like Hewitt, Gilbey and Hoare.[74] Such
pieces draw upon anxieties over female sexuality understood as disorder which belong to a longstanding anti-feminist tradition in order to
defend the monarchy as a patriarchal institution against Diana as an
unruly female. Benson's piece went so far in this direction that it presented the Diana/Charles antithesis at full force. There was no way of
accommodating Diana within or proximate to the world of the royal

and she must be expelled. The article ended with a quotation from an unnamed friend of Charles who spoke of the separation as like 'being unchained from a monster'.[75]

The extremity of this position was in fact rare, and was contained in this case by the multi-perspectival debate structure of the *Tatler* within which the piece is embedded. The more neutral tonality of Hoey's work was much more common. What was at stake here was less a straightforward issue of gender and sexuality than a more complex set of overlapping conflicts and connections in which gender and sexuality functioned as signs and symbols as well as for themselves. In this context, the notion of Diana as enigma worked more than anything to contain the disruptivity of the Diana/Charles antithesis and to stabilize the romance and familial narratives through which the royal fulfils its function as exemplifying identities of various sorts. This is not to divert attention from the use of anti-feminist material by Hoey and others, but to see its use as being strategic, overdetermined as it is by considerations other than those based on gender relations.

The cross-cutting of discourses of royalty and gender complexifies the significance of this material. Negative representations of Diana such as those by Benson and Hoey offered opportunities to play out anti-feminist traditions with general implications. However, the primary struggle here is over control of royal cultural space, and gender difference is deployed symbolically on the part of rival combatants. Put into the historical context of royal representations, this material can be seen to be engaged in a retrospective masculinization of the monarchy as the 'other' of Diana.

More recently, the most commonly framed objections to Morton's biographies have focused on their emphasis on victimization at the expense of an empowerment narrative. *Diana: Her True Story* has always been more popular than *Her New Life* and perhaps surprisingly this remained so in the immediate aftermath of the death. In the USA, for example, one million copies of the former were reprinted, in comparison to only 400,000 of the later book.[76] Morton's decision to publish transcripts of Diana herself from 1991–2 in the revised *Diana: Her True Story – In Her Own Words* intensified the association of his name with an understanding of Diana as victim. The *Daily Mail* headlined its coverage 'Anger at betrayal of Diana'.[77] Rival biographers and commentators were quick to define themselves in opposition to this element of Morton. When the *Sunday Mirror* serialized revelations from Diana's hairdressers Tess Rock and Natalie Symons it mimicked the title and cover format of Morton's book on its front and inside pages. In large typeface that took up almost half a page, it was announced that 'Diana was not the bitter, unhappy woman portrayed by Andrew Morton. She was full of love and laughter.'[78] The three-week serialization presented itself as delivering specifically feminized knowledge in the form of gossipy details of sexual relationships and appearance. Like Morton, Diana's femininity was presented as transcending class difference, but unlike Morton this was done in emphatically non-mythic terms, by stressing the 'all-girl bond' between 'the ultimate Uptown Girl' and 'her down-to-earth soul sisters'.[79] As with the *News at Ten* and *Star* pieces described earlier, the Rock and Simons material demythologized Diana only by reference to a normative femininity defined through a trivializing discourse of personal relationships. However, this was directed towards a female audience and positioned itself with respect to a public culture of female solidarity, as opposed to the private confessional of the Diana-Morton relationship.

Richard Kay and Geoffrey Levy similarly positioned themselves in opposition to Morton in their *Diana: The Untold Story*, first published as a part-work in the *Daily Mail* from January to April 1998. According to Kay, in his introduction to the first part, 'to really know Diana was to discover a woman of much greater depth and complexity than the bitter bulimic portrayed by biographer Andrew Morton'. As in the 'Diana Diaries' serialization, Morton was used here as exemplifying an overly downbeat and victimized version of Diana. Kay and Levy presented themselves as correcting what they called Morton's 'bleak picture' of a 'rancorous, loveless union that was doomed from the start'.[80] Again, like the hairdressers Rock and Symons, they sought to rehabilitate both Charles and the Charles/Diana relationship. Where the 'Diana Diaries' had emphasized romance and sexuality, after having assured readers that 'A special part of Diana's heart always belonged to Charles', Kay and Levy operated in a discourse that was both more serious and more mythic.[81] The 'untold story' turned out to be that Diana's achievement of maturity, via motherhood, a stable and warm friendship with her ex-husband, and at last the fulfilment of a public role and personal happiness ('landmines and love', as part ten was entitled), enabled the Cinderella myth to be reworked successfully after all.

As these last examples demonstrate, *Diana: Her True Story* casts a long shadow. The biographical details of Diana's last year, involvement in the land-mines campaigns, the Dress Sale and the reaction to her death raised the possibility of a definitive break with the structures set up by Morton. Yet these developments had been made possible by the ideological shift in the relationship between royalty and gender popularized in the 1992 biography. From *Diana: Her True Story* to *Panorama* to *Her True Story – In Her Own Words* the romantic myth of Diana as latter-day Cinderella was superseded by a quasi-feminist narrative of personal empowerment. This was accompanied by reversing the relationship between gender and power in the realm of the royal. The patriarchal structures of the royal family, in relation to which Diana's femininity had been constructed in terms of supplementarity, were displaced by an overtly feminized understanding of what royalty should be.

The Diana myth produced by Morton effected this move by eliding considerations of social and economic class. This narrative and descriptive strategy was put into visual terms by the cover illustrations on the successive editions of the biography, the earlier versions of which were discussed in Chapter 1 above. The paperback edition of the *Her True Story – In Her Own Words* (1998) bore on its cover a cropped shot from the Demarchelier studio session heavily utilized in the first edition. Here the popular response to Diana's death was taken as validating her complete transcendence of class, so the polo-necked jumper was at last deemed appropriate for the front cover, in an image tightly cropped to maximize Diana's head and to obviate recognition of the jumper as a designer item. Even this was not the final point on the trajectory. The latest version of Morton's biography, another 1998 paperback reissue with yet another chapter, bore on its front cover a photograph of Diana in the same white evening dress seen on the 1992 US edition, with Diana in black polo-neck on the back. This combination made visible Diana's status as the 'people's princess' in markedly simpler form than the earlier covers; it is also the first British edition to emphasize the latter half of the formulation. Perhaps this reiteration of Diana's uniqueness was a response to the proliferation of readings of Diana beyond the discourse of royalty.

Many representations of Diana have adopted these structures with comparatively little revision, offering them in a variety of discourses from the avowedly realist, in the *Mirror*'s 'Diana – the business' and the *Mail*'s 'Diana: her own woman', to the more mythic. Some readers and commentators (Burchill, Campbell and Robinson) understood this inversion outside the context of the royal, and for them Diana became an icon of empowered femininity, placed in opposition to patriarchy and 'the establishment'. Others, who considered themselves opposed to Morton and to Morton's Diana (such as Hoey, Benson and tabloid editors) sought to preserve the authority of the royal by containing the Diana/Charles antithesis within frameworks of debate and flow, and through reference to patriarchal notions of dissembling and enigmatic femininity. Both pro- and anti-Diana commentators engaged in a process of remasculinizing the monarchy in contradistinction to Diana's symbolic and actual femininity.

Several factors have militated against the resolution of these overlapping conflicts. In part they are mixed up in the long-lasting relationship between feminist identity politics and the mass media, for which neither co-option, appropriation nor recuperation is a fully adequate description.[82] We have seen how in the Morton books and in the *Panorama* interview tropes from feminist and pre-feminist culture were invoked to present as exemplary a privatized empowerment narrative. Despite the compromises of these articulations, it was more than possible to re-read them strategically and reconnect them with feminist traditions. But gender difference alone is an insufficient basis for understanding these developments. As well as activating appeals to both female solidarity and paternalistic care, this material also offered a notion of the princess ambassador as a feminized alternative to traditional understandings of the royal. Thus at base the instability of 'Diana' is generated by the complex and shifting relation between femininity and the royal, terms which in 1992 became simultaneously antithetical (Diana vs. Charles) and coextensive (the people's princess). This relation is further complicated by the ways that in the discursive constructions of Diana described above, femininity is presented at various levels of signification: as signifier of gendered identity, itself defined in multiple ways, and as sign within a system of national and familial myth.

Almost all the material under discussion here has registered the proliferation of 'Dianas' and sought to stabilize its meaning. This has been, as we have seen, a self-defeating process leading to further proliferation and further instability. The key moves in this argument have all been reversals. To put it crudely, the popular media first celebrated a Diana feminized in terms of deference, lack of intellectual and cultural authority, and supplementarity, then vilified the same qualities. Morton reversed the polarities once again, and elicited direct responses which denied the accuracy or the significance of Diana as a warm caring female, and indirect responses which sought to contain both these oppositional positions. In all these cases Diana's femininity was so much at stake that few stopped to consider how and why Diana had come to emblematize femininity at all. In the previous chapter I outlined the importance of understanding the production of Diana's femininity in relation to notions of the royal. In the next, we shift our attention to the ways in which visual images of Diana played into and across gender difference.

4
A Life in Images

How is she ever – short of abandoning her blonde highlights, gaining a couple of stone and slobbering [sic] around in unprincesslike clothes – to be taken as anything more than an exquisitely coiffed airhead?

Sunday Times, 1985[1]

Iconicity

The use of the term 'icon' to describe Diana in popular and academic discourses suggests both the power and the ambivalence of her image.[2] Visual images of Diana are widely understood as making identity present, but there is much less agreement on the status and the significance of such processes of figuration. If indeed as Suzanne Moore has put it, 'Diana became a blank screen available for all kinds of projection',[3] an historical explanation of how and under what conditions this blankness has been filled in, is long overdue. Images of Diana are the sites of multiple and often contradictory investments, calling up notions of royal and non-royal, ordinary and extraordinary, Englishness, Britishness, nationality and the international, of feminist icon and patriarchal phantasm, femininity as lived experience and Woman as abstract symbol. This chapter therefore examines the relays between images of Diana and constructions of identity. It combines critical and historicist approaches, showing in detail how images of Diana function as sites of contest over identity, and bringing to light the hidden processes of displacement that constitute the cultural meanings of Diana as an icon.

Visual representations of Diana make identity present in two main ways. At one level, visual images of Diana are taken as direct evidence of the feelings, thoughts and identity of a real person At another level, Diana images circulate as privileged signifiers of femininity, maternity, white racial identity, Englishness, Britishness, Commonwealth identity, humanity, (post)modern mediated subjectivity, and so on. Investments of both kinds – in Diana images as revealing a particular selfhood, and in 'Diana' (the sign) incarnating a range of identities – are made meaningful by processes of displacement predicated on resemblance. On the one hand, photographs are almost always seen as expressing Diana's 'inner reality', whether in terms of deferent heterosexual white femininity in 1980–1, or as self-assured campaigner against land-mines in 1997. On the other hand, this photographic expressivity underwrites the status of 'Diana' as emblem. Whether the identities to which Diana gives specific form are apprehended as ahistorical essences or as historical variables, in the first, and often in the last instance, Diana stands for them because she looks like them. For the most extreme partisans and also many acerbic critics of Diana's significance as a cultural icon, her selfhood and her significance can be read off from her image.

The first images of Diana to be widely disseminated publicly were already freighted with mythic significance. These were the well-known press photographs taken in September 1980 at the 'Young England' kindergarten, which showed Diana holding a couple of children as sunlight filtered through her dress, silhouetting her legs. Such images called up a series of meanings informed by mythic constructions of gender, race, and national identity, which can be conceptualized in terms of a series of semiotic chains, for example:

The sun shining through Diana's dress – innocence – virginity – control of sexuality – English rose.

Children by her side or in her arms – ideal maternal femininity – English rose.

Blonde hair, white skin – glowing in light reflected from the sun – ideal romantic femininity – English rose.

These are not the only semiotic structures by which it is possible to read the kindergarten photographs, but they were and to a large extent still are dominant ones. In such readings Diana's image naturalizes certain notions of ideal female, familial, racial and national identity. Still, even these powerful readings (made dominant in part by the successful presentation of Diana as their exemplum) have been destabilized by certain versions of the empowerment narratives described in the previous chapter. The kindergarten photographs have come to mark the starting point of a trajectory of victimization, recovery, empowerment and self-realization, whose culmination is marked variously by the photographs of Diana next to an Angolan minefield taken in January 1997, or the images of Diana's dresses associated with the Sale the following June, or the paparazzi photographs of an embrace with Dodi Fayed published in August. This trajectory has even made it possible, as we will see, to re-read the kindergarten image so as to release a notion of female sexuality repressed in its original context. Visual representations of Diana thus emerge as sites of contestation and objects of ambivalent investment, whose significance remains dynamic.

The reliance of these empowerment narratives on largely visual evidence points up a significant tension. Assumptions of her photographic expressivity tend to confine Diana within the realm of the visual, the to-be-looked-at, yet have been crucial in constructing her as a positive image of female transformation. In general, the only commentators to deny that images of Diana directly express her identity do so from anti-feminist positions. The perceived lack of fit between Diana and her image is used to open up an attack on her fakery and media manipulation. By contrast, celebratory writing tends to reiterate the notion that Diana's feelings, thoughts and identity can be directly 'read off' from her image. The valency of this belief changes over time. The notion that by 1997 Diana came to forge an expressive language of images which constituted a kind of self-representation bears a very different meaning from investing directly in her symbolic significance as national mother in the 1980s. Yet readings of Diana images as expressive can end up reiterating objectifying discourses of female visuality and the ideological syntheses of royal femininity. The question asked rhetorically in 1985 by the *Sunday Times*, quoted at the head of this chapter, remains unresolved.

The main task of this chapter is to trace a history of investments in the expressivity of Diana images. In the concluding sections, I will go on to argue that Diana's involvement in land-mines campaigns in 1996–7 and particularly the Dress Sale of 1997 can be read as reconfiguring, dislodging or at least showing up the limits of expressive discourse. What is key here is to link representations of Diana as an active agent, bringing ethics and values associated with femininity into the political sphere, with what appear to be strategic moves on her own part to rework her cultural meaning. The point is to make a connection between Diana's visibility as an agent in the public realm, and traces of intentional interventions in her self-representation which destabilize the expressivity of her image.

Expressivity

Although the notion of the expressivity of Diana's image is almost as old as her media profile, it was only developed into its most intense form immediately after her death. Then, a combination of mourning practices and a felt need to emphasize her personal empowerment gave rise to the belief that Diana had developed the ability, perhaps beyond that of any other human being, to utilize the dissemination of her image via mass media to communicate at the level of the personal. One of the most extreme statements of this belief was made by Irène Frain in her 1998 book of Diana photographs. According to Frain,

> photographs of Diana should not be looked at as if one were leafing through a souvenir album, misty-eyed with nostalgia. These photos need to be interpreted as one would a deathbed confession. Whether consciously or unconsciously, Diana said everything there was to say through them.[4]

This way of putting it may be unusually explicit, but Frain here articulated an assumption that grounds the popular consumption of Diana images. It goes back in one form or another to 1980, but is especially visible in television representations of Diana and in the memorializations published shortly after her death in glossy magazines, part-works, newspaper supplements and picture books such as *Diana, The People's Princess* (1997) by *Sun* journalists Arthur Edwards and Charles Rae, Anthony Holden's *Diana: A Life and a Legacy* (1997) and Michael O'Mara's *Diana: A Tribute in Photographs* (1997). Frain's explicitness makes clear the way in which a sense of the expressivity of Diana images enables all of these forms to present her as transcending distinctions between public and private, personal identity and mass consumption. Frain rejects a viewing of Diana images as simple photographic records. As mere souvenirs, such images could only summon up the pain of loss. Instead she understands the photographs dynamically, as communicative acts on the part of Diana, a mass-mediated 'deathbed confession'. Whereas the 'souvenir album' circumscribes the emotional charge of photographs within the bounds of personal memory, Diana images, according to Frain, communicate both emotion and biographical narrative across mass media. Moreover,

Frain imagines these acts of communication to be independent of intentionality ('consciously or unconsciously'), complete, and perfectly transparent ('Diana said everything there was to say'). This is a powerful fantasy of pure communication beyond the contingencies of the linguistic.

Commemorative books and magazines took for granted this logic of expressivity. Typically they are composed of images of Diana, glossed by short, portentous captions. Frain's book and Holden's *Diana: A Life and a Legacy* push at the limits of this logic, presenting large numbers of images without immediate comment.[5] The former takes this to an extreme by reproducing the photographs across the whole page, and deferring commentary until the very end of the book. On the final few pages the images are reproduced in miniature, with captions stating factual information concerning date and place, and iconic explication such as 'To conquer the kingdom of hearts, she begins by subjugating the body', and 'The spectre of depression'.[6] Through this separation Frain's text enacts the redundancy of description which is the logical end of a belief in photographic expressivity: Diana's image communicates without need of words. Emanating from outside Britain – the book developed from a series of articles in *Paris-Match* – Diana's iconicity is derived here without explicit reference to royal status. Instead, Frain presents Diana as transcending the distinction between public and private through what she calls (in translation) 'style'.[7]

When in the week after her death, British television presented moving and still images of Diana without verbal commentary,[8] and in the ensuing months photograph-heavy newspaper supplements and hastily assembled picture books appeared, all these forms drew upon long-standing assumptions about the expressivity of Diana's image. Previously unpublished photographs had provided both authentication and, according to Andrew Morton, major selling points of the 1992 *Her True Story*. Images of Diana as a girl from the Spencer family album and the Demarchelier photograph 'from her study' testified to a life before the Windsors, and independent of them. Later, the paperback version boasted on its cover of 'a new chapter and 28 new photographs'.[9] For a period after Diana's death, beliefs that her self was spontaneously invested in and available from her image were strongly enforced by the popular press. To analyse the ways in which such a belief had come about, via a discourse of cultural meaning, was deemed tasteless, ridiculous or even heretical.[10] Yet such analysis is made necessary by the complex and important role played by ideas that Diana's image was directly revelatory in authorizing different viewing positions and different investments.

In the late 1980s and early 1990s, the notion that Diana successfully expressed herself through images validated populist understandings of her unhappiness, over and against the deployment of expert and insider royal knowledge. Thus for instance images of Diana's emaciated body were seen to make available to ordinary readers the truth that she was suffering from the eating disorder bulimia, while this was being denied by the explanations of royal experts. Examples such as this and the ill-fated tours to Canada and India in 1991–2, especially when glossed in the ways offered by Morton, presented Diana as someone trapped within an alienating cultural environment, using the dissemination of her image via mass media to somehow get out messages to the public. Later, Diana came to be celebrated for signalling empowerment through the development of a muscular body and deployment of clothes, as for example when her glamorous appearance at the Serpentine Gallery on 29 June 1994 upstaged Charles's admission of adultery televised on the same evening. Hence, for those with a positive investment in Diana, her ability to express herself through image can be viewed as the subject of a long struggle for control over self-representation, or more dangerously, used directly to read off her condition at any given moment.[11]

However, the sense of Diana's image as being expressive can work to undermine the biographical empowerment narrative and to maintain patriarchal assumptions and objectifying practices of representation. The notion that Diana communicated through her image 'consciously or unconsciously', as Frain put it, substitutes a kind of mystical immanence for any sense of a real person who might exercise agency over acts of communication, and may wish to maintain a distinction between personal and private. This sense of expressivity draws on a long history of Enlightenment thought about truth, evidence and representation. Sandra Kemp has shown how, especially in relation to faces, Western culture retains assumptions about the relationship of appearance to coherent identity which are ultimately unsupportable. It is these structures that account for what she calls the 'wellnigh magical or religious power' of Diana's face, whose image effectively materialized a persona. Kemp's point is to highlight the problematic at the centre of Diana's iconicity: the moment of apparently purest self-revelation, in which words are transcended by image, is also the moment where Diana is most entirely dehumanized, turned into 'a mixture of news commodity and marketing tool.'[12]

As Kemp's formulation suggests, the trajectory of Enlightenment representations of selfhood is given a decisive, intensifying twist by modern technologies. The photographic expressivity attributed to Diana is a cultural product of two major developments in the recent history of the mass media in Britain. The successful international celebrity photograph magazine *Hello!*, launched in 1988, followed by imitators such as *OK!* provided important cultural spaces in which Diana's trajectory could be traced in terms of combining royalty with celebrity. More significant to begin with were the effects of shifts in newspaper technology and working practices subsequent to the launch of the *Today!* daily and the moving of News International plant from Fleet Street to Wapping in the 1980s. The reproduction of colour photographs in these mass-circulation publications gave renewed impetus to the genre of features predicated upon and built around such photographs. It was this genre which reinvigorated speculation over Diana's health and tensions in her marriage, within the form of sensational journalism. The popularity of such material empowered the 'paparazzi' and hostile or indifferent 'royal watchers', over and against those who, like Penny Junor, portrayed themselves as insiders, who were dependent on royal patronage for information.

A decisive period for the relationships between Diana, royal representation and mass media was 1991–2, especially the visits to Canada (October 1991) and India (February 1992) and subsequently, after the publication of Morton's *Her True Story*, to South Korea in November 1992. During this time photographers accredited by and dependent upon the royal establishment found it, as one of them wrote later, 'extremely difficult to get a smiling picture of them both'.[13] They ended up instead with a series of images of Prince and Princess looking embarrassed to be together and Diana looking unhappy, and most expressively the infamous picture of Diana turning away her head rather than kiss after the polo match in Jaipur. In addition, the India visit generated for accredited and unauthorized photographers alike a series of images of Diana alone, reaching out to the underprivileged.[14]

The consequent shift in power over royal representation is demonstrated by the careers of male journalists such as Anthony Holden, James Whitaker and even Andrew Morton, all of whom moved through a period of being within the loop of official royal patronage, to define themselves as critics of the Windsors and Diana partisans. Diana's own trajectory paralleled theirs while making it possible, not least by generating a market in royal biographies for anti-royalists. *Diana: Her True Story* was followed within a year by Whitaker's *Diana v.*

Charles and Holden's *The Tarnished Crown*. In turn, notions of Diana's photographic expressivity were deployed in such books as a means of defusing criticism of intrusive journalism. Hence in the laudatory *Diana: A Life and a Legacy*, Holden captioned a series of images with the assertion that 'of the unauthorised pictures inevitably taken of her, wherever she went, there were many which captured her private self charmingly enough to win her eventual approval.'[15] Such formulations negate distinctions between official and unofficial, private and public photography. They erase the complicated – and often gender inflected – relationship between Diana as a person and the production and consumption of her image by media workers and publics. The aggressive and often sexually objectifying discourse of some actual photographers, of 'the chase', 'the hunt', 'shots', 'aimed lenses' and 'blitz' have been rigorously repressed.[16]

Ever since 1981 the notion of Diana's expressivity has proved particularly useful to the popular press in framing stories based on photographic images while forestalling criticism of the invasive practices of such journalism. Most notoriously, in November 1993 the *Sunday Mirror* and *Mirror* printed secretly taken photographs of Diana exercising in a private gym. The images were accompanied by textual commentary which presented Diana's body as a direct index of her persona:

> Diana's body language at the gym was a telling barometer of her moods.
> In the pictures she is stunning.
> Although they were taken in secret, she could not have looked better if she was posing for a designer exercise video.
> Never before has the world so plainly been shown that – far from being ill – she is in magnificent shape.[17]

In this case, the presumed ability to 'read off' from Diana's appearance is used to try to naturalize the objectifying discourse of the photographs and their presentation in the newspaper. The photos on the cover and inside page, in both of which Diana's pelvis occupies a central position with her legs spread, directly evoke pornographic representations, as do the strapline comments 'How the Throne shaped Di's sex appeal' and 'And the best is yet to come'.[18] The explicitness of this example is rare, and notorious, but it illustrates how the notion of the expressivity of images of Diana's body can readily function in objectifying fashion. The intention is no doubt to sanitize the pornographic elements of the *Mirror* gym photograph features by employing the language of revelation. In this case, the images were so clearly objectifying and their publication so contradictory to Diana's intentions that it was not possible to obscure the inherent voyeurism. Still, in general the discourse of Diana's photographic expressivity successfully masks its objectifying tendencies.

Beatrix Campbell's very ambivalent sense of 'tabloid democracy'[19] catches well the combination of republicanism and anti-feminism that characterizes many Diana representations in the popular press. It was the invocation of the notion of expressivity that in large part enabled the press to sustain the practical contradictions of pursuing and glamorizing Diana. From very different perspectives, woman-centred and feminist workings of Diana's iconicity are themselves caught in something of a double bind. Given the need for visual confirmation of an empowerment narrative, how is it possible to avoid reiterating patriarchal definitions of femininity in terms of spectacle and immanence? Before focusing on this question in detail, it is important to review how historically a range of iconic registers has been employed to present images of Diana as indicators of biographical truths and transformations.

Her life in images

Notions of Diana's photographic expressivity are articulated at their least intense in what might be called the 'fashion princess' genre exemplified by scores of picture books and video cassettes which presented Diana as blossoming through the 1980s into the most glamorous member of the royal family.[20] This was achieved, it is explained, by her taking control of her self-presentation with the help of advisers from *Vogue* and, later, a close relationship with designers such as Giovanni Versace and Catherine Walker. The 1980s fashion princess books maintained a sense of Diana as both ordinary and extraordinary through a variety of formations. These included the assimilation of Diana into the structures of royal femininity and positive representations of Diana as a consumer whose tastes and interests are comparable with most women. Typically, coverage of casual dress alternated with high fashion, and Diana was presented as bridging high street and haute couture. Above all, in narrative terms, she was depicted having to develop a sophisticated fashion sense from a low base. An extreme example of the genre promised to enable readers to 'discover for yourself what makes Princess Diana look so good', which turned out to be a combination of fitness routines, diets, make-up tips and fashion advice.[21] Here, in Ann Chubb's *Royal Fashion and Beauty Secrets* Diana's trajectory was presented as a metamorphosis any girl could emulate, provided she had the money.

Diana's marital separation and divorce, and the Dress Sale of June 1997, produced ideological shifts in this material which were further elaborated posthumously. For the fashion princess books of the mid-1980s such as Martina Shaw's *Princess of Fashion* and Jane Owen's *Diana Princess of Wales: The Book of Fashion*, Diana's empowerment through clothes functioned implicitly to sustain and strengthen her supplementary position within the royal family according to traditional gender hierarchies. The 1992 publication of *Her True Story* opened up the possibility of a revised narrative. In this story Diana turned away from an unhappy marriage in which her behaviour and status were circumscribed by monarchical structures often recognized as oppressively patriarchal, to generate a redeeming and empowering relationship with the public through her image. Posthumously published picture books and newspaper coverage often intensified the iconic register of this trajectory, not only presenting Diana's use of fashion as indexing empowerment but also reading Diana images as expressing a wordless communication with the public. A series of books appeared at the time of the first anniversary of Diana's death, which registered this intensified iconicity while also maintaining the technical and stylistic preoccupations of the earlier fashion princess genre. These included Georgina Howell's *Diana: Her Life in Fashion*, Graham and Blanchard's *Dressing Princess Diana*, and the autobiography of the couturier Catherine Walker, all of which were also widely circulated in the form of part-works given away with newspapers, Jackie Modlinger's *Diana: Woman of Style*, and the American-published *Diana: The Secrets of Her Style* by Diana Clehane. All of these attempted to explain how Diana employed fashion to produce cultural meanings, and constructed her relationship with clothes in terms of a biographical trajectory of empowerment.

While these various works have all taken Diana's relationship with photographic and television images as paramount, they have made it meaningful by reference to a range of notions of gendered identity. In the simplest and most direct form of this trajectory, the iconic innocence associated with the Young England kindergarten photograph is contrasted with Diana's later development of control over her appearance, primarily through her clothing but also metonymically her image more generally. The earliest examples of this in the early and mid-1980s began to chart the overcoming of early mistakes and public criticism by the more sophisticated choice of dress.[22] Although Diana's status as a consumer played a major part in normalizing her, the fashion transformation never made her a suitable Thatcherite heroine, since it was too readily attributable to inherited wealth and privilege rather than enterprising individualism. No doubt in the late 1980s and early 1990s the negative press accorded the royal family in general contributed to the decline in the genre, and it was only revitalized after the iconic shift associated with Morton in 1992, and intensified posthumously. In these later forms, the maturation narrative is elaborated in terms of a variety of more obviously ideologically inflected forms of empowerment, culminating in the celebratory discourses of the 1997 *Her True Story – In Her Own Words*. Yet in its concentration on personal consumption, taste and the material technicalities of dress design, the fashion princess genre has always tended to moderate the intensity of Diana's iconicity. These emphases meant that the 1998 'fashion icon' books restrained the tendency to present Diana images as directly expressive which is apparent in the immediately posthumous material. Even at its most intense, the genre still registered the importance of authorial intention in Diana's self-presentation, or, as Rebekah Warren's review of the Clehane volume put it, set out to explain how 'Diana harnessed the power of glamour to achieve humanitarian goals'.[23]

This tendency to remain low-key is exemplified in *Dressing Diana* (1998) by Tim Graham and Tamsin Blanchard, which emphasized Diana's strategic use of dress to make style statements. These are glossed primarily by reference to the technicalities of cut and the language of fashion, within a vaguely defined empowerment narrative. The back cover signals 'the transformation of Diana, Princess of Wales into an icon of style and beauty', but this is presented in the book proper as a succession of personal statements made through the deployment of clothing styles, rather than as a progressive narrative.[24] It is essentially a retrospective of fashion successes looking back from the perspective of the 1997 Dress Sale, images from which figure prominently.

Bridging between this documentary genre and more explicitly ideological work was *Diana: Her Life in Photographs*, edited by Andrew Morton's publisher Michael O'Mara in 1995. The empowerment narrative promised but largely undelivered in the early editions of *Her True Story* and *Her New Life* is here figured in the terms of the fashion icon genre. O'Mara's brief captions signal a trajectory from weakness and naïveté to strength through the control of appearance. Thus the transparent skirt image is glossed with 'The young kindergarten teacher who had innocently posed for the photograph was mortified'. Seventy pages later, 'Her tall, slim figure perfectly suits the intricate and sophisticated gowns she chooses to wear'. A few pages on another caption is only a little more explicit. '"Shy Di" she may have been in her early days, but once the confidence came, Diana knew how to make the most of her assets', it begins, going on to quote an unnamed fashion critic as saying that the Princess 'knows that if clothes are going to talk, less says more'.[25] This last comment relates to the elaborate styles worn by Diana in the early 1980s, primarily associated with the design team of David and Elizabeth Emanuel and later regarded as further examples of a kind of romantic immaturity. (The huge train of Diana's wedding dress, designed by the Emanuels, was seen to be badly crushed as she emerged from her carriage outside St Paul's Cathedral. The misjudgement helped to cement Diana's status as an ordinary woman who had not quite adjusted to a fairy-tale existence, whose romantic investment in the monarchy was matched by a lack of familiarity with the cramped conditions within royal coaches.) *Her Life in Photographs* presents images in documentary fashion, as direct representations of the trajectory suggested by Morton in 1992–4. The instability of Diana's empowerment in the Morton biographies of this period is paralleled by O'Mara's inclusion towards the end of the book of a series of images of Diana in the street, clearly distressed by the attentions of 'paparazzi'.[26]

After Diana's death, O'Mara published a considerably revised version of the book under the title, *Diana Princess of Wales: A Tribute in Photographs* (1997). This edition reiterated the combination of triumph and tragedy in the 1997 *Diana: Her True Story*. Captions were subtly altered to put more distance between Diana and her images, and to suggest that her control of them went further back. Thus, '"Shy Di" she may have been' in one of the above examples, became '"Shy Di" was her label'. More strikingly, the 1997 edition excised the discomfiting paparazzi images, replacing them with photographs of the 1997 visits to Angola and Bosnia in support of the campaign to ban land-mines, and the funeral. This editorial decision clearly demonstrates the predisposition of self-consciously memorializing texts to locate any problematic distance between Diana and her image firmly in the bad old days when she remained within the ambit of royalty. As a result, the consciousness of the complex and ambivalent processes of representation provoked by the paparazzi photographs in the 1995 edition, is negated in the later, celebratory text. While the first version articulated in documentary style a trajectory of increased knowledge and power, made a little precarious by the continued pressures of press and public interest, the posthumous edition cast this biographical shift in terms of coming to power over self-representation. While the former is more realist, its scope is limited. It implies a contest for control of Diana's public image, but tends to present this contest within the privatized and individualistic form of a pre-feminist 'battle of the sexes'. The latter more intense sense of Diana's iconicity raises the stakes. It reworks mythic structures of Diana as Woman to produce a transcendent figure which is no doubt more inspirational, but tends to isolate later Diana images from a sense of the material and ideological processes that produced them. Diana is presented as effortlessly transcending the distinction between public and private, in ways that mystify the discursive means by which this effect is produced.

Feminist iconicity?

The problems magically resolved by O'Mara's editorial selection and reliance on notions of expressivity are exposed more prominently in the accounts of Diana by Julie Burchill and Beatrix Campbell. Yet even this more sophisticated work has been subjected to somewhat reductive summary, as in the following passage from a review in the *Sunday Times*:

> The Burchill–Campbell storyline is a version of riches to rags: poor little rich girl, reared for top-drawer biological functions, confronts disillusion, abandonment and loneliness, before finally discovering fulfilment in a love affair with the public and in her own good causes.[27]

In fact, both Burchill and Campbell are more wary of the romance elements of such a narrative than this implies, and neither takes up celebratory positions as wholeheartedly as is suggested here. What remains in this summary is the nucleus of Diana's appeal at its most populist. What is left out is that which must be repressed in order to facilitate a fully positive investment in her as a heroic figure. Complex issues of representation are compressed into a one-dimensional narrative. Relations of cultural production and consumption are expressed metaphorically as a 'love affair' between star and public. The tricky question of Diana's cultural exemplarity, as for example in relation to modelling national identity and perhaps a 'new Britain', is sidelined by the affective power of a quest for fulfilment within the personal sphere. It is only by reversing these displacements and compressions that a balanced critical assessment of the gender politics of Diana images can be made.

The notion of Diana's photographic expressivity offers a magical resolution of these complexities, or rather displaces them so that a spectacle of female empowerment can be fully enjoyed, and/or used as the basis for a process of cultural/political 'feminization'. Thus an iconic Diana comes to seem an adequate substitute for a speaking one. Yet this very manoeuvre allows her significance to be circumscribed within 'feminized' realms of visual appearance (as opposed to reality or meaningful content) and culture (rather than politics). It is no coincidence that Diana is habitually compared to the iconic women of the 1950s and 1960s, Marilyn Monroe and Brigitte Bardot, and infrequently to a more powerful figure such as Madonna whose star persona postdates second-wave feminism.[28] While the iconic significance of all such figures lies in their performance of self, Madonna has insisted more successfully than most on the autonomy of such performances as cultural products. Madonna has deliberately and even aggressively policed the distinction between a self that produces and a self that is performed. The combination of power and weakness in Diana's iconicity largely derives from the blurring of such distinctions. Just as in postwar constructions of royal femininity, to which Diana's iconic figuration remains indebted, this produces a powerful ideological effect of bridging public and private. Yet though this power is exercised in the name of femininity, it tends to construct gender difference in terms of symbolic oppositions rather than lived experience.

An investment in expressivity papers over these complexities and oversimplifies the relationship between Diana, the public, the monarchy and the mass media. Diana and her popular constituency are defined together against the monarchy, while the media are simple conduits for the images she used to communicate with 'us'. As a result, the monarchy itself is understood as some kind of shadowy, patriarchal establishment rather than the highly mediated and multivalent cultural formation that it is. As the power of the monarchy is exaggerated, the often intrusive, objectifying and sometimes highly anti-feminist practices of representation in the mass media are concealed.

Readings of Diana's cultural meaning in terms of the bringing of 'female values' into cultural and political prominence are far from nullified by this problematic, but they cannot afford to ignore it. Crucial here are the different frameworks within which Diana is understood as an emblem of caring humanity. At one extreme she serves as the inspiration for an active project inflected by a dynamic reformulation of gender roles. According to this logic, the example of Diana shifts the boundaries between the political and the personal, such that human affective relations (defined in terms of 'female values' of caring and mutuality) are validated in the realms of politics and public life. At the other extreme Diana's significance is merely symbolic; its affective force is contained within the realm of culture in the narrowest sense of symbolic representation, defined in opposition to a (putatively 'masculine') material or political 'real life'. Although this distinction appears to criticism – as here – in terms of a polar opposition, in most posthumous representations of Diana these formations are inseparable.

In large part this fusion is due to the multivalent relations between feminism and mainstream culture, such that the figuration of Diana drew upon various notions of gender identity, some of which were antithetical. It can therefore be seen that the valency of Diana's iconicity is largely determined by the extent to which the formation of royal femininity is transformed or supplanted, so as to re-present its ethic of care in terms of a demand for political transformation. The issue is complexified by the multivalence of notions of royal femininity already deployed in royal representations to bridge across public and private, rather than in any simple way policing patriarchal gender distinctions. The 'feminine side' of royalty personifies both domesticity and the centripetal forces of social amity, as against the formal, public and military symbolism associated with royal males. It is constructions of royal femininity that have largely enabled the monarchy to present itself as a vision of social ties and responsibilities at odds with the logic of the market, rather than the site of established power and privilege. In Diana's case, might not a similar operation be taking place in the service of maintaining the symbolic power of a specifically heterosexual, white, and aristocratic model of femininity? If Diana is to be successfully claimed for an emergent process of feminization, such claims must find ways to evade containment within the already ambivalently feminized typology of the British monarchy.

These questions lead us back to a concern with the emblematic and symbolic significance of Diana's biography. In some posthumous constructions of Diana as icon, the processes of symbolic appropriation outlined by Warner in *Monuments and Maidens* penetrate and colonize female biography. The representation of maternity and heterosexual romance in emblematic terms, that was seen to characterize her initial representation within patriarchal and monarchical forms, is intensified in many constructions of Diana as 'media saint'.[29] In 1984 Diana Simmonds insisted on understanding Diana not only as a model of femininity, 'the magical size Ten', but also as fulfilling a wider social function, 'the soothing Mentholatum for a bruised national physique'. In a valuable corrective to one-dimensional celebrations of Diana's 'glamour', she emphasized the construction of 'Diana' in the press as a means of 'mass psychic renewal' during a period of economic depression and social atomization under Margaret Thatcher, and the weakness of the Labour Party.[30] A sense that Diana posthumously came to emblematize a very different kind of femininity associated with the somewhat different politics of New Labour should not completely obscure that both processes utilize mechanisms of symbolic appropriation. It remains important to dismantle the mythic appropriation of femininity in the service of other symbolic discourses, and to think of femininity as one site of the formation of identity and as an agent of transformation. The need for such critical work is sharpened by the Labour government's commitment to a project of 'modernizing' the monarchy, in which the ideological formation of royal femininity may be consolidated or transformed.

A range of critical approaches to Diana can be positioned as counter-arguments and counter-strategies to these problematics. For example, the basic issue of the gendering of visuality can be reformulated in ways that emphasize its historical contingency. Rather than as a specifically feminist heroine, Diana can thereby be viewed in a more limited way as figuring the costs and possibilities of 'the new media-derived subject', in Kemp's phrase, which are made especially apparent by being positioned as female.[31] This allows a nuanced sense of the interaction of various gender discourses in relation to other codes of identity (such as race and class) in the construction of 'Diana'. The importance of femininity can be concretized by reference to lived experience, exemplified by the negatives of objectification and media harassment and the positive development of personal agency, and as sets of representational conventions and symbolic codes, rather than as a master category grounding an inspirational trajectory of empowerment.

An alternative strategy has been to place Diana's inspirational significance in the service of a tactical shift in media discourse. Hence, for example, some critics have viewed the Diana events as bringing about a reversal in the hierarchizing of 'hard' and 'soft' news according to gender difference. Such positions are summarized by Carter, Branston and Allen in their edited volume *News, Gender and Power* (1998). In their introduction, the editors refer to arguments that coverage of the Diana funeral events highlights ways in which

> the representation of certain highly privileged news celebrities allows a range of feminist debates to be articulated, and in a way which retains an emphasis on expressive feelings and emotions that would otherwise be disallowed under the constraints of 'objective' reporting or 'dispassionate' and 'detached' commentary. Feminized forms of reporting this tragic event received worldwide tributes from women for whom certain personal concerns (bulimia, the experience of divorce, very gender-specific feelings of worthlessness) had been given a greater public voice.[32]

The argument here completes a trajectory begun by John Hartley's contribution to the same volume. In 'Juvenation: News, Girls and Power', Hartley described the trivializing and infantilizing presentation of Diana news in the British press. According to Hartley, before her death Diana's association with 'emotion, expressiveness, and heart-over-head "populism"' was treated with 'cynicism and even contempt'. What is being appealed to in both sections of the book is a distinction between on the one hand the enlightenment heritage of modernist 'hard' news values, implicitly androcentric and individualistic, and on the other hand what Hartley calls 'postmodern, "Diana" journalism [that] teaches care'.[33] While clearly this distinction affords a position from which to critique androcentric journalistic practice, the invocation of an inspirational Diana risks leaving unremarked an essentialist sense of gender difference. Hartley's claim that 'Diana's crime was that she operated via sight, touch, and talk, not thought, reason and critique' successfully highlights the misogynistic practices of the mainstream press, but it allows the expressivity imputed to Diana to reproduce a potentially essentialist gender difference of female caring *versus* male critique.[34] Because of this, the affective power of Diana works against the sophisticated and detailed sense of journalistic practice apparent in the *News, Gender and Power* volume as a whole. Although the editors' introduction proceeds with admirable caution, its argument seems distorted by a felt need to make an unequivocal response to the Diana events, which pulls it towards an implicitly once and for all binaric distinction between 'feminized' and presumably androcentric forms.

The urgency of transforming, rather than directly reversing hierarchical gender binaries is underlined by Elizabeth Wilson's impassioned critique of inspirational constructions of Diana. For her, the most excessive celebrations of Diana as avatar of 'new Britain'

> reaffirmed a reactionary stereotype of women as the only sex with tear ducts, the only ones who 'care'. We could only become a more 'caring' society, went the argument, if we were a 'feminized' society. This is one of the worst pseudo-feminist clichés in the book: the idea that men are incapable *ever* of feeling, or caring or of nurturing.[35]

How is it possible to develop the positive affective sense of Diana as modelling femininity in terms of caring that Carter, Branston and Allen demonstrate in some women's consumption of reportage, while avoiding the reactionary implications pointed out by Wilson? Some key strategies revolve around the form and the scope of Diana's empowerment narrative. Andrew Morton influentially positioned Diana on a trajectory from 'being', understood as fulfilling the purely symbolic and reproductive functions demanded by the royal family, to 'doing', thought of in pro-, quasi- or post-feminist terms as the desire for a career, as activity which is directly useful.[36] Most Diana biographies present this trajectory as incomplete. It is the significance accorded to this incompleteness that is crucial. For example, Julie Burchill reworks the Morton narrative to reject outright the possibility that Diana could escape the condition of 'being'.[37] In a more politically thoughtful manner, Beatrix Campbell closes her critical biography by comparing the failure to translate the potential of the Diana events into a political programme with the Carolinian controversy of 1820.[38]

What I want to emphasize here is the importance of problematics of *representation* in arresting the progressive political valency of Diana's iconicity. Diana can be seen as having adopted a series of strategies to overcome the objectifying tendencies of her representation, as for example the use of emblematic gestures such as touching and 'reaching out', the use of the semiotics of clothes, the appropriation of therapeutic feminist discourses in the *Panorama* interview, the implicit and explicit addressing of her public image to a female audience, and finally, the Dress Sale and the adoption of the land-mines cause. Yet even when these strategies are successful, to celebrate them unequivocally would be to reinforce the confinement of both Diana and 'feminine values' within discourses of visual expressivity. The purely inspirational construction of Diana turns on her ability to speak through her clothes and her body image, so that she seems not to need a voice. In order to resolve this impasse, it is necessary to rewrite the privatized, abstracted narrative of *Her True Story* so as to highlight the multiple representational terrains on which struggles for selfhood and over meaning take place. Such a project necessitates two critical moves. One is a decoding, which investigates – and aims to undo – the symbolic discourses of race, class and heteronormativity that constructed a specific white and royal/aristocratic subject position as a universal feminine identity. The other seeks to restore a sense of active agency to Diana herself by picking away at the assumption of her expressivity. This involves attending to historical moments when the expressive power of Diana images cracked open, and to the visible traces of her own intentionality.

Kindergarten Madonna

Diana's first mass photo-call resulted in press photographs of an innocent, yet ambivalently sexualized Madonna. This took place on 18 September 1980, at the beginning of the period of rumour, speculation and intense media scrutiny touched off by Nigel Dempster's suggestion in the *Daily Mail* that she might become Charles's bride. Taken at the Young England kindergarten where she worked, these images showed a young woman holding one child aloft in the crook of her elbow, and holding the hand of another, as the light shone through her skirt silhouetting her legs. Julie Burchill has made explicit what is implicit in the contemporary newspaper coverage and the situation of the image near the beginning of vast numbers of Diana picture books: this was the 'first iconic image of Diana'.[39]

In his account of the iconography of white racial representation, *White*, Richard Dyer remarks that the early history of Diana's public image could be told through the imagery of 'the glowingly pure white woman ... demure, looking down, luminously sweet ... at heart illuminated with the pure desire of love for children'.[40] The key element is 'glow', identified by Dyer as the signal of ideal white femininity and bound up with notions of romance and reproduction. His point is confirmed by a photograph of Diana reproduced in *White*, a head-and-shoulders shot from the kindergarten session, in which ambient light falling on Diana's hair and shoulder creates the effect of a halo. Dyer has, it seems to me, successfully described the iconic discourse through which Diana was disseminated in the early 1980s, not just in the kindergarten session but through the wedding and the photographs of her with the newly-born William and Harry. As Dyer points out, one of the effects of this discourse is to naturalize the responsibilities of white femininity in terms of reproducing the race. One might add that, as Dyer's choice of images implies, the kindergarten photographs produce that iconicity even more strongly than those of Diana as a bride and the more denotative images of her with the newly born William and Harry. What remains unconsidered though in his account is the significance of the transparent skirt.

In a powerful contemporary reading, the image served to normalize Diana as an ordinary person on the basis that she lacked the sophistication and power which would enable her to take control of her image. Her status as everywoman was reiterated, in a way that also reinforced Diana's emblematic and mythic status. Here was a potential royal who represented 'us' back to ourselves, not yet through the iconic discourse of royal femininity, but on the basis that she, like us, was not quite in control of her appearance. This sense of the kindergarten photographs as revealing a lack of ultimate power over self-representation initiated the trajectories of Diana's subsequent empowerment and her status as figuring the problems and possibilities of western subjectivity in the later twentieth century.

Still, gender and sexuality remain crucial elements in the meaning of this image of inadvertent display. Perhaps for most contemporary viewers, Diana's mistake most served to guarantee the truth of the iconic discourse decoded by Dyer. Diana's apparent naïveté reinforced her presentation not just as 'virgin of the century', in Ailbhe Smyth's phrase,[41] but also as ideal *white* female, that is, both as a model of what white women should be and as incarnating ideal femininity as racially white. Even in posthumously published material the kindergarten photographs are repeatedly associated with Diana's virginity.[42] Clearly, the terms in which Diana is produced here as ideal (white) female depend upon privileging reproduction and maternity as most desirable female activities, while keeping them totally separate from sexuality. Interlocking with this was the symbolic elaboration of Diana as what Anthony Burgess termed 'an icon of cleanliness'.[43] As such, her lived experience of gendered identity was effaced by symbolically feminized discourses of Innocence, Chastity and Virtue.

What made the image so powerful were the multiple levels on which Diana literally incarnated these abstractions. In her they were made flesh but not fleshly. The sight of her lower body, solid and dark beneath its gauzy covering, was the ideal at the point of being made corporeal, the abstract in the process of becoming visible. The embodiment of the ideal cannot help, it would seem, but generate at least a trace of irony. There is always a potential slippage between the nude and the naked. But Diana's inadvertent sexual display anticipated such ironies and drained them away. Yes, this was a body capable of being sexualized. But unconscious of its own sexuality, it both signified and enacted innocence.

Yet (of course) such readings themselves enacted a repression and disavowal of sexuality. In most accounts of the kindergarten photo-call published before Diana's death, self-conscious sexual feelings are made explicit only by being deflected on to male viewers of the image. Charles's alleged comment to Diana that 'I didn't know you had such good legs' is frequently quoted. The sexual interest of the photographers and other journalists involved in pursuing Diana at the time was acknowledged, trivialized and disavowed in much contemporary material.[44] What would become known as the 'Shy Di' persona was taken as authentic and as proof against considering Diana as a sexual being. All of this is later seamlessly incorporated into the fashion-oriented transformation narratives and helps to secure the notion of Diana as an innocent, unsophisticated nineteen year old, whose subsequent maturation can then be described.

After Diana's death, commentators influenced by feminism have returned to early photographs of Diana in public to undo some of the sexual repressions enacted in them. The sexualization of the young Diana plays a doubly symbolic function in Julie Burchill's biography. Burchill delights in reading Diana as confusing the virgin/whore dichotomy central to patriarchal discourses of femininity, and emphasizes Diana's sexual warmth in contrast to the coldness and remoteness of her husband, the villain of the piece. For Burchill, the kindergarten photographs constitute an iconicity of 'sweet docile face, a way with children, and legs like expressways to delirium', and bear comparison with the Marilyn Monroe 'leg shot' in *Seven Year Itch*. She subsequently sums up the image as 'the nursery school Madonna with the Betty Grable legs backlit by her last summer of freedom'.[45] This is something of a provocative formulation. It licenses the libidinous investment of the usually male photographers, which was at the time often semi-sublimated into the language of the chase, the hunt and the stake-out, but was also sometimes made explicit.[46] Yet it also suggests a more complex understanding of the photograph as marking a certain point on the trajectory of Diana's relation with her image. Burchill's reading introduces a sense of Diana's body and sexuality into this relationship. This means that her subsequent transformation is not just a matter of the development of skills at self-presentation. Instead, in the transparent skirt photo, Diana is thought of as having been surprised by her own body. The sexuality out of her conscious control here will later be deployed triumphantly in the presentation of an empowered self.

A similar process is outlined by Beatrix Campbell, for whom Diana's subsequent appearance at her first official engagement in a low-cut black ball-gown is particularly significant. Again, this incident was often historically presented in terms of embarrassment and misjudgement, but Campbell re-reads it as evidence for the deliberate deployment of an erotic charge in Diana's self-presentation.[47] Like Burchill, Campbell draws upon second-wave feminist critiques of patriarchal culture to highlight the ways in which discourses of respectability and the royal acted to repress female sexuality. Campbell does more, though, to distinguish between individualistic and communal counter-strategies.

The implications of these various readings of Diana, fashion and self-representation are complex, not least in these more sophisticated writers. Burchill recognizes the limited nature of the empowerment through clothes narrative, and argues that Diana sought to distance herself from such strategies when she found more substantial charitable roles.[48] Campbell's account often reiterates a sense of conflict and complexity in the deployment of image. More populist discourses can also have complex implications. Thus, for example, one newspaper part-work carries the iconic notion of Diana communicating through her clothing back as far as the kindergarten photographs. In the *Daily Mail's Diana: A Life in Fashion* it was argued that the obsessive focus on Diana's legs has diverted attention from a message she had intended to transmit:

> What went unnoticed, however, was the pattern of Diana's mauve-and-white printed skirt ... In a choice that already marked out her wish to communicate a message without committing herself to words, Diana had chosen to wear a skirt printed with hearts. It was her first signal, her first communication through fashion.[49]

An enlarged detail of the photograph reveals that the famously transparent skirt is patterned with hearts. While at one level this is simply bathetic, such a contention does open up a more complex relation between Diana as performer and as expressive icon on one hand, and the gendered and sexualized structures through which her representation was mediated on the other. One does not have to strain too hard in order to read this item as displacing a viewing position patterned on male heterosexual desire and patriarchal discourse, by a sense of clothes as direct communication which has little to do with sexuality. There is a triple positioning of femininity in this reading: Diana as performed self and as performing self, and as viewing position. The latter defines the purely representational discourse of clothes as style in terms of a non-sexualized female reading community, defined against an implicitly male heterosexual interest in female sexual display.

What structures all these treatments of the image is the tension with which we have become familiar between a sense of celebrating Diana as an inspirational figure, and the critical analysis of her representation. By concentrating on the latter, it is possible to reverse the dominant reading of the transparent skirt as reinforcing the ideological discourse of white femininity described by Richard Dyer. Part of Dyer's argument is that 'glow' is naturalized as part of the discourse of ideal white femininity. The semi-visibility of Diana's legs in the kindergarten photographs, then, could be read as calling attention to the disclosure of the body by light falling upon it, and hence potentially as defamiliarizing the presentation of the ideal white woman as the source of light. In turn, the inadvertent sexualization could be read back into the production of the image, to demonstrate the internal inconsistencies of Western and patriarchal discourses of ideal femininity. Thus, in parallel with Burchill's account, the visibility of Diana's legs might be understood as a kind of resistance to the patriarchal discourses that have sought to regulate female sexuality, reminding viewers of the presence of a real body at the moment of its sublimation into an iconic image. It is not only the virgin/whore dichotomy which can be put at stake by such a reading. In a wider sense, the transparency of the skirt could be taken as calling attention to the conventional confinement of femininity within the realm of the visual, and highlighting the material and discursive production of such conventions.

These subversive senses of the transparent skirt as 'something wrong' could still be contained by Platonic and/or monarchical frameworks in which individuals are not necessarily expected to embody ideal forms completely successfully. A sense of flaws reinforces the successful construction of Diana as humanizing the ideal. Yet they have the virtue of directing attention to the discursive structures used to produce Diana's iconicities, as against reproducing the inspirational but objectifying notion that images gave direct access to Diana's identity, state of mind or significance. The productive possibilities of such readings are redoubled by the later images of Diana that seemed to reveal that there was 'something wrong' with her, with her treatment, and with the discourses used to present her.

'Something wrong': the limits of the image

Conservative and monarchical ways of constructing Diana's iconicity were initially challenged, not directly by rival modes of representation, but by reading images of Diana as suggesting that there was 'something wrong'. These began to be disseminated as early as the royal tours to Italy and to Australia in April and October 1985. On the former, Diana's use of previously seen clothes, allegedly to counter criticism of her expenditure, attracted adverse comment in the popular press; on the latter it was her startlingly thin body that would eventually start speculation over eating disorders.[50] Especially with hindsight, and with the biographical gloss provided by Morton, the negative expressivity of these images powerfully subverts conservative discourses of ideal and royal femininity. Yet the retrospective incorporation of such images into empowerment narratives, as, like the kindergarten photographs, the inadvertent starting points for a reinvention of self, reconstitute conservative discourses of royal femininity in all but name. The problem has been how to express positively a trajectory of empowerment without reinvigorating the very ways of seeing and being seen whose destructive effects were traced on Diana's body in the 1980s.

The significant comparison here is with the Duchess of York, Sarah Ferguson. While clearly sexist attitudes towards body shape and hair colour played a significant role in the ways the popular media differentiated between the two, a more subtle distinction lay in their relation to expressivity. Whether popular or being vilified, Sarah was presented as doing things, from flying a helicopter to writing about one to participating in 'It's a royal knockout'. Diana, by contrast, just was. Even Sarah's motherhood was consumed as much more of an individuated project, while Diana was seen to express and incarnate maternal feeling in ways symbolically linked to her royal role as national mother and, at another level, as epitome of heterosexual white femininity. Both models of female identity figured important elements of the Thatcherite *zeitgeist*. For a while it seemed possible that the more classless, because less aristocratic, individualistic mode of selfhood emblematized by Sarah Ferguson might even become pre-eminent. But whereas Diana's embodiment of personal affectivity remained firmly distanced from notions of economic productivity, in publishing a children's book for profit Sarah Ferguson put herself into the realm of economics where her privileged position was obvious. Whatever her personal qualities and failings, Sarah's consequent inability successfully to evade identification with class and other privilege significantly undermined her popularity.

The discourses of pure expressivity and of fashion princess/icon can be seen as two halves of a fractured whole. Both are embedded in the visual, and both tend to suggest readings of Diana images in terms of the materialisation of intention, in which the other components necessary to produce meaning, discursive structures and readers, are negated. While the first constructs Diana's trajectory according to an abstracted discourse of empowerment and a transcendent femininity, the latter renders Diana in highly class-specific terms and renders the empowerment narrative at a mundane level. In this sense, the counterpart to Frain's apotheosis of the immanence of 'Diana style' quoted above is Georgina Howell's description of the relationship Diana developed with the *Vogue* editorial team in *Diana: Her Life in Fashion* (1998):

> The idea was never that *Vogue* should advise or guide Diana. They only intended to provide a clothes vocabulary from which Diana could 'shop' according to her needs, and make her own fashion statements.[51]

Risking less, the notion of Diana as fashion princess or, latterly, fashion icon, by itself produces her as an interesting but unremarkable figure. Her appearance, rather than the immanent manifestation of self, is portrayed as the result of a learned and calculatedly employed vocabulary of style. To the extent that she continues to embody ideal femininity, this is defined as a matter of social status rather than transcendent embodiment.

This polarity can be exemplified in different treatments of the image in which Diana appears most saintlike, a Tim Graham photograph taken on a visit to the Al-Azhar mosque in Cairo, in May 1992. Diana is wearing a pale green Catherine Walker dress, with a chiffon scarf, and is pictured with eyes raised and head tilted slightly upward. The image is saturated in light. Everything around Diana looks white, her skin is very pale and heavy blonde highlights add to the halo effect. The photograph was reproduced widely in the immediately posthumous period, and was chosen for the front cover of the climactic part of the *Daily Mail* 'Untold Story' serialization.[52] The intensity of the mythologization achieved here was sustainable for a short period only immediately after Diana's death. Outside this immediate context, the immanence of the saintliness expressed in the photograph was overtaken by a sense of its status as self-presentation: saints do not take care over their appearance, least of all deliberately have themselves photographed in saintly pose. The image is much less prominent in the subsequent, less intensely iconic, more documentary material. It does not appear in Catherine Walker's autobiography (which is largely devoted to her dressing of Diana) or in Fincher's *Diana: Portrait of a Princess*. Where it is reproduced, either it is viewed purely in terms of its diplomatic conformity, as in Graham and Blanchard's *Dressing Diana*, or as in Howell's book, where the fashion expert distances herself from 'popular' investment in 'its saintly overtones'.[53] As elsewhere, in this instance, the documentary and technical concerns of the fashion icon discourse act to demythologize the more intensely iconic constructions of Diana.

What seems to embarrass Howell a little is the very success of the image in presenting Diana as the apotheosis of sainthood. If it was Diana's intention to be read in this way, she has succeeded too well. The image is so powerful an emblem of sainthood as to negate the importance of the specificity of the person, who becomes only the occasion or the carrier for this mythic meaning. 'Diana' is spoken by the discourse of sainthood. Alternatively, in the retrospective demythologizing of the image, the re-installation of Diana's intentionality undermines the effect of saintliness. Sainthood is spoken (or embodied) by Diana.

The sister notions of Diana's expressivity and her saintliness are perhaps best understood in the context of the intensity of unexpected grief. (I am taking it that Tony Walter and others have done enough to bracket, if not dispose of, any sense that the triggering of grief by the death of someone familiar only through mass media is by itself problematic.)[54] At any rate, it waned fairly quickly during the year after Diana's death. All the fashion books and part-works discussed above registered in some way or another a sense of the limits of the expressivity of Diana images. They point to examples of fashion 'mistakes' or direct attention to images which successfully evoke a marital harmony now generally understood to have been lacking in real life, or quote Charles Spencer's caution against regarding Diana as saint or martyr in his memorial address, or resort to the final-page conclusion that Diana most truly found herself as a 'work-horse' not a 'clothes-horse'.[55] Even

Irène Frain confesses to being unable to work out the meaning of the unostentatious fashion choices of Diana's final year.[56]

These moves to curtail the discourses of expressivity, fashion icon and saintliness are not solely a product of historical distance from the most intense phase of mourning for Diana. The last nine months of Diana's life, in particular the visits to Angola and to Bosnia in support of the campaign to ban land-mines and the Dress Sale of June 1997, bear the traces of a strategy to renegotiate the terms of her representation in the media. Clearly these were highly mediated events and cannot be understood simply as the final emergence of a real self purified from signification. Rather, in connection with the Dress Sale and the land-mines campaigns, Diana was portrayed crossing boundaries between the private, the public and the political, in ways that significantly revised the visual discourses hitherto discussed. During 1997, images of Diana in Angola and Bosnia, in London and New York began to open up a distance between intention and appearance. Representations of Diana visiting minefields, hospitals and cemeteries, and coverage of the dresses with and without her presence, worked against notions of transcendent expressivity. They enabled, for perhaps the first time, an understanding of Diana in terms of human agency in the public and political sphere that did not collapse back into royal femininity. Moreover, this dynamic mode of empowerment was coupled with a sense of class, gender and 'race' specificity that undermined recuperation into symbolic femininity. At times, television coverage of Diana's involvement in the campaign against land-mines opened up a critical distance around the symbolic forms of ideal white femininity which enabled Diana to be seen in terms that productively reworked their associations with social amity, an ethic of care and English/British national identity.

Television and land-mines

Jenny Kitzinger has demonstrated how the 'everyday familiarity and moving power of television images' adds significant dimensions to the cultural significance of Diana. As Kitzinger argues, television representations of Diana in movement contributed to her iconicity in two related ways.[57] First, they cemented Diana's attractiveness in terms of 'spontaneity' in ways impossible for still images, chiefly by capturing her eye movement in meeting the gaze of others and then looking away. Then also, television showed much more effectively than stills Diana making tactile contact with others. Her gestures of touching and above all 'reaching out' played a major part in shaping her iconicity and cultural meaning. For many, Diana's actions in deliberately touching people with AIDS are the single most significant acts in her life, having an importance in shaping mainstream attitudes both towards the transmissibility of HIV and towards people with AIDS, which extends far beyond any biographical intention or royal/national significance.[58] Diana's 'reaching out' more generally figures prominently in the celebratory and descriptive accounts of Morton, Holden, Burchill and Bradford, and is analysed as a crucial part of Diana's appeal in three highly suggestive essays by Homi K. Bhabha, Régis Debray and Naomi Segal.[59] Having registered its importance, Kitzinger shows how the time frame of television was crucial in disseminating Diana as the princess who touched, since it facilitated the representation of repeated, prolonged and reciprocated contact, whether through bodily proximity, the prolonged stroking of a child's knee or gaze into the eyes.

This emphasis on the formal modes of representation associated with the 'reaching out' motif begins to suggest ways of looking that might negotiate the familiar problems of expressivity and iconicity. Cover images of Diana's head and shoulders, and official and semi-official family photographs tell only half the story. Images of Diana touching, leaning towards, hugging and gazing at others can serve partially to deflect the look of the viewer away from Diana herself and on to the object of her attention. Time after time in the still photographs associated with celebrity magazines such as *Hello!*, one's gaze is initially drawn to Diana, and then to who is being looked at and/or touched by her. Diana's much-vaunted personal style, which included not only reaching out to touch, but also for example lowering her own headline to talk with children, can be read in such images as emphasizing the relations between identities. Diana's style brings difference into proximity, in contrast to the conventionally 'stiff' representation of the royal family on tour. In such official media events, the royal family is called upon to perform Britishness, European identity and often white racial identity, which it does by appearing separate from and in contrast to non-British, non-European or non-white Others. Hence where the royal family makes difference visible in terms of gradations and limits, images of Diana hint instead at the mutual construction of identity and difference.

Such progressive readings of Diana images, as I would regard them, are not necessarily obvious, nor are they free from problems. Most significantly, Diana's embeddedness in visual discourses of performativity tends to render her moves towards otherness complete in themselves. Her image enacts a need and a wish for reciprocation, often indeed a desire for reciprocation from positions of equality, but in the realm of the visual this dynamic remains privatized and gestural. In the mode of the mere spectacle, others become Others, merely supplementary to Diana's performance of caring white femininity. Here again the discursive structuring of Diana as emblem enables her to be represented negatively in terms of 'mere' appearance. Hence the hostile press and television coverage of Diana's attendance at a heart operation performed by her friend Hasnat Khan. As a visual problematic it has a counterpart in ironic popular views of Diana as 'Lady Bountiful', or as being ghoulishly attracted to sites of pain and suffering. This critical sense of Diana's privileged status was taken up by the popular press, as when the *Sun* published its spoof 'Diana card', which, modelled on the card carried to facilitate organ donation, expressed the wishes of the bearer that, in the event of hospitalization, he or she would prefer not to be visited by Diana. In all these cases, the double bind of Diana's status as emblem facilitates moves of disavowal which end with the rejection of any outside to masculinist and white-centred positions.

What is more significant than Diana's personal psychic needs here are the exigencies imposed by popular interest and mass media journalism, such that Diana remains the centre of short narratives, relegating others to walk-on parts on the periphery. The wordless television images played in the immediate aftermath of Diana's death exaggerated this tendency still further.[60] The visual and narrative logics of television especially reinforce Diana's visual and narrative centrality. Television representations of Diana tend to be structured by the importance of centring a single body or face in any given frame. Her relations to others are presented either iconically, for example by the look directed out of the frame or an inclined, stretched posture or through narrative forms such as sequences of shot and counter-shot. Invariably it is Diana's image on which the look comes to rest. What is significant about the coverage of the land-mines campaign is its deliberate construction of the visual as a strategic means to effect changed attitudes and affect political policy. As such seeing was subjugated explicitly to acting. It was not enough to look at her visit to Angola in January 1997; it was not enough even to feel similarly affected. What mattered was to take action, and action of a more or less political kind; to ban the manufacture and sale of anti-personnel land-mines.

Diana's involvement in the land-mines campaign is crucial for her cultural meaning because it raised the possibility of shifting the boundary between the spheres of culture and of politics. This was made apparent as much by the criticisms voiced by Conservative MPs of Diana as a 'loose cannon', as it was by Anthony Holden's celebratory assertion that having altered government policy in Britain and the USA, she 'had transformed the global menace of landmines from a political issue into a humanitarian one'.[61] Yet, as Holden's comment demonstrates in another sense, apparently supportive discourses, including Diana's own contention that the Angola visit was not political, can work to repair those boundaries in the name of her own exceptionalism.

In some respects, the images of Diana produced by the Angola visit are caught within a comparable double bind. Yet, as with Diana's 'reaching out', touching and cuddling people with AIDS, though here in more intensified form, Diana can be seen here to be inhabiting traditional symbolic discourses and reworking them. In both contexts Diana's status as modelling identity was deployed in the service of shifting dominant behaviours. In the case of AIDS work this was supplemented by the official status of her patronage. Diana's visits to the first dedicated ward in Britain clearly signalled approval of the directing of financial and institutional resources towards AIDS care and research in ways that added materially to the support signalled by touch. It has also been argued that Diana's visibility played a crucial role in the securing of funds for AIDS related projects in the United States.[62] As Jenny Kitzinger has argued, 'it was Diana's then status *within* the establishment that made her touch so powerful'.[63] But this also suggests the limits of exemplarity alone. Arguably, while the land-mines visits to Angola and Bosnia continued to work within the frame of exemplarity, there was a difference in that the trips were explicitly linked to a specific campaign to change government policy, rather than being directed towards inspiring a general cultural and personal response. As such, the iconicity of the caring princess was put in the service of a deliberate demand for political change.

This project is reflected in the ways that the 'caring princess' discourse can be seen to be revised in some of the most memorable images from the Angola visit. The widely reproduced photographs of Diana alone in tan trousers, white shirt, armoured vest and perspex helmet in a partly cleared minefield play within a traditional context in which white femininity symbolizes all that is best about English/British or European culture. In this sense such images empty out the historical specificity of white female identities and reiterate racial and national hierarchies. But they can also be seen as strategically reworking the iconic discourse of ideal white femininity exemplified in dominant readings of the 1980 kindergarten photographs. The flak jacket covers Diana's upper body in a dark block of heavy colour, whose thickness is emphasized by a white patch bearing the 'Halo trust' name and logo. Instead of being diaphanous and translucent, her body is made solid and dark. The luminescence of whiteness is still there, in the white shirt, light trousers, light skin and blonde hair, but the transparent helmet surrounds her head with a hard reflective surface. Catching the light, it makes her head shine rather than glow. This revisionist take on conservative discourses of ideal white femininity is marked ironically by the 'Halo trust' insignia. The image suggests a secularized, militant and militarized counterpart to the kindergarten madonna. Moreover, the minefield photographs appeared in an explicitly political context, in which this militant femininity was mobilized against commercial and military interests. They dominated the front page of most British newspapers on 16 January 1997, and acted as a successful counter to ministerial criticism of the trip that had been reported the previous day, both visually and by eliciting favourable editorial comment.[64]

In general, reportage of the Angola visit took forms that amounted to a reframing of Diana's iconic status by reference to a militant campaigning persona, albeit one that was validated by emotional feeling rather than a well-informed consideration of issues. Probably more significant in the long term was the crossing of borders between the social/cultural and political spheres and the shifts in relations of visibility. As Diana was often shown stating, the aim of the visit was to use the media attention she generated to focus on a global problem. This simple strategy was highly effective in bringing about the revision, at least temporarily, of the iconic framing devices habitually used when representing Diana on television. Instead of being positioned always as the object of the gaze, Diana appeared on news items in a mixture of positions, sharing the frame with a variety of other people, and even as directing the attention of camera operator and viewer.

The apotheosis of these innovative representations was the account of the Angola visit in the BBC2 programme 'Diary of a Princess', shown in the humanitarian/current affairs series *Heart of the Matter*, on 11 February 1997. The *Sunday Mirror* had anticipated 'Panorama: The Sequel', another personal testament, but instead the programme expanded and developed the position of Diana as mediating images rather than being centre-screen.[65] The format of the programme straightforwardly followed the stated intention of bringing to a global audience (though in effect a British one) the damage done by land-mines in Angola. This placed Diana in a double position. As the continuity announcer had put it while introducing the programme, she is shown simultaneously 'encounter[ing] the harrowing consequences of land-mines' and also 'draw[ing] the world's attention to the campaign to ban these weapons'. Throughout, Diana was placed as mediating the gaze of the audience. She is shown making contact with land-mine victims, care workers, officials and mine clearance experts through touching and speaking with them. She registers the impact of land-mines injuries through commentary, 'I knew the facts, but the reality was a shock.' She even, on occasion, explicitly directs the attention of camera operator and viewers. Whether due to the exigencies of filming, or to strategic planning, in the vast majority of shots the frame is shared by two or more people. Diana thus appears as both subject and object of the gaze. She is also represented ambivalently in relation to racial typologies. Her presence among hospitalized Africans can be read at one level as naturalizing colonialist racial hierarchies via the invocation of Eurocentric conventions of the white woman as ministering angel. Yet at another level her conversations with officials and those injured might be read as destabilizing such hierarchies.

This double-double positioning is resolved visually in the programme by presenting the figure of Diana as turning the first-world gaze into a sympathetic touch. Though neo-colonialist identifications of white women as nurses help to sustain this presentation, 'Diary of a Princess' also contains much material that decisively breaks with colonialist structures. Most often, in the hospital scenes a 'feminized' sense of sympathetic feeling is invoked to bridge cultural, political and power differences between Europe and Africa through personal contact. Other sections of the programme show a militant white femininity at work in Diana's conversations with Red Cross officials of various national and 'racial' identities, and more symbolically in coverage of the minefield photo-call. Ultimately, the implicitly maternal interest in the welfare of injured children evidenced in hospital visits and voice-over is called upon explicitly to demand a world-wide ban on land-mines.

The overarching structures of racial difference and post-colonial power relations, and the explicit project of the film to trace the effects of land-mines on human victims, make this a complex and deeply ambiguous piece of television. Logically, the programme is committed to presenting Angolans in the most victimized terms possible, in order to expose the ravages of land-mines. It is possible to read it as exemplifying Diana's relations with the media at their most problematic, in that the objectifying gaze is deflected from the princess to wounded and damaged Africans. Less dramatically, there remains an intractable problem in a succession of third world victims being produced for the gaze of first world viewers. In formal terms, Diana's practice of touching and seeking reciprocal communication does counteract these to an extent, since it tends to put those injured by land-mines on an equal footing within the television frame and to present them as exhibiting resilience under the most difficult circumstances, rather than as broken victims passively awaiting white aid. In addition, racial difference is further fragmented by showing numerous other figures of Black or white appearance whose precise role and identity are left vague, but who are presumably international and local Red Cross officials, medical workers and state administrators.

The persona constructed for Diana in 'Diary of a Princess' is hugely indebted to pre-existing models of royal femininity, combining elements already apparent in the representation of the Queen as mother of the Commonwealth and Princess Anne's tours for Save The Children in the early 1980s. In both of these examples, it can be seen that notions of royal femininity ultimately function to contain international affective ties and responsibilities within symbolic and charitable structures. Alongside the recapitulation of some elements of this tradition, the representation of Diana in 'Diary of a Princess' makes three significant innovations. First, the exigencies of Diana's own position as a recently divorced, 'semi-detached' member of the royal family meant that the visit to Angola was contextualized in terms of her biographical search for a fulfilling role as much as it was a fact-finding mission. Hence where Queen Elizabeth and Princess Anne were portrayed as taking abroad a perfectly stable identity, Diana's visit played out the reconstruction of a public persona and a private person by a dynamic process of relating to other people. This in turn made it possible to read Diana as figuring symbolic shifts in dominant forms of white and British identities, rather than the consolidation of conservative formations associated with the royal family. A second innovation is the articulation of caring femininity to an explicit demand for changes in political policy. In 'Diary of a Princess' the assumed maternal responsibilities of the white woman are propelled, via humanitarianism, into the political realm. Third, and linked to this, was the emphasis laid in 'Diary of a Princess', and made explicit in its title, on words rather than images. In voice-over commentary towards the end of the programme, Diana remarks that the sight of suffering children is especially moving for a mother, before modulating from personal experience into a call for humanitarian political action. She uses her final words to demand nothing but 'a total worldwide ban on anti-personnel land-mines'.

What is at stake in 'Diary of a Princess', more clearly than virtually anywhere else in popular culture, is the key problematic of Diana as icon of femininity: the possibility of developing a project of social transformation in the name of the feminine out of a formation which has its roots in patriarchal gender distinctions. It is because of this that the presentation of Diana as mediator of the gaze rather than simply being its object is crucial. The framing of a feminized gaze is important not just because it may contest the objectifying elements of iconic discourses so far as Diana representations are concerned, but also because it may challenge the gendered distinction between cultural and political which has served historically to privatize the ethic of care. Yet what the programme also demonstrates is the continued importance of racial difference and postcolonial relations in structuring relations of power and looking. Diana is shown taking up the position of power from which the first world gaze reinforces international power differentials, and taking on with it various feelings of guilt, responsibility, sympathy and determination to intervene. This is complex enough, but in a key moment just before the voice-over emphasizes the affectivity of looking 'as a mother' and goes on to enunciate the demand for a ban on land-mines, Diana is also shown seeking to ameliorate the effects of the gaze itself. At this point a very young child is partially undressed, the better to display her wounds both to the television camera and to press photographers, whose cameras can be heard clicking. After an awkward pause, Diana intervenes. She covers up the child's body with a blanket and says 'I think that's enough' to a press photographer who remains out of shot.

Dress Sale

The sale of 79 of Diana's most glamorous dresses on 25 June 1997, after they had been on display in London and New York, was a media coup. The generation of $5.6 million for AIDS and cancer charities, the bulk of which came from television rights and catalogue sales, was clearly significant. This real-world effect suggested an important biographical shift. The Dress Sale was popularly regarded as marking the end to her marriage, to her official status within the royal family, and with it to her formal symbolic status in representing Britain. Unofficially, the dresses became known as Diana's 'wardrobe of state'. The *Daily Telegraph* reported that they represented the bulk of Diana's personal collection of formal gowns, leaving only ten or so 'for evening engagements in her new simpler and more serious life style'.[66] More fully, as Cathy Horyn's feature 'Diana Reborn' in the July edition of *Vanity Fair* put it, 'Princess Diana's decision to auction 79 of the dresses she wore as the wife of England's future King is a powerful symbol of her changing life.'[67] This move cemented the trajectory of professionalization signalled after the short break from public life in 1993–4 and the reorganization of Diana's charity work epitomized in the land-mines campaign. Equally significantly, Horyn wrote of Diana as 'trying hard to craft a meaningful *and* pleasurable existence' hinting at the possibility that the sale marked a distinction between public and private life.[68] Still more than this, I want to suggest that the Dress Sale as a media event gave rise to significant ways of rethinking the relationship between Diana and Diana images.

Announced in February 1997 with a preview showing of five dresses at Christie's in London, the Dress Sale culminated in two public viewings, in London from 3 to 6 June the same year, and in New York from 19 to 25 June, with the auction itself on the final day. Most obviously, the Dress Sale signalled a shift from the iconic and the symbolic to the professional and materially useful. As the sale's widely reported motto put it, 'Sequins Save Lives'. The phrase encapsulated the notion that clothes with symbolic resonances in terms of international diplomatic relations, cultural events and of course biography were converted into real money to help real people. But of course these connotations were reiterated and reorganized rather than being cancelled by the sale and its reportage. The *Daily Mail* called them 'The Ups and Gowns of Diana's life'.[69] Hilary Alexander, fashion editor for the *Daily Telegraph*, was more specific. 'Each dress', she wrote in February 1997,

> in itself is a part of history, both fashion and royal, but taken as a whole, the collection charts the highs and lows of a marriage which crumbled before the eyes of the world.[70]

The Dress Sale marked a pivotal moment in the materialization of these histories. At the public viewings, in the catalogue and in media coverage reliant on both, the dresses were assembled in public for the first and only times, preparatory to the breaking up of the collection at the auction itself. From the first, the sale was presented in terms of disposal and fragmentation. The February *Telegraph* news story that accompanied Alexander's piece was headlined with a quotation from Diana's official statement launching the sale: 'I am delighted that these dresses, which gave me so much pleasure, may be enjoyed by others.' This was elaborated in the *Telegraph* magazine's sale preview three months later by Sarah Mower, who reviewed the collection of dresses as a 'wordless biography', before concluding that 'the decision to liquidate their difficult memories into doing good is probably Diana's most elegant gesture yet'.[71] This double movement of bringing together followed by liquidation became a crucial paradigm for the Dress Sale. In assembling the dresses in public preparatory to their dispersal, the sale materialized in them as objects the multiple histories whereby Diana's appearance was read symbolically in terms of nation, diplomacy, archetype, fashion, royal history and personal biography. The subsequent dispersal of the dresses is often read directly as a 'goodbye to all that', signalling an end to Diana's official life as a princess. I want to go further than this, to argue that the Dress Sale enacted not simply a biographical change but a break with the discourse of expressivity itself. This can be seen best through further investigation of the precise nature of its materialization of Diana's history through clothes.

The public viewings created an aura around the dresses which was elaborated into gradations of presence by media coverage. It was not just that queues formed round the block outside Christie's salerooms. More significantly, proximity to the dresses was differentiated according to a hierarchy beginning with actually being present (if possible during the gala openings attended by Diana herself), then through obtaining glossy images in printed media, preferably the £30 catalogue that bought entry to the showing, and only then through television images. It was hard to light for television the static, quite cramped display. This emphasized the limits of television coverage and privileged being there. Television photography was manifestly not nearly as good at reproducing the sensuous beauty of the dresses as the glossy still photographs reproduced in the catalogue, magazines, and, later, fashion icon books. What television could and did do was to replay the biographical moments that the *sale* of the dresses was bracketing off.

At the viewings, in the sale catalogue and in the reportage, the dresses were and are presented as isolated lots, in apparently random order. Together with their visual appeal this has the effect of emphasizing their materiality as – highly sensuous and desirable – objects, while at the same time inviting viewers to make sense of them individually.

On my own visit to the London show, I noted somewhat impressionistically three main ways in which people – mostly, but not entirely, women – made sense of the dresses. First and most obviously, individual dresses were read in terms of Diana's biography: 'This is the one she was wearing when …'. Second, the dresses were regarded with a mixture of aesthetic appreciation, desire and fantasy, attracting discussion along the lines of 'Which is your favourite?', and 'Which would you like?'. Finally, another question attracting a deal of speculation was, 'Which will sell for most money?', which often led back into discussion of the first two kinds. Almost all the comments I overheard were heavily inflected by a sense of the dresses as material objects, and did not sustain the sense of reverential, mystical and religious feelings attributed to visitors by some contemporary broadsheet articles and posthumous commentators.[72]

The presentation of the dresses both at the viewings and in the catalogue clearly separated out these ways of reading them, contrasting their materiality as objects with their biographical significance. Thus, for example, the display of dresses was supplemented with a small number of almost life-size archive photographs of Diana. Some dresses were thus presented primarily in terms of their material existence, while others were placed much more firmly in the context of specific biographical moments. At least at the London show, two dresses at either extreme were prominently contrasted with one another. As one entered, the first dress to be seen was the one most strongly inflected by biographical narrative and least significant from a design perspective, the £900 off-the-peg black cocktail dress by Christina Stambolian. This was the only prêt-à-porter dress in the collection, but it had famously been worn to the Serpentine Gallery the night of Charles's admission of adultery in the Jonathan Dimbleby ITV programme, as a large photograph reminded visitors. The dress placed at the end of the display, and the only one still visible to a backward glance from the vestibule as one left, was one of the most expensive and most interesting in fashion and design terms. This was lot 78, the 'Elvis dress' with cropped jacket edged in pearls, designed by Catherine Walker. It too was accompanied by a large photograph. But if it reminded viewers of anything, it was associated with nothing more or less biographically significant than Diana's appearance at the 1989 British Fashion awards.

The sale catalogue emphasized still further this separation of the material existence from the symbolic or narrative significance of the dresses. Each lot is shown photographed directly from the front and basic details of its design and history are given. These images were widely reproduced in colour supplements and in the tabloid press.[73] In the catalogue these definitive shots are supplemented in several ways: by archive photographs of Diana wearing the dresses, by beautifully lit close-ups of particular features, by a few designers' sketches, and by a series of photographs of Diana in a selection of the dresses that had been taken by Lord Snowdon at a specially arranged session in March 1997. Images of the last sort featured particularly prominently in print and television media, and it is one of these that appears on the front cover of the catalogue, and on the poster advertizing the sale. The photographs by Snowdon, which are in black and white, tend to dehistoricize the dresses, privileging continuity and their material existence over their connection with specific moments in a biographical narrative. This effect is cemented by the sale catalogue as a whole, in which the biographically charged power of the historical images of Diana in the dresses is redirected towards the lusciously reproduced front-on images and close-ups of the lots themselves. The purposely dry information provided in the catalogue about designers and points of stylistic interest further substantiated this process. The catalogue commentary remained so resolutely staid that its descriptions of the more biographically significant items courted incongruity. In the case of the Stambolian 'revenge dress', for example, it is hard to suppress a sense of deliberate playfulness. Opposite a full-page photograph of Diana resplendent at the Serpentine Gallery, the catalogue noted that the dress 'caused a great deal of comment at the time and subsequently, not only for its daring asymmetrical ruching, but also because it was thought not to be the work of a British designer'. When later Georgina Howell called it 'beside her wedding dress, her most famous frock', one doubts it was the ruching or the Greek-born, British-based designer she had in mind.[74]

The cumulative effect of these ways of presenting the dresses, further disseminated in printed media and via television coverage which edited together news of the sale with archive footage of Diana, is to deflect the objectifying elements of Diana's iconicity on to the clothes.[75] Their biographical symbolism is acknowledged and then suspended by their being sold for wear by others or for public show. At the time, Cathy Horyn's article in *Vanity Fair* made explicit something of this doubleness. Horyn emphasized the Dress Sale as a break, quoting from the launch interview when Diana herself stressed the dispersal of the collection; 'I am extremely happy that others can now share the joy that I had wearing them.' She went on to cite the sale organizer, Meredith Etherington-Smith, calling the dresses 'mini-biographies'. 'Well, *maybe*' is Horyn's response, but this sense of the dresses as biographically meaningful has to be placed against their separate material existence:

> Ultimately, they're empty shells – beautiful, shiny, marvellous to look at, but still ... *shells*. And the fabulous creature who once occupied them? She's packed up and moved on.[76]

This process of auratic dissolution was completed by reader competitions in the *Sun*, the *Mirror* and even the *Mail on Sunday* to win one of the dresses. Martine McCutcheon, then star of soap opera *Eastenders* and emblem of female blue-collar ordinariness, modelled the *Mirror*'s dress on the front page, headlined 'Queen of the Vic!'.[77] In addition, the catalogue and reportage just described amplified and developed the effects of the assembling and disposal of the dresses in separating out and bracketing off the iconic discourses of archetypal, national and biographical symbolism. Rather than being positioned as passive signifiers of Diana's expressivity, in this material the dresses are presented to popular audiences as a series of objects, each of which is meaningful in several ways. Iconic symbolism of various kinds takes its place here alongside stylistic analysis, the affective qualities of the clothes, personal preference, speculation about and reaction to the relative prices paid at auction, and so on.

As the comments from the *Telegraph* and *Vanity Fair* quoted above imply, the Dress Sale was at the time eminently readable in terms of a break with the specific elements of iconic discourse which portrayed Diana, like the royal family, as embodying Britishness. Such a break was made visible in the photographs by Mario Testino which accompanied the Horyn article in *Vanity Fair* and which later appeared in two special supplements to the *Mail on Sunday* magazine, *You*.[78] These are quite unlike the vast majority of Diana images. According to fashion writer Georgina Howell, they 'showed Diana more relaxed than any other photographer had caught her before'.[79] They are naturalistic, mostly monochrome, dynamic and inflected above all by the discourse of high fashion photography rather than those of royal or otherwise iconic femininity. Many of them show Diana in motion, sometimes blurred and often at least partially out of focus. It is this last quality that differentiates them from the nearest comparison, the images by Patrick Demarchelier, another *Vogue* photographer, taken for Morton's

1992 book and in subsequent sessions. Like all other classic Diana pictures, and unlike the Testino shoot, Demarchelier's images are sharp and static, inviting readings of them as having captured some kind of essential Diana-ness. The Demarchelier portfolio reproduced as a posthumous tribute in the November 1997 *Harper's Bazaar* contrasts markedly with the Testino photographs in *Vanity Fair* a few months earlier.

In terms of their iconic meaning, the Testino photographs send out a profoundly mixed set of messages. The angles and blurred effects are strongly marked by intentionality. These are high fashion shots whose artistry is paraded. Yet the effect of this is not at all to reduce Diana to a mere body, providing only the raw material for a good image. Unlike almost all other mass-disseminated Diana images, the interaction between a particular viewer (Testino) and viewed is registered directly in their composition. The variation in focus and movement blurs set up a more dynamic relationship than the standard attempts to 'capture' Diana as some static, sharp essence, in which the photographer is reduced to a generic role indistinguishable from the mass of viewers of Diana and her image. This is complemented by Diana's strong eye contact with the lens or animated glance out of shot, and her relaxed postures, all of which assert a sense of power and autonomy. The high fashion, slightly avant-garde qualities of the images break decisively with the reproduction of Diana as everywoman according to the formation of royal femininity or the romance heroine described by Morton, both of which appeal to lower middle-class identity as normative. Elaine Showalter describes how the *Vanity Fair* photos attracted the attention of stylists and customers in her 'neighbourhood hair-dresser's in London', presumably a much more sophisticated clientele than the working-class girls who, according to Angela Carter, had adopted Diana looks in the 1980s.[80] In coding female independence in terms of the high fashion model, the Testino images glamorize aristocratic identity understood in North American terms as intensified celebrity. In so doing they narrativize positively Diana's restoration to the social status she had before her marriage. Rather than a sad divorcée stripped of the title of Her Royal Highness, Diana is presented here as the fulfilled high-born cover girl.

Cathy Horyn's description in the accompanying article of Diana as 'fabulous creature' who has 'packed up and moved on' reiterates this identification with the aristocratic fashion model. Diana's career is framed here through the performance of fabulousness, in terms of

packaging and movement. There should be no mistaking the result-
ing images as the direct expression of personal or symbolically female
qualities. High fashion photography is concerned with surface, not
character; success as a model depends on the elimination of character
and sustaining the opacity of surface. In this the images reproduce
some of the elements of supermodel femininity described by Myra
Macdonald, though the combination of naturalistic and avant-garde
elements in the Testino photographs with Diana's assertive presence
and her aristocratic status suggest continuities with earlier *Vogue*
models.[81] Testino's spare monochromatic images thus dispense with
the iconic frameworks of expressive identity and symbolic femininity. If they can be read as expressing anything it is a mood, not a personality, and still less Woman. If they have a biographical
significance, it lies in marking a liberating distance between identity
and appearance.

Still, these are meaningful *images*. The minimalist chic and the
dynamism of the Testino session constitute the beginnings of a new
iconography of Diana rather than a break with iconicity altogether.
There remains a tension between understanding the Testino images
and the Dress Sale as signalling a liberating biographical moment, and
the sense that to do so is to remain within discourses of visual expressivity. As a way of negotiating this tension, I want to argue for an
understanding of the Testino images, the Dress Sale and the 'new look'
adopted by Diana in 1997 as beginning to dismantle the hitherto dominant assumptions about the expressivity of Diana images. These developments, I suggest, make available a more sophisticated and active
reading of the production of meaning in which intentionality, structures of meaning, and the activity of reading, are made evident. While
a certain critical sophistication is important here, the beginnings of
such self-reflexivity can be discerned in the presentation of Diana
images in the British celebrity news magazine *Hello!*.

The Dress Sale and the Testino session interlocked with a new
fashion look Diana adopted in 1997. This was generated by a succession of similar dresses in pastel shades, all sleeveless, with scoop necklines and short skirts, exemplified by the simple embroidered shifts
worn for the gala evenings of the London and New York sale shows.
The series of almost identical dresses were widely read as denoting
maturity, independence, self-confidence and often happiness, while at
the same time being 'minimalist'.[82] As Judy Wade put it in a June 1997
Hello! feature, it hardly mattered whether 'it's a vampy Versace or a
classic Catherine Walker', the shape was the same. Yet at the same time

that the look could be understood as having a denotative meaning, for Wade at least it cancelled the expressivity of Diana's image. All that is said by Diana's appearance in these dresses, as far as Wade can make out, is 'I know I'm on show'. She went on to finish her report with an interesting apotheosis of Diana as enigmatic female:

> She is a complex character, as mysterious as she is approachable. This dual appeal keeps the world guessing. We may think we know the Princess of Wales, but will anyone ever really know Diana?[83]

Although the invocation of enigmatic femininity is never unproblematic, this account bears the traces of a shift in Diana's iconicity in the context of the Dress Sale. In particular, it suggests a much more personally empowering negotiation of public and private than that framed by the same magazine's cover story two months earlier, which had described Diana as 'trapped between two worlds', 'no longer a royal highness but forever unable to lead a private life'.[84]

As represented in *Hello!* the shift I have been suggesting with respect to the Dress Sale is realised only intermittently. The difficulty of knowing Diana implied by Wade's article was erased in the trail for it on the magazine cover. Here, ambiguities became the singular attributes of the enigmatic 'Daring yet timid, loved but lonely/Diana/Woman of contrasts'. In the cover photograph Diana is shown expressing such a contrast. She looks to be speaking passionately and confidently, while glancing sideways anxiously and nervously intertwining her fingers. More innovatively, the sequence of photographs accompanying Wade's report made explicit both representation as a material practice and Diana's acquired skills at self-presentation. The images portrayed Diana at two recent public events, the opening of the London Dress Sale show and a gala performance of *Swan Lake* at the Albert Hall. Across the magazine's centre pages, the princess was shown demonstrating what captions call 'her skill at getting out of cars elegantly', and 'a new gesture to ensure modesty in front of the cameras' necessitated by the recently adopted scoop necklines of her 1997 look. On later pages, interior shots are accompanied by Wade's more detailed explanation of how Diana deliberately stands as fashion models are trained to do in order to ensure she photographs well.[85] Now clearly at one level the presentation of these photographs in this way functions to license their production and consumption. A potentially objectifying gaze is acknowledged, only to be disavowed. Yet this treatment does strongly demarcate public and private selves, and negates the logic of expressivity. Diana's appearance is presented here as saying absolutely nothing about a personal and private self. Moreover, the skills of self-presentation she is shown demonstrating at these public engagements are themselves circumscribed within the discourse of celebrity femininity, without mythic or other symbolic reach.

Hello! has played a significant role in configuring Diana representations. According to the magazine's tenth anniversary issue, by May 1998 Diana had featured on 61 covers, around 12 per cent of the total and more than twice as many as the next most heavily featured person, Sarah Ferguson. In addition, Diana appeared on the cover of four of the six best-selling issues. This includes the magazines issued in the weeks of her death and funeral, which sold around one million copies each.[86] Clearly marketed at an interest in celebrity which is self-consciously, though not exclusively feminized, *Hello!* always sought to distance itself from the most invasive and objectifying practices of celebrity photo-journalism as practised by the most downmarket tabloids. The magazine claims not to use the work of unaccredited or paparazzi photographers, and it is averred that its publisher bought photographs of Diana sunbathing topless in order to prevent their publication. Whether or not there is truth in these notions, their circulation suggests the ambivalent position of *Hello!* in mediating, licensing and controlling popular interest in the personal lives of others. This ambivalence is clearly visible in the feature just discussed, and in the yearly surveys of 'the most and the least elegant outfit' worn by Diana, published in the Christmas 1995 and 1996 issues.[87] Another crucial factor here is the way in which royalty is represented in *Hello!* as an intensified kind of celebrity. The international reach of the publication tends to draw the royal within the field of celebrity more generally, thus marginalizing the specific iconic discourses associated with royalty. In general it is not that *Hello!* demystifies monarchical discourses, but it allows them to be activated in varying intensities by its readers. Thus in some limited ways, the magazine anticipated certain elements of the reading of the Dress Sale offered here, in giving rise to a more normalized sense of Diana as separable into personal and public selves, whose image was meaningful but whose meanings were delimited and contingent.

The Dress Sale was a gesture of disavowing emblematic significance which was itself emblematic. This doubleness makes it important to distinguish between accounts which take for granted the wholesale liquidation of iconic readings of Diana's appearance, and those which acknowledge the persistence of expressive discourses. On the one hand the Dress Sale is incorporated into a linear narrative of empowerment, marking the obsolescence of evening wear because Diana had finished a life of formal display and moved on to a life of useful activity. On the other hand is the notion that the Dress Sale demonstrated the structural rather than the historical inadequacy of clothes, and by extension images, to convey identity.

Unequivocally celebratory accounts of Diana enshrine the first of these and thereby perpetuate the objectifying discourse of expressivity. To consider the Dress Sale as in itself dispensing with emblematic significance is to suspend rather than to cancel the iconic meaning of the dresses themselves. Hence, as in the posthumous fashion biographies, the celebratory narrative of a final liberation from the double bind of 'being rather than doing' coexists easily with a sense of the biographical significances of the dresses themselves. Thus in *Diana: Her Life in Fashion*, for example, Georgina Howell quotes Etherington-Smith's description of the dresses as 'mini-biographies', as Horyn had done in the *Vanity Fair* article. Having thus restored the authoritative status of the dresses as biographical signifiers, Howell goes on to present the assemblage of dresses as negating their material status. 'To see them for real,' according to Howell, 'conferred on them Diana's own mystique and reminded the world of each royal milestone.'[88]

Even where, as in *Vanity Fair*, commentators such as Horyn go on to qualify or contest the notion of the dresses as 'mini-biographies', this tends to be on the grounds that the Dress Sale itself makes them historically obsolete. The dresses are understood as inadequate biographical signifiers since their frame of reference remains within the purely ceremonial sphere associated with the royal family. Horyn's transatlantic, 1990s perspective translates what Bagehot called the 'dignified' constitutional role of the monarchy into 'film premieres', 'equine pageants' and 'snore-inducing banquets'.[89] As symbolized by the Dress Sale, Diana's break with the royal family is thus constructed in terms of a shift from a purely emblematic existence associated with the British monarchy into the realm of reality and practical usefulness, implicitly coded as American. Clearly, both the liquidation of the dresses into hard cash for AIDS and other charities, and Diana's embrace of landmines activism, are powerful signals of such a biographical transformation. However, they cannot help but be just signals. The Dress Sale is popularly understood as demonstrating the historical contingency of clothing – and hence appearance – in representing Diana; the point is to see it as demonstrating the structural contingency of this process.

Diana's death reimbued material objects with the power to signify her, since there was no longer any possibility of a real self making itself present. As a result, the break in signification associated with the Dress Sale has largely been closed up and flattened out. Whereas I have argued for a sense of the sale as lodging biographical meanings in inanimate objects, in the passage quoted above Howell conceptualizes this relationship in reverse. Instead of the dresses materializing Diana's history, it is Diana's 'mystique' which attached itself to the dresses. It is clear that images of Diana will continue to have iconic significance of various kinds, and to be read as denoting a biographical narrative.

Because images are as much representations as they are expressions, it is easy to pour scorn on beliefs that Diana was embodied in her image. But critical discourses that have sought to directly unmask what they portray as 'fakery', 'non-questions', *'connerie'*, 'captivat[ion]' or 'an age of dreams' in relation to Diana's iconicity have tended to replay monolithic distinctions between rationality and emotion, high culture and popular culture, and to adopt a posture of critical insight which positions the people as cultural dopes.[90] The reinscription of these binary oppositions does little to illuminate Diana's cultural significance. What matters so far as consumers of 'Diana' are concerned – and that includes those who mourned and those who were indifferent – is neither the success nor failure of an ascribed project of doing rather than being, but the shifting frameworks of meaning that made possible popular understandings of Diana as projecting the personal via mass media while, arguably, the basis for her iconicity shifted massively. Similarly, attempts to contest Diana's iconicity on the grounds that her public image was at odds with her (personal/private) self have a point, but miss *the* point.[91] What is at stake here is less the relationship between an actual person and representations of that person, than the meaningful structures by which millions of people made sense of Diana images as negotiating distinctions between personal and public.

Therefore, images of Diana should neither be rejected as disseminators of false consciousness, nor uncritically celebrated as expressions of the personal across mass media. Instead, they are complex social texts which bear the traces of multiple intentions and are subject to many readings. Thus, for example, the February 1992 photograph of Diana alone at the Taj Mahal is neither wholly an emotionally-laden 'postcard home' as one commentator has called it, nor media manipulation by Diana, nor even the sole creation of the press photographers who arranged the shot, but is produced out of a complex set of interactions.[92] The same goes for all images of Diana, whether overdetermined by iconographies of sainthood and white femininity like the Cairo photograph discussed above, or imbued with biographical significance, like the succession of photographs in black and navy evening dresses, from the off-the-shoulder ballgown of March 1981 to the blue velvet Victor Edelstein worn at the White House in December 1985, to the Stambolian 'revenge dress' selected for the Serpentine Gallery in March 1994, to the halterneck Catherine Walker taken to New York in February 1995.

5
The Mourning for Diana and the Question of National Transformation

> In our grief for Diana, there is none of that old British reserve. We are united as never before. And we want the world to know it. It is the new British spirit. The spirit of Diana, proclaimed loud and proudly throughout the land.
>
> Editorial, *Daily Mirror*, 4 September 1997[1]

The project of historicizing Diana representations cannot help but undermine the construction of Diana as a unique, transcendent figure. The emphasis on representation in the foregoing has, to some extent deliberately, rubbed against the grain of the intense affective responses to Diana's death and the exceptionalist readings of her significance they suggested, whether celebratory or dismissive or making abject. Situating 'Diana' with respect to discourses of monarchy, gender, race and figuration has provided a means of evaluating the claims and counter-claims made posthumously for Diana's significance. Yet the associations of Diana with intensity and excess still require explanation. In this concluding chapter I will try to suggest some reasons for the intensity of 'pro' and 'anti'-Diana sentiments, and to assess their significance. This is to continue the trajectory of previous chapters, in which analysis and historical description are turned increasingly towards explanation and evaluation. Moving on now to the posthumous contests over Diana's significance, questions of 'how' are further displaced by the necessity of asking 'why?' and ultimately, if it can be put so crudely, 'so what?'. Answers to these questions start with the senses of plenitude, unity and transformation associated with the 'Diana events', and end with the possibilities for reimagining national identity through the figure of Diana.

Diana as either/or: unitary representations of the Diana events

During the week of Diana's funeral, printed media and television alike presented a common sense that the mourning process was calling into being a national transformation. The *Mirror*'s editorial commentary quoted above, like one in the previous day's edition of the *Sun*, described the emergence of a new national identity which required cultural and political change, albeit focused on reform of the monarchy.[2] The broadsheet press took up a similar theme in terms that were equally if not more extreme. On the eve of Diana's funeral, 6 September 1997, in the *Guardian* newspaper, the American academic Elaine Showalter described the mass mourning for Diana as 'a political occasion, a moment of subdued, but very British, revolutionary sentiment'.[3] A day later, the *Observer* put the slogan 'The nation unites against tradition' above its masthead, following up the next week with a round-table discussion under the rubric of 'New Britain', featuring Will Hutton, Stuart Hall, A.L. Kennedy and Susie Orbach.[4]

Despite the repetition of certain key phrases, especially 'new' and 'united', a clear vision of national transformation did not emerge. By framing their perorations as reproaches to the Queen's lack of public response, the *Sun* and the *Mirror* adopted ambivalent positions, reiterating the centrality of the monarchy to national identity, while taking for granted populist authority to dictate royal behaviour. From a different political position, the right-wing journalist Simon Heffer contested the association of Diana with a demand for change. Rather, Heffer argued in the *Daily Mail* (3 September) the shared grief for Diana had 'truly united our kingdom', demonstrating the strength of national communal ties within the entity of Great Britain.[5] Heffer was enlisting the Diana events against what he saw as the centrifugal forces of devolution, a reading later forcefully rejected by Anthony Barnett, who elaborated their progressive influence on constitutional reform in *This Time*.[6] As the format of the *Observer*'s treatment implied, the details of any social change remained up for debate. In this debate, 'Diana' became a sign that naturalized competing definitions of a 'new Britain'; pro- or anti-devolution, populist and monarchist.

In the first instance, this diversity is a direct result of the multiple and conflicted iconicity associated with Diana while she was alive. Posthumously, Diana came to figure (new) Britain in still more intensified ways because representations of her gave visual or verbal form to the sense of social integration associated with the mourning events. Enfolding debates over devolution, the cultural and political significance of the monarchy, a national transformation imagined 'in the feminine', and much more besides, Diana's posthumous iconicity was elaborated on a continuum between two extremes. At one pole, whiteness and aristocratic Englishness were reproduced at the centre of national identity. At the other pole, the mourning events took up the images of Diana making contact with people of diverse racial, ethnic and sexual identity. She thereby became a figure of mutuality across ethnic and racial difference, both within the nation and in relations between Britain or Britons and others.

What made all these visions of new Britain powerful and effective was the notion that the mourning for Diana constituted a shared emotional experience. The various explicit attempts to shape the nation imagined themselves as coming after events which had united the country at the level of feeling. Journalists and academic commentators celebrated the mass mourning for Diana in terms of inclusivity, as a kind of democracy of feeling available to all without distinction of race or ethnicity, gender, generation, sexuality, education or intellectual ability. It was even, given the global reach of her iconic image, an international phenomenon, but one that was owned by the British. The project for commentators thus became one of making self-conscious the social solidarity they perceived, by elaborating its meaning. National unity could be assumed as already having been achieved, almost magically.

A combination of factors suggested this interpretation. Most obvious was the apparent diversity of those who publicly mourned, including non-white Commonwealth immigrants and their descendants, the ladies of middle England, gay men, children and also a vast range of foreign nationals around the world. It was important that these groups within Britain were seen to be composed of people who were normally underprivileged in terms of access to the media. Mourning Diana was thereby understood as a means of becoming visible in mainstream media. This emphasis on new signifiers of Britishness meshed with a general sense that the public reaction to Diana's death arose outside the mass media, which was then obliged to reconstitute itself as a carrier for the authentically popular. The coupling of this sense of the popular with notions of transformation suggested the term 'revolution' to commentators such as Showalter and Jacques.[7] Qualified, and to some extent ironized, by the adjectives 'British' and 'floral', respectively, both formulations testified to the difficulties of maintaining a critical sense of proportion on the Diana events' combination of mass emotion with shifts in national identity.

At the other extreme from celebratory responses, it was exactly their assumption of a unified nation that provoked mistrust and anxiety on the part of a minority of commentators. Ian Jack assembled in the literary magazine *Granta* the views of some of 'those who felt differently', highlighting the exclusivity of insisting on participation in mass emotions. In more deliberately ideological mode, the right-wing think tank the Social Affairs Unit associated Diana with emotionalism, moral relativism and a victim culture blamed on identity politics. In the Unit's anthology volume *Faking It: The Sentimentalisation of Modern Society*, published in April 1998, Diana's popularity and the public reaction to her death were included in a multifaceted critique of the so-called 'sentimentalization' of Britain. Anthony O'Hear attacked the Diana events as 'the elevation of feeling, image and spontaneity over reason, reality and restraint', part and parcel of the dissolution of social ties based on duty, restraint and deference to establishment authority and their replacement by mere sentiment.[8]

Drawing implicitly on conservative cultural hierarchies, and explicitly on Edmund Burke's criticism of the French revolution, O'Hear also stood for the patrician elements of academia in rejecting an explicitly feminized affectivity in the name of an implicitly masculine reason. Conversely, many on the left, including for example Elizabeth Wilson and Richard Coles, saw the Diana events as a *reductio ad absurdum* of feminism and gay activism. Wilson, Coles and other critical academics were animated by a suspicion of representations of social homogeneity that has its roots in Marxist, feminist, gay and lesbian, and anti-colonial traditions. At the same time, and overlapping with this, the plenitude and fullness attributed to the society that mourned Diana were bound to attract scepticism from critical positions influenced by psychoanalysis and poststructuralism. From these perspectives the promise of full self-presence associated with mourning Diana could appear as pathological and/or 'merely' linguistic, a discursive effect mistaken for a communal experience.

The mass media's overwhelming mobilization of national presentness in respect of the Diana events created an urgent need for demystification.[9] But the persistent ambivalence of Diana's own significance was reiterated by the mourning itself. Given that 'Diana' remained a site of continual contestation, what could it mean to reject her significance? Projects of direct critique often found themselves giving weight to the Diana phenomena even while insisting on their triviality or irrelevance. Something of this is registered in Antony Easthope's mocking apology to 'true believers' in 'Saint Diana of the pont de l'Alma', and, more productively in the title of Wilson's essay, 'The Unbearable Lightness of Diana'.[10] The ironic strategies deployed by Wilson, Easthope and others are attempts to negotiate this double bind, with varying degress of self-consciousness, but which can never quite succeed. As much as irony is used to deflate celebratory accounts of Diana, ironic exaggeration perpetuates the association of Diana with excess. The perceived triviality at the centre of the Diana phenomena paradoxically makes them deeply worrying. Hence there is a symptomatic unease in unitary and diagnostic critical responses to the Diana events. It is echoed in the overtly celebratory material, as in the use by Showalter and Jacques of qualifiers to their notion of revolution, which neither fully ironise nor precisely delineate the kind of revolution at stake.

Diana as 'both ... and': multivalent representations of the Diana events

With the benefit of further hindsight, and the decreasing intensity of populist celebratory discourses, more recent academic analyses of the Diana events have sought to avoid unitary judgements. A highly insightful essay by Nick Couldry opens up a discussion of the Diana events as offering the image of social integration rather than its reality.[11] In an effort to avoid either/or diagnosticism, but to maintain critical positioning, Couldry uses de Certeau's distinction between tactical and strategic cultural interventions. This enables critical analysis by differentiating between shifts in access to symbolic power on the basis of their duration and structural impact. The Diana events can thereby be seen in terms of a trajectory whereby, initially, the customary transparency of the media as simply fulfilling the dictates of popular interest was put at stake. Ultimately, however, this relation was not transformed. Rather, the effect was arguably to increase the concentration of media power by reinvigorating the persuasiveness of mediated representations of popular feeling. In retrospect, liminal examples such as the *volte face* performed on Diana and Dodi by the popular press, and the hostility to the mass media represented on television, could be portrayed as evidence of the mass media's honesty, accuracy, and willingness to respond to shifts in the popular mood.

Couldry's account of the relations between media representation and the popular points directly towards notions of difference, especially differential access to and power over representation. In an essay in the same volume, Mark Gibson explicitly defines the possibilities and the problems raised by Diana in terms of representing racial and ethnic difference. Gibson describes the signification of Diana, especially her association with Dodi Fayed, in terms of 'the transposition of difference onto a plane of *non*-contradiction, where transracial, transcultural social encounters are not remarked as such, but are simply "taken for granted".'[12] This is to be distinguished from a hoped-for sense of identities in contradiction, which would enable a genuine shift in the relations between political centre and margins. Gibson's formulation of this problematic, and Mica Nava's identification of celebratory Diana discourses with 'a kind of *post* anti-racism'[13] to which it is a response, suggest the importance of paying attention to the symbolic structures through which Diana figured relations of racial and cultural difference. As Gibson's work implies, the celebratory discourses of inclusivity inspired by the mourning events are structured by a double move in which difference is both acknowledged and taken for granted. This work of displacement is performed by taking up, and often taking for granted, the cultural formation of royal femininity. National identity is symbolically unified by being displaced on to Diana's personal, affective and romantic associations.

The presence of these conservative formations alongside ideas from feminist traditions ensures that Diana's posthumous iconicity is fundamentally mixed. This is not to say that the meaning of Diana is arbitrary or simply multiple, because its arbitrariness and proliferation are most often contained by syntheses which bear a strong resemblance to the familiar monarchical combinations of ordinary/extraordinary. Diana's significance is ambivalent, not plural.[14] This ambivalence inhibits the direct appropriation of 'Diana' in the name of a holistic constituency or programme, whether in terms of 'feminization' or 'conservative modernization'.

As such, Diana's posthumous signification has worked in similar ways to the Blairite Labour Party's uses of the past. Andrew Blake has coined the term 'retrolution' as a way of understanding how the reform programmes of New Labour have been presented in terms of continuity, by imagining the future in terms of the past.[15] Rather than simply regarding the 'modernization' of the monarchy achieved with Blair's help after Diana's death as a manoeuvre to preserve traditional power relations, Blake's analysis suggests a more dynamic relationship between continuity and change. If certain continuities can be deployed as a means of enabling significant change, cultural activity can play a significant role in imagining futures other than those determined by market forces and commodity fetishism. Hence the notion of retrolution provides a means to analyse critically Blairism and the Diana events, while also foregrounding the cultural sphere as a site for the imagination of political change. So far as Diana is concerned, it is less a question of the presence of the past, than of the uses to which historical formations are put. What is crucial to understanding the ambivalent and contradictory definitions of new Britain associated with Diana is a sense of how notions of femininity and whiteness are *markedly* involved in the remodelling of national identity.[16]

In pursuing these concerns I am not attempting to speak for the mourners who were otherwise marginalized. Nor do I wish to reify Diana's significance in discourses of whiteness or femininity, whether historical or innovative. Instead, my objectives are to show how Diana representations worked as imaging relations between people of different identities, to delineate the various ways in which these images of difference were synthesized to constitute national identity, and above all to demonstrate how progressive readings of Diana are enabled and constrained by the symbolic resonances of her gender, class, sexual, racial and ethnic identities.

Diana died in a state of semi-detachment from the royal family. Although she was stripped of the title 'Her Royal Highness', reserved for close members of the royal family, Diana maintained publicly a major investment in her royal or quasi-royal status. During the 1995 *Panorama* interview Diana articulated a position of strong support for the institution of monarchy, presenting the role of mother to the future king as work of national responsibility. By assuming her transcendence of royal status, celebratory accounts unselfconsciously reiterate the synthesis of ordinary and extraordinary that Diana representations inherited from monarchical ideology. In contrast, critical commentators are keenly aware of a failure to close the ideological gap between Diana as ordinary and as extraordinary. Hence they attack as mystifying the presentation of Diana as 'one of us'.[17] To regard 'Diana' as a site of contest necessitates the forgoing of such unitary explanations. What can be offered instead is an explanation of the ways in which Diana's figuration of national unity was structured by a variety of identity formations developing in relation to one another and over time. Elizabeth Wilson's critique of the conservative elements of Diana's iconicity, 'white, blonde, tall and slim, the most traditional style of beauty',[18] is undeniable, but what remains unacknowledged are the complex ways in which this identity works with and against 'colour'.

Diana's whiteness has been presented in relation to others in several registers. In the realm of official public duties, she was seen 'reaching out' to difference whether through her treatment of AIDS patients, or her trips to Angola and Bosnia on behalf of the campaign against land-mines. Such ambivalent representations combined elements of a latter-day Lady Bountiful, reconstituting the status of whiteness via traditional formations of charity, to which were added a revisionist politicization of Diana's status. In a very different context, representations of her romantic associations with men of colour such as Hasnat Khan, and especially Dodi Fayed, set up Diana's personal affective life as a model of whiteness embracing difference. Diana's emotional attachments were read as authenticating what might otherwise be con-sidered mere gestures. This trajectory was intensified still further posthumously by the imagined possibility of a mixed-race baby born to Diana and Dodi, who would be half-brother or half-sister to the princes of the blood royal. This notion has attracted a variety of invest-ments, which are further complicated by Mohammed al Fayed's own unsuccessful attempts to gain British citizenship, and his accusations that a racially motivated conspiracy was responsible for the deaths of Diana, Dodi and their driver, Henri Paul. The possibility of such a preg-nancy enables Diana to be seen both as a figure for white Englishness embracing difference, and as embodying a new Britain defined in terms of multi-ethnic synthesis. Yet this apparently progressive emblem is heavily indebted to conservative formations of gender, race and nation. On the one hand, Diana's figuration of national identity takes place through the most literal sense of embodiment. On the other hand, the continual slippage between her status as signifying English/British national identity and/or white racial identity serves ultimately to maintain the centrality of whiteness in the national imaginary.

Race, ethnicity and 'national desire'

At least since the 1960s, theorists of nation have emphasized the disjunction between the political nation-state and the cultural or ideo-logical production of national identity. 'Nationalism is not the awak-ening of nations to self-consciousness,' as Ernest Gellner forcibly put it, rather 'it invents nations where they do not exist'.[19] In the seminal *Imagined Communities*, Benedict Anderson softened Gellner's either/or formulation and investigated the antithetical notions of time associated with nationhood. As Anderson makes clear, the self-perception of a homogeneous 'folk' whose history stretches back in linear time is called into being by the political institution of the nation-state, rather than the other way round. Hence Anderson came to regard as central the question of why the nation, perhaps the defining institution of modernity, imagines itself as antique. This sense of nationhood as a combination of antiquity and modernity helps us to see how the constitutional monarchy is at the centre of the process of nation-making. Rather than some feudal remnant, it is the very status of the monarchy as an anachronism that gives it a unique ability to authenticate the nation.

The implications of this problematic exceed the scope of the analytical traditions of Marxist historiography and British empiricism that Anderson brought to bear. The priority of nation as a political entity to the cultural nation whose expression it claims to be, is not only historical but also discursive. As a focus of national identity, the British constitutional monarchy – and Diana – can be seen to naturalize the political nation in both historicist and discursive ways. Its invented traditions supply a sense of historical continuity, while the royal family performs national identity for audiences whose communal responses reproduce affective ties. In these different ways, the constitutional monarchy makes good, or makes bearable, the 'lack' at the heart of the nation.[20]

In relation to this lack, the royal family and Diana can be seen as performing national identity in significantly different forms. In broad terms, the royal family provided a continuous narrative which served perpetually to defer satisfaction of desires for national homogeneity. While the figure of Diana took part in this narrative, it also offered the overt realization of an ethnically English nation. As has been seen in chapter 2, the iconography of the 'English rose' and genealogies attesting Diana's 'English blood' presented her as the means to reinvigorate the royal family by making it more ethnically and racially English. From 1981, then, Diana was read both as ethnically English and as an actor in the narrative production of Britishness. At first this doubleness mutually reinforced that of the Windsors, as for example via the shared experiences of Charles and Diana in aristocratic country pursuits. That they met in a cornfield on the margins of a shoot made Charles more English too. Yet Diana's English blood-line was always capable of opening up a sense of lack so far as the 'Germanic' Windsors were concerned. After 1992, and especially posthumously it came to stand over and against the monarchy's personifications of the nation, which in turn came to seem one-dimensional.

Both Julie Burchill, and Kitty Kelley in *The Royals* (1997), published outside the UK in the week of Diana's funeral, are much exercised by what they perceive as the Windsors' lack of true Englishness.[21] Yet the 'non-Englishness' of the British royal family was hardly at issue from 1917, when the name Windsor was adopted to replace Saxe-Coburg-Gotha, until the late 1980s/early 1990s. Only latterly has the name change itself come to mark the royal family as inauthentic, because of the comparison with the less performative and more embodied modes of figuring the nation associated with Diana.

The powerful sense of Diana as the antithesis of the Windsors over-shadows the real continuities between royal spectacle and media repre-sentations of the Diana events. As Jatinder Verma has pointed out in an essay which shows up the ways in which Diana particularized whiteness, while Asians and 'other ethnics' shared centre-stage in the mourning events, they were conspicuously absent from positions of intellectual commentary in the media.[22] The presence of non-white people as part of the national spectacle was celebrated, as it had been in Imperial and Commonwealth parades, yet the mainstream media rarely presented non-whites as having anything to say about the new Britain that was apparently emerging. Again, as Paul Gilroy has argued, the presence of non-white mourners is remarkable more for its genera-tion of surprise than for the factual existence of racially and ethnically differentiated Britons.[23] Such professions of surprise make sense only if the whiteness of Britain has already been assumed, and surely Diana's iconicity, and the ideological formations of monarchy, had played a part in generating the assumption that exemplary Britons were white.

Royal visits and the geography of difference

In his powerfully scathing response to celebrations of the Diana events, Gilroy insisted on the double importance of monarchical ideology and mass media structures in giving form and meaning to the popular response to Diana's death. Gilroy pointed to strong similarities between the models of national unity provided by coverage of the Diana and Dodi romance and the mourning events on the one hand, and monarchical traditions, Churchill's state funeral and Victorian notions of charity on the other. Building on these connections, it is possible to place Diana representations in a long tradition of portrayals of the royal family as figuring British *and* English identity. Official royal visits enact this significance both internally and externally, through placing the royal family in relation to native people within the geography of Britain, the British Empire and Commonwealth, and of other nations. While visits within the British Isles serve to differentiate Britishness internally according to nation, region and locality, English and British identity are cohered most explicitly during official visits overseas. As was suggested briefly in the previous chapter, Diana's 1997 visits to Angola and Bosnia can be seen as revisionist versions of the royal tour. The combination of national and racial identity in the figure of Diana can be traced by returning to this comparison in more detail. Clearly there are major historical shifts between the moments of Empire, Commonwealth and multicultural Britain associated with respectively Victoria, Elizabeth II and Diana. Yet there are also continuities in the ways that Britishness and Englishness have been produced by representations of royal tours. Victoria's sojourns in Scotland, the 1901 'Royal Tour' in which the future George V and Queen Mary visited almost the whole of the British Empire, excepting India, the visit to Southern Africa undertaken by George VI and family in 1947, the 'Royal Commonwealth Tour' taken by Elizabeth and Philip in 1953–4, and Diana's trips to Angola and Bosnia, were all highly mediated events which constructed a racialized geography.

In the representation of these visits in news media and more permanent souvenirs, racial difference has historically played an important part in structuring relations between England, Britain, Empire and Commonwealth. Racial and ethnic difference was mapped onto a hierarchy of centre and margins, whereby the Empire was internally differentiated by distance from the metropole. Hence Victoria's status as Queen was confirmed by her being recognized by Scots while travelling in disguise.[24] Illustrations drew on and reinforced this hierarchical structure of difference, by making geographical distinctions visible through ethnic and racial difference. Thus, for example, in his 'lower deck account' of the 1901 tour, Petty Officer Harry Price devoted a full page to an illustrated taxonomy of 'Diferent [*sic*] Races of People met with During the Tour'.[25]

The photographs in Dermot Morrah's *The Royal Family in Africa* (1947) clearly portrayed the validation of the political authority and representative legitimacy of monarchy – and by synecdoche Britain – by its being put in the sight of Black Africans, white colonial Britons and Afrikaners. Stimulated by the centrifugal political forces that had led to a multiplication of political arrangements, the visit took in the Union of South Africa, headed by Smuts, the 'High Commission

Territories' of Basutoland, Swaziland and Bechuanaland, and the 'colonies' of Northern and Southern Rhodesia. It was by appealing to human relationships, in explicit contradistinction from 'abstract principles', that the complex relations between these political units were conceptualized, and, it was hoped, stabilized. Morrah began by invoking Protagoras's assertion that 'Man ... is the measure of all things', by way of broaching the questions of a written constitution, the role of the monarchy and the political organisation of the Empire.[26] However, even as Morrah went on to particularize King George VI as 'the man who is the measure of all British things', the rhetoric of kingly personage was giving way to the more flexible and engaging visual iconography of the royal *family*.

It was the family that was given prominence in the book's title. It was the family too whose activities provided its main interest, and whose image, in the shape of the King, Queen, their two daughters and an unidentified lady-in-waiting disembarking from a plane, occupied the centre of its dustcover. Similarly, popular souvenir booklets of the 1953–54 Commonwealth Tour presented Elizabeth and Philip in terms of the family.[27] The young Charles and Anne, who had been left at home, nevertheless were heavily featured in the account of their parents' journey homeward. Still more strikingly, many of the elements of the visit are configured by reference to the family unit, in ways that replay and extend the conventional deployment of children as innocent markers of difference. It is not just that the Queen is twice shown accepting a bouquet from a five-year old Black girl, one Tongan and the other Maori; on two occasions white local girls are presented as surrogate royal children.[28] Photographs and narrative combine to constitute the white girls as temporary members of the royal family, while the Black girls actively perform deference. It is the constitution of Britishness in terms of the family that naturalizes these asymmetrical power relations. There is no such reciprocity in comparable representations such as H.R.H. The Duke of Edinburgh's *Birds from Britannia*, the record of a 1956–7 world tour modelled after androcentric narratives of exploration, which is concerned with obtaining photographic images of birds and sea mammals, and intra-racial male-bonding.[29]

In order to fulfil the Imperialist function of consolidating English/British identity at the metropole, descriptions of royal tours necessarily conferred a certain order of ethnic and cultural identity on the 'other'. This is highlighted by the contrast between the Duke of Edinburgh's one-man adventure narrative and the Commonwealth

Tour souvenirs. When Prince Philip plays the explorer, the objects of the powerful gaze of the non-white male are reduced to the level of mere nature. Somewhat less objectifying, though still clearly asymmetrical in terms of power and centrality, is the reciprocal gaze required to consolidate British authority through what is presented as colonial deference (in the examples cited above, the exotically clothed Black girl presenting the Queen with flowers). This marking of difference also constitutes the ideal English family as white. What was and remains crucial for both these processes is the presentation of difference in terms of space. In royal visits, regional, racial and ethnic tensions are displaced to a plane of non-contradiction, in Gibson's phrase, by being settled down into stable geographic spaces. According to this logic, London, or rather Windsor, is the source and centre of Englishness and whiteness, from which Britons are displaced according to regionally located racial and ethnic identities. Within such a spatial hierarchy of difference, it is only on special occasions such as military anniversaries, coronations, marriages, and funerals, that such differences are expected to become visible at the metropole. The very exceptionalism of such gatherings serves to reconfirm the authority of the centre.

Diana's visits to Angola and Bosnia in support of the campaign to ban land-mines sent out mixed messages, in which these colonialist ideological forms were partially reworked by reference to discourses of humanitarianism and internationalism. The instability to which this combination gave rise is well exemplified by the temporary politicization of the celebrity magazine *Hello!* in October 1997. *Hello!* marked the award of the 1997 Nobel Peace Prize to the International Campaign to Ban Land Mines with a cover feature on Diana's part in the campaign, which included the following reportage:

> When the Princess walked across a stretch of ground littered with mines, at a significant risk to her own personal safety despite her body armour and protective visor, the image was shown around the world. But her courage earned her criticism, most notably from several Tory ministers, one of whom described her as a 'loose cannon' and another who declared: 'The parallel that comes to mind is Brigitte Bardot and cats.'
>
> The controversy that Diana provoked at Whitehall, which was less than enthusiastic about the ban, initially claiming that land-mines were 'legitimate defensive weapons', did not undermine her determination to 'raise the profile' of the campaign. And the claim that she was meddling inappropriately in political issues was

answered by the Princess with, 'I am not a political figure. The fact is I am a humanitarian – always have been, always will be.'[30]

The later change in government policy, and the subsequent international agreement to ban the manufacture and sale of land-mines (yet to be fully ratified) have been used to substantiate claims for the importance of Diana as bringing to bear something other than expediency and self-interest into national and global politics. But rather than positioning Diana as marking some kind of political or cultural break, nearly two months after her death *Hello!* articulated a variety of conflicting definitions of her identity and significance. Even in such a short passage, she was represented as being politically controversial, in drawing criticism from the Conservative Party and provoking 'consternation in Whitehall', but in her own words, non-political; in danger, yet not in danger; and, perhaps most significantly, so deeply understood as English that it did not need stating, but regarded as foreign 'like Brigitte Bardot', by a Tory cabinet minister.

These ambivalences were reiterated by the *Hello!* feature as a whole, which took the form of a retrospective of Diana's involvement in the International Campaign to Ban Landmines. There was no sense of incongruity in placing political and humanitarian material alongside the apparent trivia of celebrity lifestyles, suggesting both the importance of celebrity in modelling identity and the multivalent power of Diana's persona. Its photographs were familiar images of Diana reaching out and touching the injured and bereaved in Angola and Bosnia, as well as including more businesslike representations of what look like fact-finding sessions, meetings with officials and aid workers. Yet one of the most striking images, placed directly above the text just quoted, is of Diana amid a group of white soldiers in Bosnia.[31] It recalls strongly the tradition of an Imperialist, masculinized military presence, enlivened by females sent from home initially as nurses, and more recently as entertainers. Against this, the rhetoric employed in the accompanying reportage insists that Diana has entered this masculinized arena of conflict to campaign against military practices. This potentially jarring juxtaposition is left unresolved, allowing Diana's feminine presence to naturalize and sustain Western military legitimacy at the same time that it is presented as overwhelming the hidebound prejudices of male politicians.

It is not hard to see how the multifaceted presentation of Diana in popular culture exemplified here called up the either/or critical responses described above. Attempts to mobilize Diana's iconicity in the service of a major break in the cultural politics of gender and/or national identity, as for example by Beatrix Campbell and Elaine Showalter, provoked responses which considered Diana and the reaction to her death as being at best meaningless, at worst reactionary. In one of these Linda Holt is clearly right to argue that 'the expressing of feelings' by itself can be an invidious substitute for political action, but a more constructive response is found in the work of feminists such as Ruth Barcan, Sally Begbie and Rosi Braidotti, who regard Diana's femininity as an incomplete and/or ambivalent project.[32]

It is the distance between femininity as lived experience and as symbol that places gender at the centre of this debate over the reworking of, or break with, tradition associated with Diana. As Sally Begbie put it succinctly in an essay significantly titled 'Dianaland – Not a playground for the fainthearted':

> In recognising the 'feminine' in feminism there is the danger that the new recruit might just be the patriarchy in disguise, but perhaps it is one of the most effective weapons against it.[33]

The material discussed in previous chapters suggests several reasons for viewing 'Diana' as a site of continuing debate with respect to these issues rather than a stabilizing iconic presence. Diana's iconicity is compounded of a mixture of discourses of femininity and consequently has multiple implications for gender politics. Most importantly perhaps, the inspirational reading of her trajectory in terms of the fulfilment of femininity as self-presence must be tempered by a sense of the continued presence of the problematic discourse of Diana's photographic expressivity. The power of Diana's image must not be allowed to negate the importance of a speaking female subject. Such problems are compounded when Diana's performance of femininity is deployed in the service of social transformation and national identity. Diana as humanitarian can be construed either as demanding the transformation of politics or as an exceptionalist suspension of the political for a single issue: landmines.

Given the symbolic importance of notions of royal femininity long before Diana came to public attention, it is hard to sustain for long the argument that she represents the liberation of femininity against the monarchy as one of the bulwarks of patriarchal power. Similarly, the political instability of notions of the monarchy as on the one hand naturalizing established power relations or on the other hand as signalling that there is such a thing as society, make it impossible to categorize inspirational readings of Diana's trajectory as either fulfilling or displacing the royal.

The history of royal femininity also suggests the crucial importance of seeing Diana's iconicity as an incomplete reworking of Imperialist representations of white women. Images of Diana reaching out across racial and ethnic difference can be read as producing a new whiteness, which maintains a global and international role but one informed by an ethic of care rather than Imperialist or national self-interest. Yet such images also draw upon a history of racialized representations of white women as nurses to the Empire and reproducers of the nation. At the same time, the perceived immediacy of Diana's iconicity brought her own embodied identity into play much more directly than the more performative and symbolic representations of the royal family. While to a certain extent their 'true' ethnicity as German was contingent to their performance of Britishness, Diana's whiteness was indispensable to her association with national identity.

The story of Di and Dodi as multi-ethnic romance

If, as Benedict Anderson put it, the notion of monarchy had most power at a time when 'mixtures were signs of a superordinate status'[34] the modern nation-state has culturally demanded its model citizens, including the royal family, to perform the containment of ethnic and racial difference. In the typology of the British monarchy, white racial identity provided a bounded zone within which ethnic mixing could take place, fractured only by the boundaries of Protestantism.[35] The whiteness of the royal family has been maintained by European pedigrees, and made visible in the periodic tours to spaces of Blackness. As just seen, this authenticates a geographical logic which maps Englishness and Britishness on to whiteness. It is against this formation that Diana's romance with Dodi Fayed takes on oppositional force. Instead of reiterating the spatial logic of racial separation associated with royal tours, Diana could be read as bringing ethnic and racial difference home.

Arguably, it is racial and ethnic difference that have given prominence to what some insiders have insisted was a relationship of little biographical significance.[36] Diana's romance with Dodi Fayed enabled people to imagine a mixed-race relationship near the centre of the British establishment, and raised the possibility that the heir to the throne might have half-siblings brought up as Muslims, whose father's heritage lay in Egypt. There is something to be said for this as a symbolic reworking of British national identity. Certainly, as Mica Nava has pointed out, the posthumous representation of Dodi Fayed in the British popular press constituted a positive improvement in its presentation of African and Asian identity.[37] However, Emily Lomax has made a powerful case for the overdetermination of the Di–Dodi romance by a commodified economy in which the exoticization of otherness is the flipside of overt racism.[38] Even when celebratory readings of the Diana and Dodi romance are understood at the level of paradigms for national identity, they can reiterate conservative formations of whiteness and royal femininity.

In the first instance, the romance form itself personalizes and depoliticizes difference, a process compounded by Dodi's wealth and cosmopolitan lifestyle. Racial and ethnic difference are initially neutered by Dodi's membership of the international jet set, before being overcome by personal affection. If difference is being brought home here, it can still be contained within the realm of romance, defined through femininity-as-feeling. Moreover, through its very exceptionalism, the romance narrative largely reiterates the spatializing of racial difference associated with royal visits. In order to be 'brought home', difference has first to be defined as outside. Juxtaposition with an ethnic and national other reinforces Diana's status as both white and central. Englishness is consolidated as white and non-whiteness is securely defined as foreign. This suggests less progressive reasons for the marked preference shown by the popular press for material on Diana's relationship with Dodi Fayed, in whom non-whiteness and non-Britishness were congruent. The Di–Dodi romance almost completely displaced any sense of what was allegedly a longer-term relationship with Hasnat Khan, a London heart surgeon of Pakistani origin. Though there are other considerations here, dictated partly by a squeamishness over Diana's sexual life, which made it seem necessary to 'justify' her engaging in a sexual relationship by invoking the emotional intensity of a grand romance, the high profile of the Al Fayed family, and possibly also Khan's wish for privacy, it would seem that the popular press found it easier to celebrate Diana romancing an ethnic other of Egyptian heritage whose life-style transcended national boundaries than a Pakistani heart surgeon who worked at a London hospital.

Nevertheless, there are some respects in which such representations can be construed as progressive. Their blurring of difference, albeit partly through Dodi Fayed's cosmopolitanism, is a far cry from the obsession with borders and limits that characterized Thatcherite conceptions of the nation. The Di–Dodi romance can also be viewed as counterposing a positive image of sensitive and ethnically marked masculinity to Charles as dysfunctional husband. Moreover, the positioning of Diana as deriving fulfilment from actively loving a man of North African descent suggests a positive development away from the strategic use of white femininity to shore up Imperial and colonial domination, commonly figured in terms of anxiety over the sexual purity of the white woman. Still, even when Diana is configured as a means of hybridizing Britishness, her whiteness continues to be deployed to reinforce the spatial distantiation of difference.

A potential way through these very mixed resonances, as suggested by Mica Nava, is to focus attention on the possibility that Diana's relationship with Dodi may in time have produced a mixed-race child.[39] This does provide a way of imagining mixed racial and ethnic identity near the centre of traditional epitomes of English/ Britishness, in the form of a Muslim half-sister or brother to the heirs to the throne. Yet it is achieved by reactivating a potentially highly essentialist discourse of royal femininity which defines Diana's importance in terms of biological reproduction. If the later trajectory of Diana's career unmasked the colonization of her womb for the reproduction of white Englishness and monarchical continuity, how legitimate can it be to follow a similar logic in the name of a multi-ethnic nation?

Despite these reservations, Nava clearly identifies a potentially progressive reading of Diana which has its roots in a potent popular fantasy. It also has a tactical importance, as is demonstrated by the continued ability of representations of Diana and Dodi to provoke controversy. A significant example here is the July 1999 press coverage of Alison Jackson's photograph 'Diana Family Portrait'. Part of Jackson's series of large black-and-white photographs entitled 'Mental Images', the photograph shows 'Diana' and 'Dodi', posed by look-alikes, holding a mixed-race baby. It completely overshadowed reportage of the 'Temple of Diana' show at the Blue Gallery in London in July–August 1999. Several newspapers, including the London *Evening Standard*, the *Sunday Telegraph*, *Daily Star* and *Mail on Sunday* ran sensationalist pieces, branding Jackson's image and the show in general 'sick', 'offensive' and exploitative.[40] Both the *Telegraph* and the *Star* blurred distinctions between the form and content of the image, enabling an unspoken racist resistance to it as depicting miscegenation to filter through explicit objections to its status as 'fake'.

This hostility was no doubt provoked in part by the ironies that as a critical artist Jackson deliberately sought to make explicit. What is really disturbing about the photograph is the apparent ease with which it 'fakes' maternal and paternal love in the caring expressions and poses of the Diana and Dodi figures. Elsewhere, Jackson elucidated her work as a response to the mediation of mass emotional investment in Diana through visual images, and the ways that representations of (white) women are conventionally standardized.[41] While there is a danger that such ironies become dispersed into academicist and purely formal discussions of the truth-effects of photography, the photograph suggests both the possibilities and the problems of continuing to signify Diana as national mother. 'Diana Family Portrait' is a representation that explicitly courts ambivalences of various kinds. As one critic asked, 'Is this a harmless glimpse of what might have been, or tasteless exploitation?'[42] Pivoting between private family photograph and symbol of national identity, between populist investment and prurience, between exposing and desiring Diana's fetishization, it makes for a potent image of her continued ambivalence.

Notwithstanding hostile newspaper accusations of fakery, a second glance is all that is necessary to identify the figures in 'Diana Family Portrait' as look-alikes. For myself, Jackson's photograph packed an unexpected emotional force, reawakening a desire to see Diana as a happy, caring mother and partner, before reminding one of its impossibility. This double-bind is a permanent effect of the requirement that Diana represent us to ourselves, whether as living out the (post)modern human condition, as national mother, as embodiment of post-colonial whiteness or emblem of new Britain. But if this is a fundamental problematic of representation in general and photography in particular, its significance changes over time and with respect to changing ideas about gender. Historically, Diana's trajectory has undone the magical resolutions of royal femininity and English rose. Her marital unhappiness initiated the disintegration of the monarchy's deployment of family images. Revelations of her emotional distress and, arguably, the circumstances of her death fleeing paparazzi, demonstrated the personal cost exacted by media intrusion which was in turn prompted by popular investment.

Diana's image no longer enjoys the power and prestige it had up to and in the immediate aftermath of her death. Neither of the books on Diana by Burchill and Campbell bore an image of their subject on their front covers, and Campbell eschewed illustrations altogether. In contrast to the highly visually oriented coverage of the funeral week, television programmes commemorating the first and second anniversaries of Diana's death often avoided directly representing her, concentrating instead on the posthumous histories of her clothes, her charities and popular memory. It is reported that the Diana Memorial Fund has dropped plans for an enormous commemorative statue.[43] And, despite a high-profile campaign in the *Mirror* newspaper for the erection of a statue of Diana in Trafalgar Square, when outline plans for an official Diana memorial were finally announced in September 1999, a fountain was the form chosen. In stimulating desires for an ideal image of Diana and reiterating the impossibility of realizing them, Jackson's photograph makes explicit what is perhaps the most intractable double-bind of Diana representations. It suggests finally a turn away from visual representations of Diana herself, towards other forms of memorialization.

Diana's funeral and the legitimation of multi-ethnic Britain

The power of the emotional affectivity associated with Diana's femininity can be and has been worked in the service of a variety of notions of national identity. The images of Diana in Angola and Bosnia make explicit her position at the borders of Imperial history and post-colonial future. Celebratory representations construct Diana in terms of femininity-for-itself that is both marked (via the Morton myth) and unmarked, when it collapses into and is effaced by a caring humanitarianism. As a signifier of national identity, in comparison to the royal family, Diana's Englishness is strongly ethnically marked. Yet at the same time it is reformulated, in the name of the caring feminine, in terms of a postcolonial humanitarianism. Given these ambivalent formations, the figure of Diana finally emerges as a 'positive image' of postcolonial white identity, though one that is hedged around on one side by possible dissolution into an essentialist gender binary, and on the other side by its containment as the gendered other of a still dominant, masculinized realm of politics at its most *realpolitik*. What remains more problematic is Diana's status as an icon of a 'new Britain', since this, it seems, cannot help but maintain the central position of white racial identity even when used to emblematize the welcoming of difference.

The BBC coverage of the memorial service for Diana and subsequent events demonstrated this problematic. Immediately after the service, the studio anchor, David Dimbleby, introduced the presentation of 'public reaction' from two sites. Contributors in both were strongly ethnically marked. In the first, the British Asian reporter Krishnan Guru-Murthy summarized the reaction of the crowds on the Mall in London. This itself was quite remarkable, in that Guru-Murthy's normally professional presentation was punctuated by technical hitches and self-doubt. 'The atmosphere,' he said haltingly, 'although it was so public, it was also intensely private, if that makes any sense.' The second featured a series of vox pops with a small group of people in Hyde Park assembled by the white reporter Fiona Bruce. Where Guru-Murthy's solo description had implicitly cohered and spoken for a shared communal experience, Bruce solicited the personal and differential meaning of the funeral event to a series of individuals. These included a white family with Merseyside accents and, on the end of the line, a fortyish Black man in shirt, tie and a red baseball cap. First to speak was the mother/wife figure, who was followed by her partner's self-revelation that 'I shed more tears today than when I lost my father'. Several others spoke of their feelings. Then the man who was last in line was introduced by Bruce as a kind of spokesperson for Wales. He too spoke of having been bereaved, but went on to emphasize the cultural inclusiveness of the service, stretching from what he called 'opera' to Elton John, and to stake a Welsh claim over Diana's memory. He referred to an unease in Wales at the repeated use of the term 'English rose' and brought up the separate memorial service in Cardiff that was taking place simultaneously. The man seemed to have a cogent agenda, which was to stake a Welsh claim to Diana while also insisting on the integration of Welsh reponses into the national framework. As he stumbled over a few words, Bruce intervened with 'She's a Welsh rose too'. He agreed vigorously before going on '... and I think she was just a rose of our heart and Queen ...', as Bruce turned back to a previous interviewee.

It was a remarkable television moment, partly as one of those times during the coverage when the normalizing frames of competence were suspended and the limits of the media apparatus started to become visible.[44] The man's incoherence solicited a mixture of emotions: agreement, sympathy, embarrassment, and threw into relief Bruce's confident professionalism. But what was also interesting was the unspoken issue of racial and ethnic identity. Nava's essay on Diana and race concludes with a sense of the ambivalence of this moment of 'post anti-racism' tinged with hope:

A cynic could argue, that, like Barthes's photo of the Negro soldier saluting the French tricolour, the visibility of blackness in Britain today merely confirms the whiteness of the national consciousness. On the other hand, it may also signal a much more radical transformation in the cultural identifications of the people.[45]

A cynic might argue that this man's racial identity was negated or abstracted by his interpolation as everyman and spokesperson for Wales. Yet as Nava suggests, the unremarkable and unremarked sense of his Blackness also signals a moment beyond the inflection of national identities by racial difference, where the multi-ethnicity of the nation can be taken for granted. What remains problematic is that it took Diana's example to legitimate his presence. As with Diana's iconic figuration, the funeral events suggest a genuinely progressive assemblage of the nation in terms of ethnic diversity, while also recalling an Imperialist gathering of the tribes. This problematic was further sharpened by the honing of revisionist official discourses for the celebrations of the fiftieth anniversary of V.E. Day in 1995, in which such gatherings as the 1946 Victory Parade were re-imagined ahistorically, as difference without hierarchy.[46] In reconstructing images of the Empire as the precursors to a positive multiculturalism, history is rewritten and the power relations behind racial and ethnic identities are whitewashed over.

Diana's significance with respect to racial difference is re-imagined again in Onyekachi Wambu's Introduction to the anthology *Empire Windrush: Fifty Years of Writing About Black Britain* (1998). Wambu suggests that the popular reaction to Diana's death marked the birth of a new and more inclusive Britain defined explicitly as post-Imperial. In the week between her death and her funeral Wambu describes a communal experience of watching 'an unknown emotional hinterland emerge from beneath the debris of history'.[47]

Wambu goes on to argue that the emotional affectivity associated with Diana in life and in the response to her death has played a major role in the emergence of a widely shared post-Imperialist Britishness. If not necessarily a national identity independent of racial and ethnic difference, it at least represented a major step in the acknowledgement of Blackness[48] as an integral part of Britishness. As Wambu goes on to suggest:

> In amongst the tears people seemed genuinely to want to confront the past and liberate themselves from it. They called her 'great' and celebrated her as a new kind of British hero. She played to a global audience in a way one could not imagine any other contemporary

British figure doing. But the greatness attached to her was not the greatness traditionally associated with British heroes. Instead her heroism focused on soft things such as her vulnerability, charity, openness and the victimization she had suffered from the old established order. By their response to her a large number of people were acknowledging that they were comfortable with the body suit, this new identity they had awkwardly and fitfully been trying on since the loss of Empire.[49]

In an important sense what Wambu is discussing here is the development of a new kind of whiteness, a 'new identity' responsive to 'the loss of Empire' which has dispensed with Imperialist values and behaviours. But to conceive the national significance of Diana's death solely in terms of transforming whiteness would be to reproduce an understanding of Britain in terms of whiteness alone, and thus to continue to silence non-white British identity. (Here Wambu comes up against one of the continuing political difficulties attendant on the newly-found visibility of whiteness in cultural studies as elsewhere in Britain and the West in general, that this new-found visibility of whiteness can function as yet another strategy to maintain its cultural power.) Therefore he uses non-racially specific language, writing about 'people' in general and, in a striking formulation, constructing the experience of white Britons coming to terms with the emotional affectivity of Diana's death in terms of immigrant experience: becoming comfortable in 'the body suit, this new identity they had awkwardly and fitfully been trying on since the loss of Empire'. Read as 'new whiteness' this new body suit is readable in terms of the spontaneity, victimization, expressivity, associated in highly fraught ways with Blackness. More than this, the conceptualization of identity as a 'body suit' promises to break decisively with the direct forms of racial and ethnic power, while at the same time insisting upon the contingency of all ethnically-based identities. Such conceptualizations, it seems to me, fit the requirements of what Homi Bhabha has called 'the liminal figure of the nation-space [which] would ensure that no political ideologies could claim transcendent or metaphysical authority for themselves'.[50]

Wambu's mythologization of Diana reinscribes the fundamental problematics of deploying gender difference in the service of a re-envisaging of national identity, the basic problem that lies at the heart of progressive readings of the Diana myth. In the passage just quoted, he makes no direct mention of gender, though both the inspirational qualities he attributes to Diana, 'soft things such as her vulnerability, charity, openness', and her status as victim of 'the old established order' are conventionally read in terms of femininity. In avoiding explicit reference to gender, Wambu could stand accused of appropriating Diana's symbolic femininity and negating a sense of the patriarchal structures that led to her victimization. Yet if Wambu had referred to Diana's femininity explicitly, it is hard to see how he could have avoided reiterating an understanding of 'feminine qualities' according to biological essentialism.

Nevertheless, what Wambu's formulation does which is genuinely innovative, is that it construes Diana as providing a form for an overdue mainstream cultural recognition of a Black presence that is already located within Britain.[51] Here Diana is not made to be the simple bridge to a difference located outside Britain, as in the Dodi romances, nor is she the means of integrating Black Britons into a culture which retains a normative whiteness, as was arguably the case with the Welshman who featured on the BBC coverage. Rather, Wambu configures 'Diana' as both a potential model for post-colonial British identities, and as a means of undoing the cultural repressions which had enabled Britain to be thought of as white. It is by reference to a past that is known and a future as yet unknown that the ambivalent figure of Diana best enables us to re-imagine ourselves.

Epilogue

Pauline Melville's short story 'English Table Wuk', opens with a diverse group of people watching Diana's funeral on television in Georgetown, Guyana. 'People's princess, my arse,' says one. Another opines, 'She could have bought Angola, never mind havin' her picture taken with amputees.' A few pages later, as they leave, a powercut having curtailed viewing of the funeral, Melville distances the reader from such perspectives: 'The spectacle of the funeral had filled them with the mild pleasures of righteous indignation and reassured them as to the rectitude and superiority of their own rational politics.'[1] Neither Diana nor the funeral is mentioned again in the story, whose main narrative concerns the seemingly irrational appeasement of the ghosts of English colonists.

As a cultural icon Diana, Princess of Wales simultaneously points backwards and forwards. In many ways Diana fulfilled ideas about royal femininity forged during the reign of her ex-husband's great-great-great-grandmother Queen Victoria. Like Diana before her wedding, Victoria was widely represented as a rose just prior to her coronation. Both women held power precariously, by reference to an unstable discourse of ideal femininity.[2] Like Diana, Victoria was mourned by many people surprised at their grief.[3] Adrienne Munich's description of Victoria, that she 'came into the world as already an allegory, but one whose meanings changed over time',[4] is still more applicable to Diana, at whose historical moment discourses of femininity and monarchy are still less stable. In her day Victoria too was considered to be the most recognized woman on the planet, her portrait reproduced by new developments in photography and printing, and sent around the world on postage stamps. Further technological development has likewise ensured the national and global dissemination of Diana's own image. Her career spanned the introduction of colour photography into British popular newspapers and the development and consolidation of global television networks, through which an estimated audience of 700 million watched her wedding and 2.5 billion her funeral.[5]

But unlike Victoria, who had almost total control of royal spectacle,[6] Diana began to have power over her representation only when she performed the difficulty of performing the ideal. Conversely, while it was only in death that Victoria finally succeeded in perfecting the iconography of the national mother, Diana was accorded such iconic status in her early twenties, and spent the rest of her life fencing with it. While Victoria's entire 64-year reign could be seen as being dominated by the paradox of a female at the head of a state which systematically denied political agency to women, whatever power Diana had derived largely from an anachronistic discourse of ideal white femininity that hardly registered the social, political and economic changes since the Second World War.

At the same time the global reproduction of Diana's image has loosened the ties between Diana and British national identity. She is installed in the zone of celebrity, her iconicity available for appropriation on the part of multiple, differently cohesive constituencies. The notion of Diana as an inspirational model for a 'new Britain' must be placed in this context. It is no coincidence that what are regarded as the most 'free' and liberated photographs of Diana, Mario Testino's portfolio for *Vanity Fair* appeared first in an American magazine. Clearly, outside the UK and the Commonwealth, the frameworks of the royal have informed Diana's iconicity less powerfully. The circumstances of Diana's death have sustained significantly anti-British discourses in parts of North Africa and the Middle East.

Diana's iconicity remains an incomplete reworking of Imperialist traditions of representing white women. Images of Diana reaching out across racial and ethnic difference can be read as producing a new whiteness, which maintains a global and international role but one informed by an ethic of care rather than Imperialist or national self-interest. Yet such images also draw upon a history of racially inflected representations of white women as nurses to the Empire and reproducers of the nation. At the same time, the perceived immediacy of Diana's iconicity brought her own embodied identity into play much more directly than the more performative and symbolic representations of the royal family. While to a certain extent their 'true' ethnicity as German was contingent to their performance of

Britishness, Diana's whiteness was indispensable to her association with national identity. For this reason Diana's iconicity can be seen as reworking white identity more successfully than national identity.

In retrospect Diana has come to stand as the last gasp of the monarchical ideology that combined the ordinary and the extraordinary. Parallels have been drawn with Jill Dando, who also died young and violently, and Sophie Rhys-Jones, Countess of Wessex, who married the Queen's youngest son Edward in June 1999. Yet the physical similarities between these three women have only pointed up the uniqueness of Diana's iconicity in pivoting between royal mystique and everyday humanity. Dando and Rhys-Jones, both pre-eminently women who work, have emphatically been represented in terms of normativity alone. 1999, in fact, signalled the dissolution of auratic femininity in two ways. The wedding of Edward and Sophie was mundane, its reportage strikingly unable or unwilling to engage with the intense and excessive discourses that had placed that of Charles and Diana in the service of synthesizing national identity. In the same year, another biography appeared by Andrew Morton, bearing a cover photograph by Patrick Demarchelier. But rather than invigorating gender symbolism, *Monica's Story* deliberately underlined the ordinariness of Monica Lewinsky.

Yet if there is some satisfaction in seeing the dissolution of mythic identities predicated on gender essentialism and heterosexual romance, some of the most powerful elements of Diana's iconicity have reappeared in surprising and perhaps worrying contexts. When Tony Blair reiterated the term 'people's princess' on the morning following Diana's death, the cultural populism with which Julie Burchill had endowed the term was displaced by the incipient mode of address of New Labour to 'the people' as a vague but powerful political entity. Where Burchill had codified popular culture as characteristically and triumphantly feminized, Blair's speech firmly circumscribed Diana in the implicitly feminine realm of affectivity. Blair emphasized her status as mother and her 'compassion' for 'the sick, the dying, children and the needy', her 'warm[th]', and 'touch'. It was Diana's 'look' and 'gesture' that 'said so much – more than words'.[7] By implication those who now can speak, himself as Prime Minister and the newly elected Labour government, are positioned as articulating the result of these communal feelings in the sphere of politics.

Since September 1997, the covert deployment of masculinist definitions of gender has worked to defuse the potential challenges to the political and social status quo posed by the 'Diana events', such as they were. Most strikingly, a powerful strand in New Labour's political discourse has embraced a sense of the importance of feeling and emotion, while explicitly subjugating it to stereotypically masculinized appeals to reason and force. Visible in the policy enacted on benefits for single mothers and the 'targeting' of disability benefits, this has been most apparent in the context of the military action against Serbia during the Spring and Summer of 1999. In May 1999, the figure of the Prime Minister's wife Cherie Blair (as she is known outside her professional life) was shown weeping during an official visit to refugee camps for displaced Kosovars in the Former Yugoslav Republic of Macedonia. Widely reported on British television and in the press, the incident repeated and reworked the iconic motifs of Diana's juxtaposition with victimized ethnic others during her visit to Bosnia two years earlier. In doing so the significance of emotional engagement, associated with femininity, was redirected from the challenge to militarism associated with the campaign to ban land-mines, to support for a continued bombing campaign. This was achieved by retaining the feminized association of affective response but articulating it within a gender binary in which masculinity remained the dominant, though unspoken, term. At least, it remained unspoken until in a speech to the Labour Party annual conference in September 1999, with a strange echo of Diana's argument 'as a mother' in the 'Diary of a Princess' programme, Tony Blair legitimated his entire political career through his own status as a father. Comparison with Diana's visits to Angola and Bosnia on behalf of the anti land-mines campaign highlights the fragile success of the 'feminization' of politics associated with Diana. Both the cases of Diana and the Blairs throw into relief the ways that complex political and military issues are simplified by the invocation of the gender binary. It may be, in the case of the land-mines issue at least, that this kind of simplification constituted a powerful progressive intervention. Yet as Melville's laconic and slightly oblique 'English Table Wuk' suggests, the figure of Diana is also important as a signal of the intractability of similarity and difference across a range of codes of identity. The short story turns on distinctions not only between classed and racial identities, but also between English and Dutch colonial practices. For Melville, one suspects, Diana calls up historical connections in which colonial and patriarchal histories are interwoven with liberation struggles, where power relations are inescapable but remain open to change, and neither whiteness nor

Blackness is monolithic. In such a context, perhaps the wisest thing is to try to think beyond the one-dimensional celebration or rejection of the Diana events, and to view them, and her, as continuing to pose gender, race/ethnicity, the nation, and the social, as questions of relatedness.

Notes

Introduction

1. A. Holden, 'Diana: Monster or Martyr?', *Tatler* 288:12 (December 1993), pp. 150–1; p. 151.
2. A. Holden, *Diana: A Life and a Legacy* (London: Ebury Press, 1997), p. 169.
3. 'Fantasy of our own potential', attributed to Pamela Stephenson, in Sir Roy Strong, 'An Icon for the Meritocratic Age' [*Independent*], rpt. in B. MacArthur (ed.), *Requiem: Memories and Tributes* (London: Pavilion, 1997), pp. 131–5; p. 134, and adopted by MacArthur as a chapter title. 'Simpering Bambi Narcissist', in C. Hitchens, 'Princess Di, Mother T., and me', in M. Merck (ed.), *After Diana: Irreverent Elegies* (London: Verso, 1998), pp. 49–61; p. 59.
4. In the early 1990s, following the academic establishment of Cultural Studies, definitions of cultural populism themselves became the site of contestation over critical practices and cultural production more generally. In *Cultural Populism* (London: Routledge, 1992), Jim McGuigan set out to reappropriate the term against what he regards as the depoliticization of the Birmingham CCCS tradition. I echo the term here to stress the double nature of monarchical legitimation, by appeal to both deference and popular interest, and hence the crucial and ambivalent importance of forms of popular culture to the construction of royalty. This is to engage only obliquely with the cultural populism debate, to which I will return in Chapter 1 below.
5. J. Burchill, 'Di Hard: The Pop Princess', in *Sex and Sensibility* (London: Grafton, 1992), pp. 233–44; p. 244.
6. Burchill, 'Di Hard', p. 237.
7. J. Williamson, 'Royalty and Representation', in *Consuming Passions: The Dynamics of Popular Culture* ([1985], London: Marion Boyars, 1986), pp. 75–89; M. Homans, *Royal Representations: Queen Victoria and British Culture, 1837–1876* (Chicago: University of Chicago Press, 1998), pp. 3, 5, 7, 45, 55 and *passim*.
8. Homans, *Royal Representations*, pp. 46–8, 53–7.
9. J.M. Golby and A.W. Purdue, *The Monarchy and the British People 1760 to the Present* (London: Batsford, 1988), pp. 68, 70, 72.
10. G. Dangerfield, *Victoria's Heir: The Education of a Prince* ([New York, 1941] London: Constable, 1942), p. 3.
11. Homans, *Royal Repesentations*, pp. 46–57.
12. See R. Coward, 'The Royals', in *Female Desire: Women's Sexuality Today* (London: Paladin, 1984), pp. 161–71.
13. *Sunday Mirror*, 26 October 1986, front page.
14. See Golby and Purdue, *Monarchy*, pp. 50–1.
15. *London Quarterly Review* 30 (April 1868), p. 84, quoted in Homans, *Royal Representations*, p. 132.

16. M. Billig, *Talking Of the Royal Family* (London: Routledge, 1992).
17. The instinct/mechanism and intimacy/cynicism binaries are rehearsed respectively by W.F. Deedes in 'The Princess of Sorrows', *Daily Telegraph*, Monday, 1 September, 1997, p. 14, rpt. as 'A Princess Among the Landmines', in MacArthur, *Requiem*, pp. 66–70, and in W.F. Deedes, 'Diana, Princess of Wales', in *The Daily Telegraph: Diana Remembered* (Macmillan, 1997), pp. 80–6; p. 86; and by Theodore Zeldin, in T. Zeldin, 'The End of Cynicism' [*The Observer*], rpt. in MacArthur, *Requiem*, pp. 142–5. The notion that Diana built personal relationships with people she never met via the mass media is a mainstay of her representation in press and television. For one example, see Holden, *Diana*, p. 13.
18. M. Jacques, 'The Floral Revolution', *Observer*, 7 September 1997, p. 15; M. Engel, 'The British Began to Queue', in MacArthur, *Requiem*, pp. 26–9; p. 29; Anonymous (*Independent*), 'If only the Royals Could Weep with the People', in MacArthur, *Requiem*, pp. 37–40; p. 39; E. Showalter, 'Storming the Wintry Palace', *Guardian*, 6 September 1997, Special section 'The Funeral of Diana', p. 15; Holden, *Diana*, p. 13.
19. See, for example, R. Braidotti, 'In the Sign of the Feminine: Reading Diana', *Theory and Event* 1:4, http://muse.jhu.edu/journals/theory_&_event/v001/1.4.html.; Z. Sofoulis, 'Icon, Referent, Trajectory, World', in Re:Public (ed.), *Planet Diana: Cultural Studies and Global Mourning* (Kingswood: Research Centre in Intercommunal Studies, University of Western Sydney, Nepean, 1997), pp. 13–18; p. 16; W. Wheeler, 'Together Again After All These Years: Science, Politics and Theology in the New Modernity', in A. Coddington and M. Perryman (eds), *The Moderniser's Dilemma: Radical Politics in the Age of Blair* (London: Lawrence and Wishart, 1998), pp. 175–91; p. 187; M. Engel, 'After the Grief, the Moment of Truth for a Nation', *Guardian*, Special section, Saturday, 6 September 1997, pp. 1–3; p. 1; and Holden, *Diana*, p. 13.
20. See Holden, 'Monster', p. 151, further discussed in Chapter 3 below; and *Diana*, pp. 188–9. Variations on this trope proliferated after Diana's death, as, for example, in Earl Spencer's address at the memorial service and in *The Daily Telegraph: Diana Remembered 1961–97*, p. 6, but can be traced back at least as far as Morton's 1992 *Diana: Her True Story*. In her extended review of Morton's book Camille Paglia anticipated Spencer's reversal of the Diana/hunting myth, as a means of crystallizing what she called Diana's cannibalistic consumption by the multiple personae ascribed to her by popular desire and mass media. Camille Paglia, 'Diana Regina', in *Vamps and Tramps* ([1994], London: Viking, 1995) pp. 163–71; first published in *New Republic*, 3 August 1992.
21. Holden, *Diana*, p. 188.
22. J. Kitzinger, 'Image', *Screen*, 39:1 (1998), 73–9, p. 78.
23. Quoted in R. Monckton, 'Her Laughter, Her Sense of Fun', in MacArthur, *Requiem*, pp. 58–66; p. 63; and *Hello!* 481, 25 October 1997, p. 13.
24. See, for example, the work by feminists such as Showalter and Wheeler listed above.
25. Homans, *Royal Representations*, p. xx.
26. Homans, *Royal Representations*, p. xxxiv.

27. Homans, *Royal Representations*, p. xxxv. In my reading, the success of this approach is most fully realized in Homans's third chapter, 'The Widow as Author and the Arts and Powers of Concealment', pp. 100–56, which explicitly relates notions of royal being and seeming to the 1860s debates over numerical and symbolic representation surrounding electoral reform.
28. Homans, *Royal Representations*, p. 101. She elaborates further that 'for the monarchy to complete its transformation into a wholly symbolic function at the head of a representative state, the best possible occupant of the throne was a widow'.
29. See, for example, S. Moore, 'Diana – her true colours' in *Head over Heels* ([1996] London: Penguin, 1997), pp. 85–91 and 'Diana the Do-gooder versus the Bad Guys', *The Independent*, Friday, 17 January 1997, p. 17; B. Campbell, *Diana, Princess of Wales: How Sexual Politics Shook the Monarchy* (London: The Women's Press, 1998); Wheeler, 'Together Again'; and N. Segal, 'The Common Touch', in M. Merck (ed.), *After Diana: Irreverent Elegies* (London: Verso, 1998), pp. 131–45.
30. See, for example, the work by Rose, and the collections edited by Merck, Kear and Steinberg, and Walter, discussed below.

Chapter 1

1. P. Hanks (ed.), *The Collins English Dictionary*, second edition (London and Glasgow: Collins, 1986), p. 1216.
2. R. Brunt, 'Princess Diana: A Sign of the Times', in J. Richards, S. Wilson, and L. Woodhead (eds.), *Diana, The Making of a Postmodern Saint* (London: I.B. Tauris, 1999), pp. 20–39; pp. 34–7.
3. On 'fashion icon', see Chapter 4; the phrase 'trash icon' comes from the leading feature in the British Sunday newspaper the *Observer*, five weeks before Diana's death, discussed by Brunt in 'A Sign of the Times', pp. 20–2.
4. R. Dyer, *Heavenly Bodies: Film Stars and Society* (London and Basingstoke: BFI/Macmillan, 1986), p. 8.
5. On this aspect of Monroe, see Dyer, *Heavenly Bodies*, pp. 59–61.
6. Dyer, *Heavenly Bodies*, p. 8.
7. L. Blackman, 'An *Extra*ordinary Life: The Legacy of an Ambivalence', in *New Formations* 36, pp. 111–24; p. 122.
8. N. Armstrong, *Desire and Domestic Fiction: A Political History of the Novel* (New York and Oxford: Oxford University Press, 1987), p. 8. Following Homans in *Royal Representations* (especially pp. xxxiii–iv, 2), I am somewhat extrapolating here from Armstrong's argument, which retains novelistic representations of desire as the touchstone for the production of modern individuality. Kath McPhillips' 'Postmodern Canonisation' (*Planet Diana*, pp. 87–91) is one of the most suggestive of the many academic attempts to resolve this antithesis; it seems to me that such resolution, while strategically desirable from some perspectives, risks universalizing the non-gendered elements of Diana's iconicity such as middle-class identity, whiteness and heterosexuality.
9. A. Morton, *Diana: Her True Story – In Her Own Words* (London: Michael O'Mara Books, 1997), p. 19.

10. A. Morton, *Diana: Her True Story – In Her Own Words* [paperback edition] (London: Michael O'Mara Books, 1998), back cover.

11. See, for example, the artist Caroline Younger's installation 'Diana Fetish' (1999), in which a series of small metal objects are pinned to the (empty) clothes of a Diana figure. The majority of the objects are small hands.

12. T. Graham and T. Blanchard, *Dressing Diana* (London: Weidenfeld and Nicolson, 1998), p. 93.

13. Paglia, 'Diana Regina', p. 170.

14. For a suggestive distinction between British and Australian responses to Diana's death, in terms of political coherence (New Labour and feminization), as opposed to multiple appropriations by different groups, see J. Duruz and C. Johnson, 'Mourning at a Distance: Australians and the Death of a British Princess', in A. Kear and D.L. Steinberg (eds) *Mourning Diana: Nation, Culture and the Performance of Grief* (London: Routledge, 1999), pp. 142–54. The essays by William J. Spurlin and Diana Taylor in the same volume further distinguish between American workings of Diana on the grounds of sexual orientation and race/ethnicity.

15. See Graham and Blanchard, *Dressing Diana*, pp. 68–9; J. Fincher, *Diana: Portrait of a Princess* (Koln: Calloway Editions, 1998), p. 106.

16. R. Dyer, *White* (London: Routledge, 1997), pp. 82–144.

17. Sofoulis, 'Icon, Referent, Trajectory, World', p. 16.

18. For the anti-feminist history of such iconographies, see, for example, Klaus Theweleit's description of the figure of the 'white nurse', in *Male Fantasies: Volume 1: Women, Floods, Bodies, History*, trans. S. Conway in collaboration with E. Carter and C. Turner (Minneapolis: University of Minnesota Press, 1987), pp. 90–100. For a more complex sense of the race and gender politics at stake, see V. Ware, *Beyond the Pale: White Women, Racism and History* (London: Verso, 1992).

19. D. Simmonds, *Princess Di: The National Dish* (London: Pluto Press, 1984).

20. Perhaps significantly, the positive sense of Diana as feminizing influence is enunciated most unequivocally by male journalists such as Morton, Deedes and Holden, in material discussed elsewhere. Feminists such as Braidotti and Sofoulis, and even Campbell at times, are somewhat more ambivalent.

21. Besides the high-profile examples discussed below, Nicci Gerrard expressed concern at the end of 1997 that the proliferation of personalized, therapeutic notions of Diana meant that the only commonly shared sense of Diana was a meaningless transcendence, while Jon Simons discussed the 'dialectics of Diana as empty signifier'. See N. Gerrard, 'We Are All Dianas Now', *Observer* 'Life' section, 28 December 1997, p. 10; J. Simons, 'The Dialectics of Diana as Empty Signifier', *theory & event* 1:4.

22. T. Graham, *Diana, Princess of Wales: A Tribute*, (London: Weidenfeld and Nicolson, 1997), p. 9.

23. 'The Tribute by Earl Spencer', MacArthur, *Requiem*, pp. 179–82; H. Clinton, 'A Reservoir of Resilience and Determination', MacArthur, *Requiem*, pp. 93–5; p. 93.

24. 'The Queen's Speech', MacArthur, *Requiem*, pp. 51–2; p. 51.

25. T. de Lauretis, 'The Technology of Gender', in *Technologies of Gender: Essays on Theory, Film, and Fiction* (London: Macmillan, 1987), pp. 1–30; p. 3.

26. Braidotti's, 'In the sign of the feminine', which utilizes Luce Irigaray in ways similar to the above use of de Lauretis, is discussed elsewhere. Assessing the limits of Diana funerary culture, Duruz and Johnson suggest that 'Perhaps we need a Deleuzian or Lyotardian rewriting of the script?' (J. Duruz and C. Johnson, 'Appropriating the People's Princess', *Planet Diana*, pp. 45–8; p. 48). More recently, the collections of work in *New Formations* 36 and in Kear and Steinberg's *Mourning Diana* have continued to bring to bear linguistic or psychoanalytical understandings of gender on the widespread sense of Diana images at the limits of representation articulated by critics such as Peter Griffith, Paul Alberts, and Richard Wilding. See P. Griffith, '"Words cannot say what she is"', *Planet Diana*, pp. 71–4. Alberts has pointed to the global mediation of Diana's death as 'a key contemporary problem: *that which cannot be represented adequately is precisely the limit of the drive to represent*' (P. Alberts, 'Sublime and Corporeal Diana', *Planet Diana*, pp. 97–101; p. 101); while Wilding reads the quintessential Diana photograph as '*the afterimage of being itself*' (R. Wilding, 'Afterimages of Being, *Planet Diana*, pp. 145–8; p. 148).

27. See, for example, V. Hey, 'Be(long)ing: New Labour, New Britain and the "Dianaization" of Politics', in Kear and Steinberg, *Mourning Diana*, pp. 60–76; V. Walkerdine, 'The Crowd in the Age of Diana: Ordinary Inventiveness and the Popular Imagination', *op. cit.*, pp. 98–107.

28. I am indebted to Heather Nunn, Andrew Blake and Carol Smith for helping to crystallize my account of the significance of Thatcherite representations of Diana, especially Nunn's comparison of the iconographies of Diana and Margaret Thatcher, in 'Violence and the Sacred: The Iron Lady, the Princess, and the People's PM', in *New Formations* 36 (1999), pp. 92–110.

29. J. Smith, 'The Frog Princess', in *Misogynies* (London: Faber, 1989), pp. 35–43; see Chapter 3 below for further discussion.

30. Nunn, 'Violence and the Sacred', pp. 93, 97–8.

31. It is a similar problematic to this that Carol Watts seeks to work through by bringing to bear Jean-Luc Nancy's distinction between politics and the political *per se*, in C. Watts, 'Unworkable Feeling: Diana, Death and Feminization', *New Formations* 36, pp. 34–45.

32. J. Paxman, *The English: A Portrait of a People* (London: Michael Joseph, 1998), J. Barnes, *England, England* (London: Jonathan Cape, 1998), A. Easthope, *Englishness and National Culture* (London: Routledge, 1999). It may be that the certain sterility apparent in these accounts derives from their failure to confront 'race' as an issue, and consequent insulation within an unacknowledged white discourse, with little reference to the voluminous work on Englishness and Britishness by non-whites.

33. See S. Breese, 'In Search of Englishness; In Search of Votes', in J. Arnold, K. Davies, and S. Ditchfield (eds), *History and Heritage: Consuming the Past in Contemporary Culture* (Donhead St Mary: Donhead, 1998), pp. 155–67.

34. See, for example, Anthony Jay's, *Elizabeth R: The Role of the Monarchy Today* (London: BBC Books, 1992), where Jay suggests that 'the British people are not merely interested in the behaviour of the Royal Family – they are involved and implicated in it ... the Queen is uniquely placed to harness people's personal values to the state, the political system and the

government, but only so long as people see her, know about her, know what she stands for (and will not stand for), identify with her, and believe that her behaviour, her standards and her values correspond with their own' (pp. 194–5).

35. This debate is discussed in detail in Chapter 5, below. Some of the key contributions during its most intense period from September 1997 to the middle of 1998 are A. O'Hear, 'Diana, Queen of Hearts: Sentimentality Personified and Canonised', in D. Anderson and P. Mullen (eds.), *Faking It: The Sentimentalisation of Modern Society* (Social Affairs Unit, 1998), pp. 181–90; E. Wilson, 'The Unbearable Lightness of Diana', *New Left Review* 226 (1997), pp. 136–45; I. Jack, 'Those Who Felt Differently', *Guardian Weekend*, 27 December 1998, 5–6, 8, 10, and *Granta* 60; M. Hume, *Televictims: Emotional Correctness in the media AD (After Diana)* (London: InformInc, 1998), and the work in *theory & event* 1:4 at http://muse.jhu.edu/journals/theory_&_event/v001/1.4.html. On conservative modernity specifically see *New Formations* 28 (Spring 1996), and Merck, *After Diana.*

36. R. Barthes, 'Myth Today', in *Mythologies*, trans. A. Lavers (London: Paladin, 1973), pp. 109–59, p. 114. Emphasis in original.

37. Wilson, 'The Unbearable Lightness of Diana', p. 137; and in a more delimited way H. Clark, 'Fashioning Diana', in Re:Public (ed.), *Planet Diana*, pp. 133–6, p. 134; M. Nava, 'Diana, Princess of Others: The Politics and Romance of "Race"', in *Planet Diana*, pp. 19–25; p. 25; M. Nava, 'Diana and Race: Romance and the reconfiguration of the nation', Kear and Steinberg, *Mourning Diana*, pp. 108–19; p. 116.

38. Barthes, 'Myth Today', pp. 128–30, and see C. Sandoval, 'Theorizing White Consciousness for a Post-Empire World: Barthes, Fanon, and the Rhetoric of Love', in R. Frankenberg (ed.), *Displacing Whiteness: Essays in Social and Cultural Criticism* (Durham, NC and London: Duke University Press, 1997), pp. 86–106, for a productive attempt to synthesize Barthes's myth criticism with a thoroughgoing critique of 'race'.

39. See Barthes, 'Myth Today', pp. 114–31; for a recent explication of the possibilities opened up by Barthes's reading, see J. Bignell, *Media Semiotics* (Manchester: Manchester University Press, 1997), pp. 22–8.

40. Barthes, 'Myth Today', p. 118.

41. Barthes, 'Myth Today', p. 122.

42. Barthes, 'Myth Today', p. 131.

43. *Ibid.*

44. M. Warner, *Monuments and Maidens: The Allegory of the Female Form* ([1985] London: Vintage, 1996).

45. S. Burke, *The Death and Return of the Author: Criticism and Subjectivity in Barthes, Foucault, and Derrida* (Edinburgh: University of Edinburgh Press, 1992), pp. 52–4.

46. See R. Barthes, (ed. and trans. S. Heath) 'Change the Object Itself', in R. Barthes, *Image–Music–Text* (London: Fontana, 1977), pp. 165–9; p. 169, where, echoing Marx echoing Hegel, Barthes described the critical practice of *Mythologies* as attempting 'to *upend* (or *right*) the mythical message, to stand it back on its feet, with denotation at the bottom and

connotation at the top, nature on the surface and class interest deep down'.

47. Incidentally, these reasons also explain why an alternative tradition of critical analysis centred on the 'multi-accentual sign' whereby the sign is seen as embodying class struggle, cannot make up for the limitations of myth criticism as elaborated by Barthes. Even allowing for a rethinking of class struggle as power relations in general, a cursory look at the history of the 'Diana' sign suggests that direct contestations over the meaning of Diana are seldom in themselves directly related to power relations.

48. D. Chaney, *Fictions of Collective Life: Public Drama in Late Modern Culture* (London: Routledge, 1993), p. 120, *passim*.

49. D. Dayan and E. Katz, 'Electronic Ceremonies: Television Performs a Royal Wedding', in M. Blonsky (ed.) *On Signs* (Oxford: Basil Blackwell, 1985), pp. 16–32.

50. Chaney, *Fictions*, pp. 2–10, 108 and *passim*.

51. N. Couldry, 'Remembering Diana: The Geography of Celebrity and the Politics of Lack', *New Formations* 36 (1999), pp. 77–91. Couldry's comment that 'there is a myth (that the Diana events represented some unproblematic expression of "the People") that needs to be questioned' (p. 78) neatly summarizes one of the impulses behind this book.

52. Jeffrey Richards makes a similar point in more general terms; 'Part of the grief for Diana will have lain in the recognition that someone who was helping to change the nature of the monarchy, and thereby British identity, had been lost.' J. Richards, 'The Hollywoodisation of Diana', in Richards, Wilson and Woodhead, *Diana, The Making of a Media Saint*, pp. 59–73; p. 73.

53. Compare the ending of Brunt, 'A Sign of the Times', p. 37.

54. A. Renton, 'Turning Diana into an ology', London *Evening Standard*, 16 March 1998, pp. 8–9; M. Austin, 'Dons Flood Publishers with "Dianababble"', *The Sunday Times*, 5 April 1998, 1, p. 17; even the more sympathetic Roy Greenslade felt constrained to place the "meaning" of Diana in double inverted commas in a *Guardian* column, R. Greenslade, 'On the press', *Guardian*, 6 April 1998, 2, p. 4. Almost alone even in the quality press, Joan Smith identified and deplored such a tendency. J. Smith, 'Diana was Infantile and Self-indulgent. There, I've Said It', *Independent on Sunday*, 19 April 1998, p. 3.

55. J. Butler, *Bodies that Matter: On the Discursive Limits of 'Sex'* (New York and London: Routledge, 1993), pp. 45, 187 and *passim*.

56. D. Slater, 'Marketing Mass Photography', in H. Davis and P. Walton (eds), *Language, Image, Media* (Oxford: Basil Blackwell, 1983), pp. 245–63; 246, 257–61; and McGuigan, *Cultural Populism*, Chapter 2: 'Trajectories of Cultural Populism', pp. 45–85.

57. A. Kuhn, 'Preface', *Screen* 39:1 (1988), pp. 67–8; p. 67; T. Walter, 'Introduction: The Questions People Asked', in T. Walter (ed.), *The Mourning for Diana* (Oxford: Berg, 1999), pp. 19–47.

58. In R. Frances (ed.), *Dreaming of Diana: The Dreams Diana, Princess of Wales, Inspired* (London: Robson Books, 1998), so the compiler claims, 'ordinary people ... speak for themselves', without the mediation of 'psychologists ...

media pundits, political analysts or royal watchers'. The means and principles of compilation, and the reasons for the location of contributors in
terms of name, age, occupation, and geography, and not for example
gender, 'race', ethnicity, sexuality, class or other form of identity, remain
obscure. See T. Hughes, '6 September 1997', and other examples in
P. Turner and S. Pressley (compilers), *Diana Princess of Wales: A Book of
Remembrances* (Godalming: Bramley Books, 1997), n.p.; and in H.
Killingray, A. Head, C. Walton, S. Harwin (eds), *Poems for a Princess: In
Memory of Diana, Princess of Wales 1961–97* (Peterborough: Anchor Books,
1998).

Chapter 2

1. Archbishop Runcie quoted in G. Honeycombe, *Royal Wedding* (London:
   Michael Joseph/Rainbird, 1981), p. 179.
2. Campbell, *Diana*, pp. 4, 7, 193–201; J. Burchill, *Diana* (London:
   Weidenfeld and Nicolson, 1998); S. Moore, 'Diana – Her True Colours',
   and 'Diana the Do-gooder versus the Bad Guys', *Independent*, 17 January
   1997, p. 17. See also R. Brunt, 'Icon', *Screen* 39:1 (Spring 1998), pp. 68–70,
   and 'Sign of the Times', for a good summary of the tensions between
   these and other positions.
3. On Victoria, see Homans, *Royal Representations*; A. Munich, *Queen Victoria's
   Secrets* (New York: Columbia University Press, 1996).
4. *Diana: An Extraordinary Life* (London: De Agostini UK, 1997), 2, p. 54.
5. R. Braidotti, 'In the Sign of the Feminine: Reading Diana', *Theory and Event*
   1:4, http://muse.jhu.edu/journals/theory_&_event/v001/1.4.html.
6. T. Nairn, *The Enchanted Glass: Britain and its Monarchy* (London: Vintage
   [second edition], 1994), pp. 35, 27, 30, 91, 36.
7. Nairn, *Enchanted Glass*, p. 94.
8. R. Barthes, 'The "Blue Blood" Cruise', in *Mythologies*, trans. A. Lavers
   (London: Paladin, 1973), pp. 32–3; J. Williamson, 'Royalty and
   Representation'; Billig, *Talking of the Royal Family*; in Nairn's *The Enchanted
   Glass* the terms ordinary and super-ordinary are used.
9. D. Simmonds, *National Dish*; R. Coward, 'The Royals'; J. Smith, 'The Frog
   Princess', in *Misogynies* (London: Paladin, 1989), pp. 35–43; and 'To Di For:
   the Queen of Broken Hearts', in *Different for Girls* (London: Chatto and
   Windus, 1997), pp. 3–17.
10. W. Bagehot, *The English Constitution* (London: Fontana, 1963 [1867]),
    p. 85.
11. Bagehot, *The English Constitution*, p. 85; D. Cannadine, 'The Context,
    Performance and Meaning of Ritual: The British Monarchy and the
    'Invention of Tradition', c. 1820–1977', in E. Hobsbawm and T. Ranger
    (eds), *The Invention of Tradition* (Cambridge: Cambridge University Press,
    1983), pp. 101–64; D. Cannadine, *The Decline and Fall of the British
    Aristocracy* (New Haven and London: Yale University Press, 1990);
    B. Pimlott, *The Queen: A Biography of Elizabeth II* (London: HarperCollins,
    1996).
12. Pimlott, *Queen*, p. 502.

13. See J. Pearson, *The Ultimate Family: The Making of the Royal House of Windsor* (London: Grafton, 1987), A.N. Wilson, *The Rise and Fall of the House of Windsor* (London: Sinclair-Stevenson, 1993), P. Brendon and P. Whitehead, *The Windsors: A Dynasty Revealed* (London: Hodder and Stoughton, 1994).

14. Gunn's picture is in the collection of the National Portrait Gallery, London, and can also be seen in reproduction on the cover of Golby and Purdue, *The Monarchy and the British People.*

15. Pimlott, *Queen*, pp. 18, 293–301, 440, 451, 502–3; Williamson, 'Royalty and Representation', pp. 84, 76.

16. Quoted in H. Vickers, *Debrett's Book of the Royal Wedding* (London: Debretts Peerage/Book Club Associates, 1981), p. 16.

17. See Billig, *Talking Of*, Chapter 7: A Woman's Realm, pp. 172–201, for suggestions along these lines.

18. For analogous examples of maternity as public and private work in American political and televisual discourses, see J. Davies and C. Smith, 'Race, Gender and the American Mother: Political Speech and the Maternity Episodes of *I Love Lucy* and *Murphy Brown*', *American Studies* 39:2 (1998), pp. 33–63.

19. The emphasis on the so-called funeral events in attempts to understand the cultural significance of Diana, Princess of Wales is a good example of this. For earlier work on such public events in the traditions of sociology and semiotics, see respectively E. Shils and M. Young, 'The Meaning of the Coronation', *Sociological Review* 1:1 (1953), pp. 68–81, and the Dayan and Katz essay discussed below.

20. Quoted in Simmonds, *National Dish*, p. 18.

21. Dayan and Katz, 'Electronic Ceremonies', pp. 25–32.

22. Anonymous, *T.V. Times Royal Wedding Souvenir*, n.d. (August 1981), n.p. (p. 3).

23. Especially by Macmillan; see Pimlott, *Queen*, p. 273.

24. M. Chance, *Our Princesses and Their Dogs* (London: John Murray, 1936), Foreword, n.p.

25. For a more detailed sense of equivalent contemporary strategies, see Billig, *Talking Of*, and Chapters 3 and 4 below.

26. Chance, *Our Princesses*, n.p.

27. As examples of the former, in addition to the material discussed explicitly, see Lady C. Asquith, *The Family Life of Queen Elizabeth* (London: Hutchinson & Co., n.d.); L. Sheridan, *The Queen and her Children* (London: John Murray, 1953); L. Sheridan, *The Queen and Princess Anne* (London: John Murray, 1959); Foreword by J. Snagge, *Our Royal Family: The Record of a Happy Marriage* (London: Odhams Press, n.d.); and the later, blockbuster version of the genre, T. Smart, D. Gibbon, and D. Coolican, *Royal Family Album* (London?: Colour Library International, 1978).

28. *Daily Telegraph Coronation Supplement No. 1*, 11 May 1937, p. xiv.

29. *Daily Telegraph Coronation Supplement No. 1*, 11 May 1937, p. vii.

30. V.M. Synge, *Royal Guides: A Story of the 1st Buckingham Palace Company* (London: Girl Guides Association, 1948), p. 11.

31. Nairn, *Enchanted Glass.*, pp. 36–41; Pimlott, *Queen*, pp. 133–6; Pearson, *The Ultimate Family*, p. 73.
32. Pearson, *Ultimate Family*, p. 75.
33. M. Crawford, *The Little Princesses* (London: Cassell, 1950), back dustcover, pp. 28, 128.
34. *Woman's Own* 28 May 1953, p. 19.
35. *Woman's Own* 28 May 1953, pp. 30–1.
36. *Woman's Own* 28 May 1953, pp. 22–3.
37. J. Winship, *Inside Women's Magazines* (London: Pandora, 1987).
38. Campbell, *Diana*, Chapter 2, 'The Domestication of Royalty', pp. 33–40; though compare Pearson, *Ultimate Family* for a well-documented if less sophisticated counterpoint.
39. On 'England-Britain', see Nairn, *Enchanted Glass*, p. 22.
40. *Picture Post*, November 22, 1947, pp. 8–9, 16, 18–19.
41. L. Wolfe, *Elizabeth and Philip: Our Heiress and Her Consort* (London: Sampson Low, Marston & Co., 1947); B.S. Shew, *Royal Wedding* (London: Macdonald & Co., 1947). Gordon Honeycombe's 1981 book on the wedding of Charles and Diana, which originally appeared under the Michael Joseph imprint, was republished in a special album binding for Book Club members. See G. Honeycombe, *Royal Wedding* (London: Michael Joseph, 1981; London: Book Club Associates, 1981).
42. Anonymous, *Princess Elizabeth's Wedding Day* (London: H.A. and W.L. Pitkin Ltd, n.d. [1947]), n.p. (centre pages).
43. Pimlott, *Queen*, pp. 126, 132–3.
44. Anonymous, *Princess Elizabeth's Wedding Day*, n.p. (pp. 4–5).
45. Anonymous, *Princess Margaret's Wedding Day* (London: Pitkin Pictorials Ltd, 1960), p. 3; Peter Lewis, 'This most memorable and glorious day', in Anonymous (ed.) *The Prince and Princess of Wales' Wedding Day* (London: Pitkin Pictorials Ltd, 1981), p. 15.
46. Sir Arthur Bryant, 'The Royal Marriage', in Various, *The Wedding of Her Royal Highness The Princess Anne and Captain Mark Phillips* (London: King George's Jubilee Trust, 1973), p. 9.
47. *Ibid.*
48. K. Spink, *Invitation to a Royal Wedding* (New Malden: Colour Library International Ltd, 1981), pp. 91, 11.
49. This latter synthesis was widely remarked upon; see also G. Honeycombe, *Royal Wedding* (London: Book Club Associates, 1981), p. 177; T. Hall, *Royal Wedding Album* (Leicester: Windward, 1981), n.p.
50. See also for example Lewis, 'Most Memorable', p. 27.
51. Spink, *Invitation*, p. 67; Hall, *Royal Wedding*, n.p.s.
52. J. Craven, *Charles and Diana* (London: Arrow Books, 1982), p. 76.
53. *Sunday Times* Magazine, 21 June 1981, p. 34.
54. For further discussion of this material see J. Davies, 'The Media Iconicity of Diana, Princess of Wales, 1981–1996', in J. Arnold, K. Davies and S. Ditchfield (eds), *History & Heritage: Consuming the Past in Contemporary Culture* (Donhead St Mary: Donhead, 1998), pp. 51–64.
55. B.R. Lewis, *HRH The Princess of Wales* (Loughborough: Ladybird Books, 1982), p. 4.

56. Spink, *Invitation*, p. 75.
57. *Daily Express* 29 July 1981, p. 1.
58. See, for example, R. Lacey, *Princess* (London: Hutchinson, 1982), p. 127.
59. *Vogue*, January 1997, pp. 73–127.
60. Making a rather different point, Diana Simmonds traces back the trajectory of male royals in uniform via a 1913 photo of cousins George V, Tsar Nicholas II and Kaiser Wilhelm. See Simmonds, *National Dish*, p. 15.
61. Longford, in 'In Love with Elizabeth', BBC 1, 27 December 1998.
62. Pimlott, *Queen*, pp. 160–1, 412–7, 464–6.
63. Vickers, *Royal Wedding*, p. 84.
64. Bagehot, *The English Constitution*, p. 100. Bagehot's phrase is used as a chapter title in S. Bradford, *Elizabeth II: A Biography of Her Majesty the Queen* (London: Mandarin, 1996 [1995]), pp. 353–91, and this and other references to Bagehot figure prominently in B. Pimlott, *The Queen: A Biography of Elizabeth II* (London: HarperCollins, 1997), M. Billig, *Talking of the Royal Family* (London: Routledge, 1992), and T. Nairn, *The Enchanted Glass: Britain and its Monarchy* (London: Vintage, 1994).
65. Bagehot, *The English Constitution*, pp. 100, 96. On the need to avoid consideration of the 'domestic virtues' or otherwise of royal personages, and the debate over monarchy-as-disguise and royal intervention in politics, see Crossman's introduction to the same volume, pp. 33–7.
66. Homans, *Royal Representations*, pp. 110–15.
67. Attenborough compared the film with tribesmen looking inside the hut of the chief and told its producer-director Richard Crawston that the film was 'killing the monarchy', while Shulman warned in the London *Evening Standard* of the dangers of empowering the television camera as the mediator of familial intimacy, and expressed concern like Bagehot at the impossibility of sustaining indefinitely the image of the royals as models of domestic virtue. Quoted in Bradford, *Elizabeth II*, pp. 353, 360.
68. Pimlott, *Queen*, pp. 411, 386–7, 382; Bradford, *Elizabeth II*, p. 354.
69. K. Kelley, *The Royals* (New York: Warner Books, 1997), p. 212; Bradford, *Elizabeth II*, p. 359; Pimlott, *Queen* passim.
70. On Kantorowicz, see Nairn, *Enchanted Glass*, pp. 28–9.
71. Simmonds, *National Dish*, pp. 70–2, remarks on the coupling of the immediate deprivation of privacy from Diana and the continuing inability to find much information about her.
72. B.R. Lewis, *Queen Elizabeth II and Diana Princess of Wales* (London: Purnell, 1983).
73. M. Simpson, *Male Impersonators: Men Performing Masculinity* (London: Cassell, 1994).
74. On Charles as 'action man', see, for example, A. Whiting, *Family Royal* (London: W.H. Allen, 1982), pp. 211–12; M. Clifford, *Charles & Diana: A 10th Anniversary Celebration* (Cambridge: W.H. Smith/Book Connections, 1991), p. 102.
75. D. Keay, *Royal Wedding: A Celebration for the Marriage of Prince Charles to Lady Diana Spencer* (London: IPC Magazines, 1981), pp. 147–8; E-H. Breil

(ed.), *The Royal Wedding: Prince Charles and Lady Diana* (London: Seymour Press Ltd, 1981), n.p.
76. P. Junor, 'Must He Wait for History to be His Judge?', *Mail on Sunday*, 25 October 1998, p. 7.
77. P. James, *Anne: The Working Princess* (London: Judy Piatkus, 1987), p. 184.
78. See, for example, G. Talbot, *The Country Life Book of the Royal Family* (Richmond-upon-Thames: Country Life Books, 1980), pp. 203–4.
79. For further work on this issue see Richard Dyer on white women, Imperialism and reproduction, in *White*.
80. Just such a juxtaposition is made in P. Donnelly, *Diana: A Tribute to the People's Princess* (Godalming: Bramley Books, 1997), p. 41.
81. M. O'Mara (ed.), *Diana: Her Life in Photographs* (London: Michael O'Mara Books, 1995), p. 77.
82. J. Hartley, *The Politics of Pictures* (London and New York: Routledge, 1992), pp. 76–83.
83. Hartley, *Pictures*, p. 80.
84. Quoted in Hartley, *Pictures*, pp. 82–3.
85. J. Berger, *Ways of Seeing* (Harmondsworth: Penguin, 1972), p. 107.

Chapter 3

1. Lacey, *Princess*, p. 127.
2. A. Kear and D.L. Steinberg, 'Ghost Writing', in A. Kear and D.L. Steinberg (eds) *Mourning Diana: Nation, Culture and the Performance of Grief* (London: Routledge, 1999), pp. 1–14; p. 11.
3. The disciplinary and procedural distinctions between Kear and Steinberg's interest in theoretical specificity exemplified in *Mourning Diana*, as opposed to Tony Walter's focus on historical specificity in *The Mourning for Diana* (Oxford: Berg, 1999), generate significantly different critical projects. My own focus on the ideological import of Diana representations is an attempt to synthesize both historicist and theoretical tendencies.
4. In *Mourning Diana*, for example, Richard Johnson is careful to define the ambivalent signification of the 'later Diana', Valerie Hey discusses the political appropriations of Diana's 'post-divorce profile', Arvind Rajagopal focuses on Diana's public persona as a figure mediating tensions within British society, and William J. Spurlin suggests the multiple trajectories of Diana's iconicity generated from 'heteronormative', 'gay' and 'queer' investments. R. Johnson, 'Exemplary Differences: Mourning (and not Mourning) a Princess', in Kear and Steinberg, *Mourning Diana*, pp. 15–39; pp. 25–6;. Hey, 'Be(long)ing', p. 63; A. Rajagopal, 'Celebrity and the Politics of Charity: Memories of a Missionary Departed', *op. cit.*, pp. 126–41; p. 130; W.J. Spurlin, 'I'd Rather be the Princess than the Queen! Mourning Diana as a Gay Icon', *op. cit.*, pp. 155–68.
5. Kear and Steinberg. 'Ghost Writing', p. 10.
6. J. Kelleher, 'Rhetoric, Nation and the People's Property', in Kear and Steinberg, *Mourning Diana*, pp. 77–97.

7. A. Kear and D.L. Steinberg, 'Preface: Mourning Diana and the Scholarly Ethic', in *Mourning Diana*, pp. ix–xi; p. x.
8. See P. Junor, *Charles: Victim or Villain?* (London: HarperCollins, 1998), its serialization in the *Mail on Sunday* beginning 25 October 1998 as *Charles: The Prince's Story*, and especially the accompanying story in the main part of the newspaper 'Diana First to be Unfaithful' (*Mail on Sunday* pp. 2–3); and press comment on the same day, for example the front-page headlines in the *Express*, 'Charles Accused of Diana Smear', and the *Sunday People*, 'Charles in Vile Attack on Diana'.
9. Spurlin, 'I'd Rather be the Princess than the Queen!', p. 165.
10. Pimlott, *Queen*, p. 554.
11. J. Wicke, 'Celebrity Material: Materialist Feminism and the Cult of Celebrity', *South Atlantic Quarterly* 93:4 (Fall 1994) pp. 751–78; see also J. Shattuc, '"Go Rikki": Politics, Perversion and Pleasure in the 1990s', in C. Geraghty and D. Lusted (eds), *The Television Studies Book* (London: Arnold, 1998), pp. 212–25, for an account of the dynamics between various identity politics and the more downmarket personal revelation shows.
12. See M. Lauret, *Liberating Literature: Feminist Fictions in America* (London: Routledge, 1994), Chapter 3: Liberating Literature, pp. 74–96.
13. J. Radway, *Reading the Romance* (London: Verso, 1987), p. 8; J. Radway, 'Interpretive Communities and Variable Literacies: The Functions of Romance Reading', *Daedalus: Journal of the American Academy of Arts and Sciences*, 113:3 (1984), reprinted in J. Munns and G. Rajan (eds), *A Cultural Studies Reader: History, Theory, Practice*, 334–50; p. 336. Subsequent quotations from the essay are referenced to Munns and Rajan in the belief that this is most widely available.
14. Radway, 'Interpretive Communities', p. 340.
15. *Ibid.*
16. Radway, 'Interpretive Communities', p. 341.
17. Radway, *Reading the Romance*, pp. 119–56.
18. Radway, 'Interpretive Communities', p. 341.
19. See for example Campbell, *Diana*, pp. 6, 118–19, Simmonds, *National Dish*, pp. 85–6.
20. I. Ang, *Living Room Wars: Rethinking Media Audiences for a Postmodern World* (London: Routledge, 1996), Chapter 6; especially p. 96.
21. See, for example, *Diana: Her True Story* (1992), p. 136. This thematic juxtaposition of warmth and coldness is also noted by Pimlott; see Pimlott, *Queen*, p. 554.
22. Smith, 'Frog Princess', p. 41.
23. P. Junor, *Charles and Diana: Portrait of a Marriage* (London: Headline, 1991), 'Author's note and Acknowledgements' n.p.; R.M. Clifford, *Charles & Diana: A 10th Anniversary Celebration* (Cambridge: W.H. Smith/Book Connections, 1991) pp. 124–33.
24. Pimlott, *Queen*, p. 453.
25. Lacey, *Princess*, p. 128.
26. Smith, *Misogynies*, p. 36.
27. Lacey, *Princess*, p. 126.

28. Homans, *Royal Representations*, Chapter 3: The widow as author and the arts and powers of concealment, pp. 100–56, and see Chapter 2 above.
29. Lacey, *Princess*, p. 127.
30. Junor, *Charles and Diana*, p. 115.
31. Junor, *Charles and Diana*, n.p., pp. 52–3, 151–9.
32. Junor, *Charles and Diana*, pp. 38–43.
33. Junor, *Charles and Diana*, p. 181.
34. C. Campbell, *Diana in Private: The Princess Nobody Knows* (London: Smith Gryphon, 1992), pp. 2–4, 162–3, 234–5, 194.
35. N. Davies, *Diana: A Princess and Her Troubled Marriage* (New York: Birch Lane Press, 1992), pp. 94–5.
36. This vagueness extends as far as the description of the relationship between Charles and Camilla Parker-Bowles in *Diana: Her True Story* (1992), p. 127.
37. See especially C. Campbell, *The Royal Marriages: Private Lives of the Queen and Her Children* (London: Smith Gryphon, 1993), pp. 1–5, 107–15.
38. J. Burchill, *Diana* (London: Wiedenfeld and Nicolson, 1998), pp. 149, 178.
39. Campbell, *Diana,* pp. 202–10.
40. Campbell, *Diana*, pp. 205, 186–201.
41. *Sunday Times*, 7 June 1992, p. 1.
42. Billig, *Talking passim.*
43. Billig, *Talking*, p. 203.
44. Billig, *Talking*, pp. 200–1.
45. J. Burchill, 'Di Hard: The Pop Princess', in *Sex and Sensibility* (London: Grafton, 1992), pp. 233–44.
46. R. Scully, 'Princess attracts record 21.1 million viewers to Panorama', http://www.pa.press.net/princess/lead14.html.
47. L. Blackman, 'An Extraordinary Life: Diana and the Fantasy of Ordinary Suffering', paper at *An Era of Celebrity and Spectacle – Diana: A One Year Retrospective* Conference, Goldsmith's College, London, 27 August 1998.
48. A. Pasternak, *Princess In Love* (London: Bloomsbury, 1994).
49. Hey, 'Be(long)ing', p. 69.
50. Quoted in Lauret, *Liberating Literature*, pp. 90–1.
51. Compare S. Moore, 'Diana – Her True Colours' (first published December 1993), with 'Diana the Do-gooder versus the Bad Guys', of January 1997.
52. See Chapter 4 for further discussion of this formation.
53. E. Wurtzel, *Bitch* (London: Quartet, 1998), pp. 16–17, 280–1.
54. Paglia, 'Diana Regina', p. 171.
55. Davies, *Diana*, pp. 272–7; 275.
56. See the feature 'Diana – the business', *Daily Mirror* 20 February 1995, pp. 21–3 and a later and more conservative version in the supplement 'Diana: her own woman', *Mail on Sunday*, 2 and 9 July 1995, especially part 2 (9 July) 'A New Look for a New Life'. Burchill, *Diana*, pp. 169–70.
57. 'Diana: her own woman' part 2, pp. 12–15.
58. J. Whitaker, *Diana v. Charles* (London: Signet, 1993), inside jacket; Kelley, *The Royals*, p. 502.
59. N. Blundell and S. Blackhall, *Fall of the House of Windsor* (Chicago: Contemporary Books, 1992), Wilson, *The Rise and Fall of the House of*

Windsor, A. Holden, *The Tarnished Crown* (London: Bantam, 1993), Brendon and Whitehead, *The Windsors: A Dynasty Revealed*; for the more serious Stephen Haseler, Diana, the 'unwitting catalyst' was still important enough to feature as the cover illustration of *The End of the House of Windsor: Birth of a British Republic* (London: I.B. Tauris, 1993).

60. J. Rose, 'The Cult of Celebrity', *London Review of Books*, 20 August 1998, pp. 10–13, and *New Formations* 36 (1999), pp. 9–20.
61. Billig, *Talking*, pp. 116–71, 204, 213–16.
62. Various, 'Diana: Monster or Martyr?', *Tatler* 288:12 (1993), pp. 148–55, 218–19; p. 150.
63. 'Monster', p. 150.
64. 'Anne Robinson joins the Sun', *Sun* 20 November 1995, p. 3,; see also pp. 1–6.
65. *Sun*, 22 November 1995, p. 6; Hewitt and *Panorama* supplements paginated separately.
66. *Sun*, 20 November 1995, p. 2, *Sun*, 22 November 1995, p. 8, ITV Teletext poll, September 1996.
67. Davies, 'Media Iconicity of Diana'.
68. *News at Ten*, ITV, 31 January 1995; *Daily Star,* 1 February 1995, pp. 1–3.
69. B. Hoey, 'Diana is just a shrewd and selfish media manipulator', *Daily Express'* 16 November 1995, p. 9.
70. *Daily Express*, 16 November 1995, p. 9; *Sun*, 20 November 1995, p. 5.
71. E. Kaplan, (ed.) *Women in Film Noir* (London: BFI, revised edition 1980); Warner, *Monuments and Maidens*; M. Macdonald, *Representing Women: Myths of Femininity in the Popular Media* (London: Arnold, 1997), pp. 1, 105–31.
72. Kaplan, *Women in Film Noir*, pp. 2–3.
73. Macdonald, *Representing Women*, p. 106.
74. Hoey, 'Manipulator', p. 9; Benson, 'Monster', p. 218.
75. Benson, 'Monster', p. 218.
76. C.A. Haney and Davis, 'America Responds to Diana's Death: Spontaneous Memorials' in Walter, *Mouring for Diana*, pp. 227–39; p. 223.
77. *Daily Mail*, 30 September 1997, p. 1.
78. 'Our Diana Diaries: Her True Story', *Sunday Mirror*, 2 November 1997, pp. 1–7, 47–50; p. 3.
79. *Sunday Mirror*, 2 November 1997, p. 2.
80. R. Kay and G. Levy, 'Diana: The Untold Story', Part One, pp. 3, 6, *Daily Mail*, 24 January 1998.
81. *Sunday Mirror*, 2 November 1997, pp. 4–5.
82. For introductions to this pervasive theme in contemporary cultural studies, see M. Foucault, *Power/Knowledge: Selected Interviews and Other Writing* (Brighton: Harvester-Wheatsheaf, 1980), pp. 56–7, and as a constant concern in C. Brunsdon, (ed.) *Films for Women* (London: BFI, 1986), T. Modleski, *Feminism without Women: Culture and Criticism in a 'Post-feminist' Age* (New York and London: Routledge, 1991), Macdonald, *Representing Women*, C. Patton, 'Refiguring Social Space' in L. Nicholson and S. Seidman (eds) *Social Postmodernism: Beyond identity politics* (Cambridge: Cambridge University Press, 1995), pp. 216–49, and J. Davies and C.R. Smith, *Gender,*

Ethnicity and Sexuality in Contemporary American Film (Edinburgh: Keele University Press, 1998).

Chapter 4

1. Quoted in J. Fincher, *Diana: Portrait of a Princess* (Koln: Calloway Editions, 1998), p. 78.
2. The proliferation of popular understandings of Diana as icon is also noted by Rosalind Brunt, to whose masterful summaries in, 'Icon', and 'Princess Diana: A Sign of the Times' the current discussion is indebted.
3. Moore, *Head over Heels*, p. 88.
4. I. Frain, *Diana* (Paris: Assouline, 1998), p. 6.
5. See especially the final section, 'Memories', Holden, *Diana*, pp. 170–91.
6. Frain, *Diana*, pp. 78–9, *passim*.
7. Frain, *Diana*, p. 5.
8. See J. Kitzinger, 'Image', *Screen* 39:1 (1998), pp. 73–9; and in a longer version J. Kitzinger, 'The Moving Power of Moving Images: Television Constructions of Princess Diana', in Walter, *The Mourning for Diana*, pp. 65–76.
9. Morton, *Her True Story* 1997, p. 19; *Her True Story*, 1993, front cover.
10. Renton, 'Turning Diana into an ology', p. 8; Austin, 'Dons Flood Publishers with "Dianababble"', p. 17; see also R. Greenslade, 'Diana: Now the Press Gets off its Knees', *Guardian*, 6 April 1998, 2, p. 4.
11. See, for example, Burchill, *Diana*, pp. 115, 119, 126, 129, 161, 199 and most obviously the caption on p. 224 to the photograph opposite, 'Diana, single, happy and in love'.
12. S. Kemp, '"Myra, Myra on the Wall": The Fascination of Faces', *Critical Quarterly* 40:1 (1998), pp. 38–69; pp. 45, 44.
13. Fincher, *Diana*, p. 186.
14. See Fincher, *Diana*, pp. 174–81.
15. Holden, *Diana*, p. 114.
16. G. Harvey and M. Saunders, *Dicing with Di* (London: Blake Publishing, 1996), quoted in Kemp, 'Myra', p. 55.
17. 'Ups and Downs of Moody Princess', *Sunday Mirror*, 7 November 1993, p. 13.
18. 'Di Spy Sensation', *Sunday Mirror*, 7 November 1993, pp. 1, 3, 13.
19. Campbell, *Diana*, Chapter 14, pp. 186–201.
20. See, for example, T. Hall, *Diana, Princess of Wales* (Guildford: Colour Library Books, 1982); M. Shaw, *Princess: Leader of Fashion* (Guildford: Colour Library Books, 1983), also published for book clubs; J. Owen, *Diana, Princess of Wales: The Book of Fashion* (Guildford: Colour Library Books, 1983), also published in a special edition for BHS; D. Hanmer and T. Graham, *Diana: The Fashion Princess* (London: Park Lane Press/Marks and Spencer, 1984); A. Janaway and D. Levenson, *Diana: Princess of Fashion* (Guildford: Colour Library Books, 1984); *Diana: Model Princess* (dir. A. Scales, London: Imagicians/Odyssey, dist. Virgin Video, 1992); *Diana: Fashion Icon* (London: BBC Worldwide, [distributed with the part-work *Diana: An Extraordinary Life*, De Agostini, 1997]).
21. A. Chubb, *Royal Fashion and Beauty Secrets* (London: Vermilion, 1992).

22. See, for example, Janaway and Levenson, *Princess of Fashion*, p. 2.
23. R. Warren, review of D. Clehane, *Diana: The Secrets of Her Style* at http://www.amazon.com.
24. T. Graham and T. Blanchard, *Dressing Diana* (London: Weidenfeld and Nicolson, 1998), back cover, *passim*.
25. M. O'Mara, *Diana: Her Life in Photographs* (London: Michael O'Mara Books, 1995), pp. 42, 113, 115.
26. O'Mara, *Her Life*, pp. 149, 154–5.
27. B. Pimlott, 'Royal Doormat or Dear Doyenne?' *The Times*, 25 June 1998, p. 43.
28. See, for example, Pimlott, *Queen*, p. 475. An exception is Julie Burchill, who compares Diana to both Monroe and Madonna, but with the latter at more length in *Diana*, pp. 62, 111, 152, 159.
29. See Chapter 1 above, Simmonds, *National Dish*, S. Lowry, *Cult of Diana: The Princess in the Mirror* (London: Chatto and Windus, 1985), and Richards, Wilson and Woodhead, (eds), *Diana, The Making of a Media Saint*.
30. Simmonds, *National Dish*, pp. 108, 76, 67.
31. Kemp, 'Myra', p. 44; on Diana as victim of the sexualizing male gaze see Campbell, *Diana*, Chapter 14, especially pp. 192–4.
32. C. Carter, G. Branston and S. Allen (eds), *News, Gender and Power* (London and New York: Routledge, 1998), p. 8.
33. J. Hartley, 'Juvenation: News, Girls and Power', in Carter, Branston, and Allen, *News*, pp. 47–70, p. 69.
34. Hartley, 'Juvenation', p. 69.
35. Wilson, 'The Unbearable Lightness of Diana', p. 140 (emphasis in original). A slightly revised version of the essay appears in M. Merck, *After Diana: Irreverent Elegies* (London: Verso, 1998), pp. 111–26. In the revised version, Wilson registers the ambivalence of gender typology associated with Diana by omitting the second and third sentences of the passage quoted above. I have retained the original form here out of a conviction that the point still needs to be forcibly made.
36. See previous chapter, and Morton, *Her True Story*, 1992, p. 76.
37. Burchill, *Diana*, p. 211.
38. Campbell, *Diana*, pp. 251–3; see also Davies, '*Princess*: Diana, Femininity and the Royal', p. 141.
39. Burchill, *Diana*, p. 62.
40. Dyer, *White*, pp. 131–2.
41. Smyth quoted in Campbell, *Diana*, p. 122.
42. See, for example, Richard Kay and Geoffrey Levy, *Diana: The Untold Story. Part One: A Very Real Love*, part-work distributed with the *Daily Mail*, 24 January 1998, pp. 16–17.
43. Burgess quoted in Burchill, *Diana*, p. 63.
44. See O'Mara as just discussed, and also for example Lacey, *Princess*, pp. 16–17.
45. Burchill, *Diana*, pp. 62, 117.
46. See Lacey, *Princess*, pp. 16–17, and the critique of the libidinal investment in photographing Diana of the mostly male press photographers throughout Campbell, *Diana*.

47. Campbell, *Diana*, pp. 119–22.
48. Burchill, *Diana*, pp. 131ff.
49. G. Howell, *Diana: A Life in Fashion*, part-work distributed with the *Daily Mail* June–July 1998, *Part One*, pp. 20–1.
50. Fincher, *Diana*, pp. 84–5, 90–1.
51. G. Howell, *Diana: Her Life in Fashion* (London: Pavilion, 1998), p. 28.
52. Kay and Levy, *Untold Story, Part Eleven: Diana's Legacy*, p. 177.
53. Graham and Blanchard, *Dressing Diana*, p. 63; Howell, *Her Life in Fashion*, p. 197.
54. Walter, 'The Questions People Asked', in *Mourning for Diana*, pp. 19–47.
55. Holden, *Diana*, p. 19; Graham and Blanchard, *Dressing Diana*, p. 205.
56. Frain, *Diana*, p. 18.
57. Kitzinger, 'Image', pp. 76, 78.
58. See D. Smith, 'The revolution of the flowers', *Gay Times*, October 1997, pp. 7–9, 51–2.
59. Morton, *Her True Story*, 1997, pp. 243–4; Holden, *Diana*, 'Reaching Out' chapter title, pp. 78–95; Burchill, *Diana*, p. 142; Bradford, *Elizabeth*, p. 434; H. Bhabha, 'Designer Creations', in Merck (ed.) *After Diana*, pp. 103–10, pp. 106–7; R. Debray, 'Admirable England', *After Diana*, pp. 127–30, p. 130; N. Segal, 'The Common Touch', *After Diana*, pp. 130–45.
60. Compare the memorializing sequences shown on television described by Kitzinger in 'Image', and the still photographs in *Hello!* No. 462, 14 June 1997, pp. 61, 64–8.
61. Holden, *Diana*, p. 147.
62. Rabbi H. Berman, 'The Public Mourning and Funeral of Diana: A Religious Perspective', paper at *An Era of Celebrity and Spectacle: Diana: A One Year Retrospective* conference, Goldsmith's College, London, 27 August 1998.
63. Kitzinger, 'Image', p. 75.
64. See *Daily Telegraph*, 15 January 1997, p. 1 headline 'MoD anger at Diana's call to ban mines'; *The Times*, 15 January 1997, p. 1 headline 'Princess's call for mines ban upsets ministers'; and positive coverage led by the minefield photographs on the front pages of the *Daily Mail, Daily Telegraph, Guardian, Mirror* and *Sun* on 16 January.
65. *Sunday Mirror*, 2 February 1997, pp. 1, 6.
66. Graham and Blanchard, *Dressing Diana*, p. 200; H. Alexander, 'Life and Death of a Royal Marriage Told in Sequins and Satin', *Daily Telegraph*, 26 February 1997, p. 7.
67. C. Horyn (report) and M. Testino (photography), 'Diana Reborn', *Vanity Fair*, July 1997, pp. 82–91, 148; p. 83.
68. Horyn, 'Diana Reborn', p. 90 (emphasis added).
69. Quoted in Howell, *Diana*, p. 188.
70. Alexander, 'Life and Death', p. 7.
71. S. Mower and M. Yates, 'Goodbye To All That', *Telegraph* Magazine, 17 May 1997, pp. 32–6; pp. 33, 36.
72. See, for example, H. Clark, 'Fashioning Diana', in Re:Public, *Planet Diana*, pp. 133–6. In fact, Clark demonstrates a concern with the specific implica-

tions of the dresses as materializing Diana's history but leaves them tanta-
lizingly unexplored. Also suggestive is a brief comment in F. Mackie,
'Conspiracy? Treason? Truth?', in *Planet Diana*, pp. 137–8.

73. See among many others Mower and Yates, 'Goodbye', and *The Sun*, 27 June
1997, pp. 26–7.

74. *Dresses from the Collection of Diana, Princess of Wales* (New York: Christie's,
1997), pp. 12–13; Howell, *Diana*, p. 154.

75. See press material discussed above and below, 'Larry King Live' on *CNN*,
25–26 June 1997, *Lunchtime News from ITN*, ITV 26 June 1997, *Lunchtime
News*, BBC1 26 June 1997.

76. Horyn, 'Diana Reborn', p. 84.

77. *The Sun*, 27 June 1997 and 28 June 1997; *The Mirror*, 28 June 1997, p. 1.

78. *Mail on Sunday: You* magazine supplement, 3 August 1997, 'Sequins Save
Lives'; *Mail on Sunday: You* magazine supplement, 23 August 1998, 'Diana: a
celebration of her beauty and her life'.

79. Howell, *Diana*, p. 188.

80. E. Showalter, 'Temple of Diana', *The Times Higher Education Supplement*,
28 August 1998, pp. 13–14; p. 14; Carter quoted in A. McRobbie,
'Second-Hand Dress and the Role of the Ragmarket', in *Zoot Suits and
Second-Hand Dresses: An Anthology of Fashion and Music* (Basingstoke:
Macmillan, 1989), pp. 23–49; p. 31.

81. Macdonald, *Representing Women*, p. 112.

82. *Mirror* supplement, 'Diana: A Tribute to the People's Princess' *Part One*,
16 August 1998, p. 14.

83. J. Wade, 'Diana: The Enigma behind the Picture-perfect Princess of Wales',
Hello!, 14 June 1997, 60–8; pp. 60, 64, 67.

84. Front cover, *Hello!*, No. 453, 12 April 1997.

85. *Hello!*, 14 June 1997, pp. 62–5.

86. *Hello!* No. 509, 16 May 1998, pp. 80–1.

87. See *Hello!* Nos. 387, 30 December 1995, and 439, 4 January 1997.

88. Howell, *Diana*, p. 188.

89. Bagehot, 'English Constitution', p. 61; Horyn, 'Diana Reborn', p. 84.

90. O'Hear, 'Faking It', G. Newey, 'Diarrhoea', in Merck (ed.), *After Diana*
pp. 147–58; pp. 148, 157, 158; R. Coles, 'Feelin's', in Merck, *After Diana*,
pp. 169–82, p. 174.

91. See, for example, Kathleen Parker's syndicated article, 'Diana was never
"one of us"', Eau Claire *Leader-Telegram*, 14 September 1997, p. 3F.

92. For the direct 'postcard home' reading, see Holden, *Diana*, pp. 104–5; the
Sunday Mirror, 'Diana: The People's Princess' *Part Two*, 2 May 1998,
pp. 30–1; and T. Hanlon, 'It was obvious things were wrong as she sat there
alone', in the *Sunday Mirror*, 'Diana: A Tribute to the People's Princess',
Part Three, 30 August 1998, p. 22; for an account which emphasizes
the conflicted, antagonistic and collaborative role of the press in producing
the image, see Campbell, *Diana*, pp. 190–1.

Chapter 5

1. Voice of the Mirror, 'Your People Have Spoken … Now YOU Must, Ma'am',
Mirror, 4 September 1997, p. 11.

2. *The Sun* Speaks its Mind, 'Show us There's a Heart in the House of Windsor', *Sun*, 3 September 1997, p. 8. See also the paired articles in this issue of the *Sun*, Lord Blake, 'The Palace must rebuild the traditional virtues of the Monarchy', and D. Starkey, 'Diana's death may have signalled the end of the Monarchy', *ibid.*, p. 10.
3. Showalter, 'Storming the Wintry Palace', p. 15.
4. See M. Merck, 'Introduction: After Diana', in Merck (ed.), *After Diana*, pp. 1–14, for a summary and critique of 'New Britain' press material.
5. S. Heffer, 'How Diana Has Truly United Our Kingdom', *Daily Mail*, 3 September 1997, p. 8.
6. A. Barnett, *This Time: Our Constitutional Revolution* (London: Vintage, 1997), and A. Barnett and J.B. Taylor, 'Diana and the Constitution: A Conversation', in *New Formations* 36 (1999), pp. 47–58.
7. Jacques, 'The Floral Revolution', p. 15.
8. O'Hear, 'Diana, Queen of Hearts', p. 184. In an argument that owed a large unacknowledged debt to Teodor Adorno, O'Hear went much further than leftist commentators such as Gilroy and Wilson in portraying a Britain changed by public reaction to Diana's death (see especially pp. 183, 190), if only to stress the urgency of contesting it.
9. Of the initial academic responses to Diana's death, the special issue of *theory & event*, 1.4 (1997), and Merck's *After Diana* are largely constituted around projects of demystification, while Re: Public's *Planet Diana* presents Diana's significance in more dynamic terms.
10. Easthope, *Englishness and National Culture*, p. 100. Compare also the tonal disjuncture between the cover design of Merck's *After Diana*, whose appropriation of Roman Catholic iconography invites mockery of Diana's presumed sanctification, a tone maintained by contributors such as Hitchens and Newey, and Sarah Maitland's serious and well-considered critique of the 'colonisation' of Catholic discourse by the Diana mourning events, in the same volume.
11. Couldry, 'Remembering Diana: The Geography of Celebrity and the Politics of Lack'; see especially pp. 84–5.
12. M. Gibson, 'The Temporality of Democracy: The Long Revolution and Diana, Princess of Wales', *New Formations*, 36, (1999), pp. 59–76; p. 62. The ambivalence of Diana's significance, and the consequent problematisation of critical apparatuses, is a theme which runs throughout this collection of essays.
13. Nava, 'Diana, Princess of Others,' p. 22.
14. Compare Walter, 'The Questions People Asked', pp. 42–3.
15. A. Blake, 'Retrolution: Culture and Heritage in a Young Country', in A. Coddington and M. Perryman (eds), *Moderniser's Dilemma*, pp. 143–56.
16. On the significance of marking racial difference in a rather different context, that of blackness, whiteness and American national cinema, see J. Snead (ed. C. MacCabe and C. West), *White Screens Black Images: Hollywood from the Dark Side* (London: Routledge, 1994).
17. The phrase is the American critic Kathleen Parker's, but it serves to summarize a variety of critical positions which refuse the logic of Diana as a direct representative of identity. Parker, 'Diana Was Never One of "Us"', p. 3F.

18. Wilson, 'Unbearable Lightness', p. 140.
19. E. Gellner, *Thought and Change* (London: Weidenfeld and Nicolson, 1964), p. 169, quoted in B. Anderson, *Imagined Communities* (London: Verso, [second edition] 1991), p. 6. In fact the second edition of Anderson's seminal text is animated by a sense that a consciousness of this disjuncture is discernible in nineteenth-century formulations of nation by Renan and others.
20. For a Lacanian framing of this lack, and also the general notion of 'national desire', see Easthope, *Englishness*, p. 48 and *passim*. Compare also the sense of Diana's death as producing 'a collective sense of loss for something the collective never possessed', in 'Introduction: Saint Diana', in Richards, Wilson and Woodhead (eds), *Diana: The Making of a Media Saint*, pp. 1–19; p. 2.
21. Burchill, *Diana*, pp. 137, 185, 203; Kelley, *The Royals* , pp. 5–19.
22. J. Verma, 'Mourning Diana, Asian Style', in Kear and Steinberg, *Mourning Diana*, pp. 120–5; p. 124.
23. P. Gilroy, 'Elton's Crooning, England's Dreaming', *theory & event* 1:4 (1997), http://muse.jhu.edu/journals/theory_&_event/v001/1.4.html.
24. On Victoria's journals see Homans, *Royal Representations* and Introduction and Chapter 1 above.
25. H. Price, *The Royal Tour 1901, Or The Cruise of H.M.S. Ophir, Being a Lower Deck Account of their Royal Highnesses the Duke and Duchess of Cornwall and York's Voyage around the British Empire* (Exeter: Webb & Bower, 1980), n.p.
26. D. Morrah, *The Royal Family in Africa* (London: Hutchinson and Co., 1947), p. 7.
27. Brigadier S.F. Clarke, O.B.E., *The Royal Tour* (in four parts; London: Pitkin Pictorials Ltd, Jan.–May 1954).
28. Clarke, 'The Memorable Visit to Tonga', *The Royal Tour* Part One: Outward Bound, p. 27; '"Goddess of the Sea" and "God of War"', *The Royal Tour* Part Two: New Zealand, p. 8; '"Come and sit by me" said the Queen', *The Royal Tour* Part Two: New Zealand, p. 14; 'The Queen Opens the State Parliament', *The Royal Tour* Part Three: Australia, p. 31.
29. H.R.H. The Duke of Edinburgh, *Birds from Britannia* (London: Longmans, 1962).
30. *Hello!* 481, October 25, 1997, pp. 10–18; pp. 12–13.
31. *Ibid.*
32. L. Holt, 'Diana and the Backlash', in Merck (ed.), *After Diana*, pp. 183–97; p. 190.
33. S. Begbie, 'Dianaland – Not a Playground for the Fainthearted', in Re:Public (ed.), *Planet Diana*, pp. 121–6, p. 124.
34. Anderson, *Imagined Communities*, p. 21.
35. On Protestantism as the key to producing a nation of Scots, English, Welsh and Irish in the eighteenth and nineteenth centuries, see L. Colley, *Britons: Forging the Nation 1707–1837* (London: Vintage, 1996).
36. Diana's friends Rosi Boycott and Lucia Flecha de Lima have firmly rejected the notion that Diana planned to marry Dodi Fayed. See, for example, de

Lima's comments in G. Posner, 'Al Fayed's Rage', *talk* (September 1999), pp. 121–30; p. 125.

37. Nava, 'Princess of Others', pp. 22–3; Nava, 'Diana and Race, pp. 113–15.
38. E. Lomax, 'Diana Al-Fayed: Ethnic Marketing and the End(s) of Racism', in Richards, Wilson and Woodhead (eds), *Diana, The Making of a Media Saint*, pp. 74–97.
39. Nava, 'Diana, Princess of Others', pp. 24–5; Nava, 'Diana and Race', pp. 115–16.
40. C. Milner, 'Charity Outraged by "Sick" Diana Art Show', *Sunday Telegraph*, 11 July 1999; 'Sick and Offensive', *Daily Star*, 12 July 1999.
41. See A. Chaudhuri, 'Is This a Harmless Glimpse of What Might Have Been, or Tasteless Exploitation?', *Guardian*, 17 July 1999, Review, p. 3.
42. *Ibid.*
43. J. Freedland, 'Diana is Dead', *Guardian*, 25 August 1999, p. 23.
44. Couldry, 'Remembering Diana', p. 79.
45. Nava, 'Diana, Princess of Others', p. 25; the passage is slightly revised in Nava, 'Diana and Race', p. 116, where the final words are 'the cultural identifications and fantasies of the people'.
46. See, for example, J. Keegan, 'End of the Empire', in M. Dewar (ed.), *The Official Government Programme to Mark the 50th Anniversary of the End of World War II* (London: Whitehall Publications and Marketing, 1995), pp. 22–7, which begins by enumerating some 23 different racial and ethnic groups among the soldiers of the 1946 Victory Parade in London, and goes on to assert that 'The British Empire dissassembled piece by piece, almost without violence ...' (p. 22).
47. O. Wambu, 'Introduction', in *Empire Windrush: Fifty Years of Writing About Black Britain* (London: Gollancz, 1998), pp. 19–29; p. 19.
48. Although he is concerned with the moment of the fiftieth anniversary of the beginning of migration from the Caribbean, Wambu's definition of Blackness also includes people from areas in Africa and Asia colonized by the British Empire.
49. Wambu, 'Introduction', p. 21.
50. H.K. Bhabha, 'DissemiNation: time, narrative, and the margins of the modern nation' in H.K. Bhabha (ed.), *Nation and Narration* (London: Routledge, 1990), pp. 291–322; p. 299.
51. On the long history of Black people within Britain, see G. Gerzina, *Black England: Life Before Emancipation* ([1995] London: Allison and Busby, 1999).

Epilogue

1. P. Melville, 'English Table Wuk', in *The Migration of Ghosts (Stories)* (London: Bloomsbury, 1998), pp. 197–209; pp. 197, 200.
2. Homans, *Royal Representations*, pp. 11, 22.

3. Munich quotes the American novelist Henry James as writing of Victoria that 'I felt her death much more than I had expected'. A. Munich, *Queen Victoria's Secrets*, p. 220.
4. Munich, *Queen Victoria's Secrets*, p. 221.
5. Holden, *Diana*, pp. 48, 168.
6. Homans, *Royal Representations*, pp. 62–9; 110–11.
7. T. Blair, speech 31 August 1997, rpt. in MacArthur, *Requiem*, pp. 17–18. Blair's media adviser Alastair Campbell is widely credited with supplying the speech's terminology.

Bibliography

Alberts, P., 'Sublime and Corporeal Diana', in Re:Public (ed.), *Planet Diana: Cultural Studies and Global Mourning* (Kingswood: Research Centre in Intercommunal Studies, University of Western Sydney, Nepean, 1997), pp. 97–101.

Alexander, H., 'Life and Death of a Royal Marriage Told in Sequins and Satin', *Daily Telegraph*, 26 February 1997, p. 7.

Anderson, B., *Imagined Communities* (London: Verso, [second edition] 1991).

Ang, I., *Living Room Wars: Rethinking Media Audiences for a Postmodern World* (London: Routledge, 1996).

Anonymous (*Independent*), 'If Only the Royals Could Weep with the People', in B. MacArthur (ed.), *Requiem: Memories and Tributes* (London: Pavilion, 1997), pp. 37–40.

Anonymous, *Daily Telegraph Coronation Supplement No. 1*, 11 May 1937.

Anonymous, *Dresses from the Collection of Diana, Princess of Wales* (New York: Christie's, 1997).

Anonymous, *Princess Elizabeth's Wedding Day* (London: H.A. and W.L. Pitkin Ltd, nd [1947]).

Anonymous, *Princess Margaret's Wedding Day* (London: Pitkin Pictorials Ltd, 1960).

Anonymous, *T.V. Times Royal Wedding Souvenir*, n.d. (August 1981).

Anonymous, *Diana: An Extraordinary Life* (London: De Agostini UK, 1997).

Armstrong, N., *Desire and Domestic Fiction: A Political History of the Novel* (New York and Oxford: Oxford University Press, 1987).

Asquith, C., *The Family Life of Queen Elizabeth* (London: Hutchinson & Co., n.d.).

Austin, M., 'Dons Flood Publishers with "Dianababble"', *Sunday Times*, 5 April 1998, p. 17.

Bagehot, W., *The English Constitution* ([1867] London: Fontana, 1963).

Barnes, J., *England, England* (London: Jonathan Cape, 1998).

Barnett, A., *This Time: Our Constitutional Revolution* (London: Vintage, 1997).

Barnett, A. and J.B. Taylor, 'Diana and the Constitution: A Conversation', in *New Formations* 36 (1999), pp. 47–58.

Barthes, R., 'Myth Today', in *Mythologies* trans. A. Lavers (London: Paladin, 1973), pp. 109–59.

Barthes, R., 'The "Blue Blood" Cruise', in *Mythologies*, trans. A. Lavers, (London: Paladin, 1973), pp. 32–3.

Barthes, R., 'Change the Object Itself', in R. Barthes, *Image–Music–Text* (ed. and trans. S. Heath), (London: Fontana, 1977), pp. 165–9.

Begbie, S., 'Dianaland – Not a Playground for the Fainthearted', in Re:Public (ed.), *Planet Diana: Cultural Studies and Global Mourning* (Kingswood: Research Centre in Intercommunal Studies, Univ. of Western Sydney, Nepean, 1997), pp. 121–6.

Berger, J., *Ways of Seeing* (Harmondsworth: Penguin, 1972).

Berman, H., 'The Public Mourning and Funeral of Diana: A Religious Perspective', paper at *An Era of Celebrity and Spectacle: Diana: A One Year Retrospective* conference, Goldsmith's College, London, 27 August 1998.

Bhabha, H., 'Designer Creations', in M. Merck (ed.) *After Diana: Irreverent Elegies* (London: Verso, 1998), pp. 103–10.

Bhabha, H., 'DissemiNation: Time, Narrative, and the Margins of the Modern Nation', in H. Bhabha (ed.), *Nation and Narration* (London: Routledge, 1990), pp. 291–322.

Bignell, J., *Media Semiotics* (Manchester: Manchester University Press, 1997).

Billig, M., *Talking Of the Royal Family* (London: Routledge, 1992).

Blackman, L., 'An *Extra*ordinary Life: Diana and the Fantasy of Ordinary Suffering', paper at *An Era of Celebrity and Spectacle – Diana: A One Year Retrospective* Conference, Goldsmith's College, London, 27 August 1998.

Blackman, L., 'An *Extraordinary* Life: The Legacy of an Ambivalence', in *New Formations* 36, pp. 111–24.

Blake, A., 'Retrolution: Culture and Heritage in a Young Country', in A. Coddington and M. Perryman (eds), *The Moderniser's Dilemma: Radical Politics in the Age of Blair* (London: Lawrence and Wishart, 1998), pp. 143–56.

Blake, Lord, 'The Palace Must Rebuild the Traditional Virtues of the Monarchy', *Sun*, 3 September 1997, p. 10.

Blundell, N. and S. Blackhall, *Fall of the House of Windsor* (Chicago: Contemporary Books, 1992).

Bradford, S., *Elizabeth II: A Biography of Her Majesty the Queen* (London: Mandarin, 1996).

Braidotti, R., 'In the Sign of the Feminine: Reading Diana', *Theory and Event* 1:4, http://muse.jhu.edu/journals/theory_&_event/v001/1.4.html.

Breese, S., 'In Search of Englishness; In Search of Votes', in J. Arnold, K. Davies and S. Ditchfield (eds), *History and Heritage: Consuming the Past in Contemporary Culture* (Donhead St Mary: Donhead, 1998), pp. 155–67.

Breil, E-H. (ed.), *The Royal Wedding: Prince Charles and Lady Diana* (London: Seymour Press Ltd., 1981).

Brendon, P. and P. Whitehead, *The Windsors: A Dynasty Revealed* (London: Hodder and Stoughton, 1994).

Brunsdon, C. (ed.), *Films for Women* (London: BFI, 1986).

Brunt, R., 'Icon', *Screen* 39:1 (1998), pp. 68–70.

Brunt, R., 'Princess Diana: A Sign of the Times', in J. Richards, S. Wilson and L. Woodhead (eds.), *Diana, The Making of a Postmodern Saint* (London: I.B. Tauris, 1999), pp. 20–39.

Bryant, A., 'The Royal Marriage', in Various, *The Wedding of Her Royal Highness The Princess Anne and Captain Mark Phillips* (London: King George's Jubilee Trust, 1973), p. 9.

Burchill, J., 'Di Hard: The Pop Princess', in *Sex and Sensibility* (London: Grafton, 1992).

Burchill, J., *Diana* (London: Weidenfeld and Nicolson, 1998).

Burke, S., *The Death and Return of the Author: Criticism and Subjectivity in Barthes, Foucault, and Derrida* (Edinburgh: University of Edinburgh Press, 1992).

Butler, J., *Bodies that Matter: On the Discursive Limits of 'Sex'* (New York and London: Routledge, 1993).

Campbell, B., *Diana Princess of Wales: How Sexual Politics Shook the Monarchy* (London: The Women's Press, 1998).

Campbell, C., *Diana in Private: The Princess Nobody Knows* (London: Smith Gryphon, 1992).

Campbell, C., *The Royal Marriages: Private Lives of the Queen and Her Children* (London: Smith Gryphon, 1993).

Cannadine, D., 'The Context, Performance and Meaning of Ritual: The British Monarchy and the "Invention of Tradition", c. 1820–1977', in E. Hobsbawm and T. Ranger (eds), *The Invention of Tradition* (Cambridge: Cambridge University Press, 1983), pp. 101–64.

Cannadine, D., *The Decline and Fall of the British Aristocracy* (New Haven and London: Yale University Press, 1990).

Carter, C., G. Branston and S. Allen (eds), *News, Gender and Power* (London and New York: Routledge, 1998).

Chance, M., *Our Princesses and Their Dogs* (London: John Murray, 1936).

Chaney, D., *Fictions of Collective Life: Public Drama in Late Modern Culture* (London: Routledge, 1993).

Chaudhuri, A., 'Is This a Harmless Glimpse of What Might Have Been, or Tasteless Exploitation?', *Guardian*, 17 July 1999, Review, p. 3.

Chubb, A., *Royal Fashion and Beauty Secrets* (London: Vermilion, 1992).

Clark, H., 'Fashioning Diana', in Re:Public (ed.), *Planet Diana: Cultural Studies and Global Mourning* (Kingswood: Research Centre in Intercommunal Studies, Univ. of Western Sydney, Nepean, 1997), pp. 133–6.

Clarke, S.F., *The Royal Tour* (in four parts; London: Pitkin Pictorials Ltd, Jan.–May 1954).

Clifford, M., *Charles & Diana: A 10th Anniversary Celebration* (Cambridge: W.H. Smith/Book Connections, 1991).

Clinton, H., 'A Reservoir of Resilience and Determination', in B. MacArthur (ed.), *Requiem: Memories and Tributes* (London: Pavilion, 1997), pp. 93–5.

Coles, R., 'Feelin's', in M. Merck (ed.), *After Diana: Irreverent Elegies* (London: Verso, 1998), pp. 169–82.

Colley, L., *Britons: Forging the Nation 1707–1837* ([1992] London: Vintage, 1996).

Couldry, N., 'Remembering Diana: The Geography of Celebrity and the Politics of Lack', *New Formations* 36, (1999), pp. 77–91.

Coward, R., 'The Royals', in *Female Desire: Women's Sexuality Today* (London: Paladin, 1984), pp. 161–71.

Craven, J., *Charles and Diana* (London: Arrow Books, 1982).

Crawford, M., *The Little Princesses* (London: Cassell, 1950).

Daily Star, 1 February 1995, pp. 1–3.

Daily Telegraph, 15 January 1997, p. 1 headline 'MoD anger at Diana's call to ban mines'.

Dangerfield, G., *Victoria's Heir: The Education of a Prince* ([New York, 1941] London: Constable, 1942).

Davies, J., 'The Media Iconicity of Diana, Princess of Wales 1981–1996', in J. Arnold, K. Davies and S. Ditchfield (eds), *History and Heritage: Constructing the Past in Contemporary Culture* (Donhead St Mary: Donhead, 1998), pp. 51–64.

Davies, J. and C.R. Smith, *Gender, Ethnicity and Sexuality in Contemporary American Film* (Edinburgh: Keele University Press, 1998).

Davies, N., *Diana: A Princess and Her Troubled Marriage* (New York: Birch Lane Press, 1992).

Dayan, D. and E. Katz, 'Electronic Ceremonies: Television Performs a Royal Wedding', in M. Blonsky (ed.), *On Signs* (Oxford: Basil Blackwell, 1985), pp. 16–32.

de Lauretis, T., 'The Technology of Gender', in *Technologies of Gender: Essays on Theory, Film, and Fiction* (London: Macmillan, 1987, pp. 1–30).

Debray, R., 'Admirable England', in M. Merck (ed.), *After Diana: Irreverent Elegies* (London: Verso, 1998), pp. 127–30).

Deedes, W.F., 'The Princess of Sorrows', *Daily Telegraph*, 1 September, 1997, p. 14.

Deedes, W.F., 'Diana, Princess of Wales', in *The Daily Telegraph: Diana Remembered* (Macmillan, 1997), pp. 80–6.

Diana: Fashion Icon (London: BBC Worldwide, [distributed with the part-work *Diana: An Extraordinary Life*, De Agostini, 1997]).

Diana: Model Princess (dir. A. Scales, London: Imagicians/Odyssey, dist. Virgin Video, 1992).

Donnelly, P., *Diana: A Tribute to the People's Princess* (Godalming: Bramley Books, 1997).

Duruz, J. and C. Johnson, 'Mourning at a Distance: Australians and the Death of a British Princess', in A. Kear and D.L. Steinberg (eds), *Mourning Diana: Nation, Culture and the Performance of Grief* (London: Routledge, 1999), pp. 142–54.

Duruz, J. and C. Johnson, 'Appropriating the People's Princess', in Re:Public (ed.), *Planet Diana: Cultural Studies and Global Mourning* (Kingswood: Research Centre in Intercommunal Studies, University of Western Sydney, Nepean, 1997), pp. 45–8.

Dyer, R., *Heavenly Bodies: Film Stars and Society* (London and Basingstoke: BFI/Macmillan, 1986).

Dyer, R., *White* (London: Routledge, 1997).

Easthope, A., *Englishness and National Culture* (London: Routledge, 1999).

Edinburgh, Duke of, *Birds from Britannia* (London: Longmans, 1962).

Elizabeth II, 'The Queen's Speech', in B. MacArthur (ed.), *Requiem: Memories and Tributes* (London: Pavilion, 1997), pp. 51–2.

Engel, M., 'After the Grief, the Moment of Truth for a Nation', *Guardian*, Special section, 6 September 1997, pp. 1–3.

Engel, M., 'The British Began to Queue', in B. MacArthur (ed.), *Requiem: Memories and Tributes* (London: Pavilion, 1997), pp. 26–9.

Fincher, J., *Diana: Portrait of a Princess* (Koln: Calloway editions, 1998).

Foucault, M., *Power/Knowledge: Selected Interviews and Other Writing* (Brighton: Harvester Wheatsheaf, 1980).

Frain, I., *Diana* (Paris: Assouline, 1998).

Frances, R. (ed.), *Dreaming of Diana: The Dreams Diana, Princess of Wales, Inspired* (London: Robson Books, 1998).

Freedland, J., 'Diana is Dead', *Guardian*, 25 August 1999, p. 23.

Gerrard, N., 'We are all Dianas now', *Observer* 'Life' section, 28 December 1997, p. 10.

Gerzina, G., *Black England: Life Before Emancipation* ([1995] London: Allison and Busby, 1999).

Gibson, M., 'The Temporality of Democracy: The Long Revolution and Diana, Princess of Wales', *New Formations*, 36 (1999), pp. 59–76.

Gilroy, P., 'Elton's Crooning, England's Dreaming', *theory & event* 1:4 (1997), http://muse.jhu.edu/journals/theory_&_event/v001/1.4.html.

Golby, J.M. and A.W. Purdue, *The Monarchy and the British People: 1760 to the Present* (London: B.T. Batsford, 1988).

Graham, T., *Diana, Princess of Wales: A Tribute* (London: Weidenfeld and Nicolson, 1997).

Graham, T. and T. Blanchard, *Dressing Diana* (London: Wiedenfeld and Nicolson, 1998).

Greenslade, R., 'Diana: Now the Press Gets off its Knees', *Guardian*, 6 April 1998, 2, p. 4.

Griffith, P., '"Words cannot say what she is"', in Re:Public (ed.), *Planet Diana: Cultural Studies and Global Mourning* (Kingswood: Research Centre in Intercommunal Studies, University of Western Sydney, Nepean, 1997), pp. 71–4.

Hall, T., *Diana, Princess of Wales* (Guildford: Colour Library Books, 1982).

Hall, T., *Royal Wedding Album* (Leicester: Windward, 1981).

Haney, C.A. and D. Davis, 'American Responds to Diana's Death: Spontaneous Memorials', in T. Walter (ed.), *The Mourning for Diana* (Oxford: Berg, 1999), pp. 227–39

Hanks, P. (ed.), *The Collins English Dictionary* Second Edition (London and Glasgow: Collins, 1986).

Hanlon, T., 'It Was Obvious Things Were Wrong As She Sat There Alone', in the *Sunday Mirror* 'Diana: A Tribute to the People's Princess', Part Three, 30 August 1998, p. 22.

Hanmer, D. and T. Graham, *Diana: The Fashion Princess* (London: Park Lane Press/Marks and Spencer, 1984).

Hartley, J., 'Juvenation: News, Girls and Power', in Carter, Branston and Allen, *News*, pp. 47–70.

Hartley, J., *The Politics of Pictures* (London and New York: Routledge, 1992).

Haseler, S., *The End of the House of Windsor: Birth of a British Republic* (London: I.B. Tauris, 1993).

Heffer, S., 'How Diana Has Truly United Our Kingdom', *Daily Mail*, 3 September 1997, p. 8.

Hello! 387, 30 December 1995.

Hello! 439, 4 January 1997.

Hello!, 453, 12 April 1997.

Hello! 462, 14 June 1997.

Hello! 481, 25 October 1997.

Hello! 509, 16 May 1998.

Hey, V., 'Be(long)ing: New Labour, New Britain, and the "Dianaization" of politics', in A. Kear and D.L. Steinberg (eds), *Mourning Diana: Nation, Culture and the Performance of Grief* (London: Routledge, 1999), pp. 60–76.

Hitchens, C., 'Princess Di, Mother T., and me', in M. Merck (ed.), *After Diana: Irreverent Elegies* (London: Verso, 1998), pp. 49–61.

Hoey, B., 'Diana is Just a Shrewd and Selfish Media Manipulator', *Daily Express*, 16 November 1995, p. 9.

Holden, A., *Diana: A Life and a Legacy* (London: Ebury Press, 1997).

Holden, A., 'Diana: Monster or Martyr?', *Tatler* 288:12 (December 1993), pp. 150–1.

Holden, A., *The Tarnished Crown* (London: Bantam, 1993).

Holden, A., R. Benson, *et. al.* 'Diana: Monster or Martyr?', *Tatler* 288:12 (1993), pp. 148–55, 218–19.

Holt, L., 'Diana and the Backlash', in M. Merck, (ed.), *After Diana: Irreverent Elegies* (London: Verso, 1998), pp. 183–97.

Homans, M., *Royal Representations: Queen Victoria and British Culture, 1837–1876* (Chicago: University of Chicago Press, 1998).

Honeycombe, G., *Royal Wedding* (London: Book Club Associates, 1981).

Honeycombe, G., *Royal Wedding* (London: Michael Joseph/Rainbird, 1981).

Horyn, C. (report) and M. Testino (photography), 'Diana Reborn', *Vanity Fair*, July 1997, pp. 82–91.

Howell, G., *Diana: A Life in Fashion*, part-work distributed with the *Daily Mail*, June–July 1998.

Howell, G., *Diana: Her Life in Fashion* (London: Pavilion, 1998).

Hughes, T., '6 September 1997', in P. Turner and S. Pressley (compilers), *Diana Princess of Wales: A Book of Remembrances* (Godalming: Bramley Books, 1997).

Hume, M., *Televictims: Emotional Correctness in the media AD (After Diana)* (London: InformInc, 1998).

ITV Teletext poll, September 1996.

Jack, I., 'Those Who Felt Differently', *Guardian* Weekend, 27 December 1997, pp. 5–6, 8, 10, and in *Granta 60: Unbelievable* (1998).

Jacques, M., 'The Floral Revolution', *Observer*, 7 September 1997, p. 15.

James, P., *Anne: The Working Princess* (London: Judy Piatkus, 1987).

Janaway, A. and D. Levenson, *Diana: Princess of Fashion* (Guildford: Colour Library Books, 1984).

Jay, A., *Elizabeth R: The Role of the Monarchy Today* (London: BBC Books, 1992).

Johnson, R., 'Exemplary Differences: Mourning (and not mourning) a Princess', in A. Kear and D.L. Steinberg (eds), *Mourning Diana: Nation, Culture and the Performance of Grief* (London: Routledge, 1999), pp. 15–39.

Junor, P., 'Must He Wait for History to be His Judge?', *Mail on Sunday*, 25 October 1998, p. 7.

Junor, P., *Charles and Diana: Portrait of a Marriage* (London: Headline, 1991).

Junor, P., *Charles: Victim or Villain?* (London: HarperCollins, 1998).

Kaplan, E.A. (ed.), *Women in Film Noir* (London: BFI, revised edition 1980).

Kay, R. and G. Levy, 'Diana: The Untold Story', *Daily Mail*, January–April 1998.

Kear, A. and D.L. Steinberg, 'Ghost Writing', in A. Kear and D.L. Steinberg (eds), *Mourning Diana: Nation, Culture and the Performance of Grief* (London: Routledge, 1999), pp. 1–14.

Kear, A. and D.L. Steinberg, 'Preface: Mourning Diana and the Scholarly Ethic', in A. Kear and D.L. Steinberg (eds), *Mourning Diana: Nation, Culture and the Performance of Grief* (London: Routledge, 1999), pp. ix–xi.

Keay, D. *Royal Wedding: A Celebration for the Marriage of Prince Charles to Lady Diana Spencer* (London: IPC Magazines, 1981).

Keegan, J., 'End of the Empire', in M. Dewar (ed.), *The Official Government Programme to Mark the 50th Anniversary of the End of World War II* (London: Whitehall Publications and Marketing, 1995), pp. 22–7.

Kelleher, J., 'Rhetoric, Nation and the People's Property', in A. Kear and D.L. Steinberg (eds), *Mourning Diana: Nation, Culture and the Performance of Grief* (London: Routledge, 1999), pp. 77–97.

Kelley, K., *The Royals* (New York: Warner Books, 1997).

Kemp, S., '"Myra, Myra on the Wall": The Fascination of Faces', *Critical Quarterly* 40:1 (1998), pp. 38–69.

Killingray, H., A. Head, C. Walton and S. Harwin (eds), *Poems for a Princess: In Memory of Diana, Princess of Wales 1961–97* (Peterborough: Anchor Books, 1998).

Kitzinger, J., 'Image', *Screen*, 39:1 (1998), pp. 73–9.

Kitzinger, J., 'The Moving Power of Moving Images: Television Constructions of Princess Diana', in T. Walter, *The Mourning for Diana* (Oxford: Berg, 1999), pp. 65–76.

Kitzinger, J., 'Image', *Screen* 39:1 (1998), pp. 73–9.

Kuhn, A., 'Preface', *Screen* 39:1 (1988), pp. 67–8.

Lacey, R., *Princess* (London: Hutchinson, 1982).

Larry King Live, CNN 25–26 June 1997.

Lauret, M., *Liberating Literature: Feminist Fictions in America* (London: Routledge, 1994).

Lewis, B.R., *HRH The Princess of Wales* (Loughborough: Ladybird Books, 1982).

Lewis, B.R., *Queen Elizabeth II and Diana Princess of Wales* (London: Purnell, 1983).

Lewis, P., 'This Most Memorable and Glorious Day', in Anonymous (ed.), *The Prince and Princess of Wales' Wedding Day* (London: Pitkin Pictorials Ltd., 1981), p. 15.

Lomax, E., 'Diana Al-Fayed: Ethnic Marketing and the End(s) of Racism', in J. Richards, S. Wilson and L. Woodhead (eds), *Diana, The Making of a Media Saint* (London: I.B. Tauris, 1999), pp. 74–97.

Lowry, S., *Cult of Diana: The Princess in the Mirror* (London: Chatto and Windus, 1985).

Lunchtime News from ITN, ITV, 26 June 1997.

Lunchtime News, BBC1, 26 June 1997.

Macdonald, M., *Representing Women: Myths of Femininity in the Popular Media* (London: Arnold, 1997).

Mackie, F., 'Conspiracy? Treason? Truth?', in Re:Public (ed.), *Planet Diana: Cultural Studies and Global Mourning* (Kingswood: Research Centre in Intercommunal Studies, Univ. of Western Sydney, Nepean, 1997), pp. 137–8.

Mail on Sunday: You magazine supplement, 23 August 1998, 'Diana: A Celebration of her Beauty and Her Life'.

Mail on Sunday: You magazine supplement, 3 August 1997, 'Sequins Save Lives'.

McGuigan, J., *Cultural Populism* (London: Routledge, 1992).

McRobbie, A., 'Second-Hand Dress and the Role of the Ragmarket', in *Zoot Suits and Second-Hand Dresses: An Anthology of Fashion and Music* (Basingstoke: Macmillan, 1989), pp. 23–49.

Melville, P., 'English Table Wuk', in *The Migration of Ghosts (Stories)* (London: Bloomsbury, 1998).

Blair, T., speech, 31 August 1997, rpt. in B. MacArthur (ed.), *Requiem: Memories and Tributes* (London: Pavilion, 1997).

Merck, M., 'Introduction: After Diana', in M. Merck (ed.). *After Diana: Irreverent Elegies* (London: Verso, 1998), pp. 1–14.

Milner, C., 'Charity Outraged by "Sick" Diana Art Show', *Sunday Telegraph*, 11 July 1999.

Mirror supplement, 'Diana: A Tribute to the People's Princess' Part One, 16 August 1998.

Mirror, 28 June 1997.

Modleski, T., *Feminism without Women: Culture and Criticism in a 'Post-Feminist' Age* (New York and London: Routledge, 1991).

Monckton, R., 'Her Laughter, Her Sense of Fun', in B. MacArthur (ed.), *Requiem: Memories and Tributes* (London: Pavilion, 1997), pp. 58–66.

Moore, S., 'Diana the Do-gooder versus the Bad Guys', *Independent* 17 January 1997, p. 17.

Moore, S., 'Diana – Her True Colours' (1993), in *Head Over Heels* (London: Penguin, 1997), pp. 85–91.

Morrah, D., *The Royal Family in Africa* (London: Hutchinson and Co., 1947).

Morton, A., *Diana: Her New Life* (London: Michael O'Mara Books, 1992).

Morton, A., *Diana: Her True Story* [Paperback edition] (London: Michael O'Mara Books, 1993).

Morton, A., *Diana: Her New Life* (London: Michael O'Mara Books, 1994).

Morton, A., *Diana: Her True Story – In Her Own Words* (London: Michael O'Mara Books, 1997).

Morton, A., *Diana: Her True Story – In Her Own Words* [Paperback edition] (London: Michael O'Mara Books, 1998).

Mower, S. and M. Yates, 'Goodbye to All That', *Telegraph* Magazine, 17 May 1997, pp. 32–6.

Munich, A., *Queen Victoria's Secrets* (New York: Columbia University Press, 1996).

Nairn, T., *The Enchanted Glass: Britain and its Monarchy* (London: Vintage [second edition], 1994).

Nava, M., 'Diana, Princess of Others: The Politics and Romance of "Race"', in Re:Public (ed.), *Planet Diana: Cultural Studies and Global Mourning* (Kingswood: Research Centre in Intercommunal Studies, University of Western Sydney, 1997), pp. 19–25.

Nava, M., 'Diana and Race: Romance and the Reconfiguration of the Nation', in A. Kear and D.L. Steinberg (eds) *Mourning Diana: Nation, Culture and the Performance of Grief* (London: Routledge, 1999), pp. 108–19.

New Formations, 28 (1996).

Newey, G., 'Diarrhoea', in M. Merck (ed.), *After Diana: Irreverent Elegies* (London: Verso, 1998), pp. 147–58.

News at Ten, ITV, 31 January 1995.

Nunn, H., 'Violence and the Sacred: The Iron Lady, the Princess, and the People's PM', in *New Formations* 36 (1999), pp. 92–110.

O'Hear, A., 'Diana, Queen of Hearts: Sentimentality Personified and Canonised', in D. Anderson and P. Mullen (eds.), *Faking It: The Sentimentalisation of Modern Society* (Social Affairs Unit, 1998), pp. 181–90.

O'Mara, M. (ed.), *Diana: Her Life in Photographs* (London: Michael O'Mara Books, 1995).

O'Mara, M. (ed.), *Diana: A Tribute in Photographs* (London: Michael O'Mara Books, 1997).

Owen, J., *Diana Princess of Wales The Book of Fashion* (Guildford: Colour Library Books, 1983).

Paglia, C., 'Diana Regina' (1992), in *Vamps And Tramps* ([1994], London: Viking, 1995) pp. 163–71.

Parker, K., 'Diana Was Never "One of Us"', Eau Claire *Leader-Telegram*, 14 September 1997, p. 3F.

Pasternak, A., *Princess In Love* (London: Bloomsbury, 1994).

Patton, C., 'Refiguring Social Space', in L. Nicholson and S. Seidman (eds), *Social Postmodernism: Beyond Identity Politics* (Cambridge: Cambridge University Press, 1995), pp. 216–49.

Paxman, J., *The English: A Portrait of a People* (London: Michael Joseph, 1998).

Pearson, J., *The Ultimate Family: The Making of the Royal House of Windsor* ([1986] London: Grafton, 1987).

Picture Post, 22 November 1947.

Pimlott, B., 'Royal Doormat or Dear Doyenne?' *The Times*, 25 June 1998, p. 43.

Pimlott, B., *The Queen: A Biography of Elizabeth II* (London: HarperCollins, 1996).

Polan, B. *et al.*, 'Diana – Her Own Woman', *Mail on Sunday* 2 and 9 July 1995.

Posner, G., 'Al Fayed's Rage', *talk* (September 1999), pp. 121–30.

Price, H., *The Royal Tour 1901, Or The Cruise of H.M.S. Ophir, Being a Lower Deck Account of Their Royal Highnesses the Duke and Duchess of Cornwall and York's Voyage around the British Empire* (Exeter: Webb & Bower, 1980).

Radway, J. 'Interpretive Communities and Variable Literacies: The Functions of Romance Reading', rpt. in J. Munns and G. Rajan (eds), *A Cultural Studies Reader: History, Theory, Practice*, pp. 334–50.

Radway, J., *Reading the Romance* (London: Verso, 1987).

Rajagopal, A., 'Celebrity and the Politics of Charity: Memories of a Missionary Departed', in A. Kear and D.L. Steinberg (eds), *Mourning Diana: Nation, Culture and the Performance of Grief* (London: Routledge, 1999), pp. 126–41.

Renton, A., 'Turning Diana into an ology', London *Evening Standard* 16 March 1998, pp. 8–9.

Richards, J., S. Wilson and L. Woodhead, 'Introduction: Saint Diana', in J. Richards, S. Wilson and L. Woodhead (eds), *Diana: The Making of a Media Saint* (London: I.B. Tauris, 1999), pp. 1–19.

Richards, J., 'The Hollywoodisation of Diana', in J. Richards, S. Wilson and L. Woodhead, *Diana, The Making of a Media Saint* (London: I.B. Tauris, 1999), pp. 59–73.

Robinson, A., 'Anne Robinson joins the *Sun*', *Sun*, 20 November 1995, p. 3.

Rose, J., 'The Cult of Celebrity', *London Review of Books*, 20 August 1998, pp. 10–13.

Sandoval, C., 'Theorizing White Consciousness for a Post-Empire World: Barthes, Fanon, and the Rhetoric of Love', in R. Frankenberg (ed.), *Displacing Whiteness: Essays in Social and Cultural Criticism* (Durham and London: Duke University Press, 1997), pp. 86–106.

Scully, R., 'Princess Attracts Record 21.1 million Viewers to *Panorama*', http://www.pa.press.net/princess/lead14.html.

Segal, N. 'The Common Touch', in M. Merck (ed.), *After Diana: Irreverent Elegies* (London: Verso, 1998), pp. 130–45.

Shattuc, J., '"Go Rikki": Politics, Perversion and Pleasure in the 1990s', in C. Geraghty and D. Lusted (eds), *The Television Studies Book* (London: Arnold, 1998), pp. 212–25.

Shaw, M., *Princess: Leader of Fashion* (Guildford: Colour Library Books, 1983).

Sheridan, L., *The Queen and her Children* (London: John Murray, 1953).

Sheridan, L., *The Queen and Princess Anne* (London: John Murray, 1959).

Shew, B.S., *Royal Wedding* (London: Macdonald & Co., 1947).

Shils, E. and M. Young, 'The Meaning of the Coronation', *Sociological Review* 1:1 (1953), pp. 68–81.

Showalter, E., 'Storming the Wintry Palace', *Guardian*, 6 September 1997, supplement 'The funeral of Diana', p. 15.

Showalter, E., 'Temple of Diana', *The Times Higher Education Supplement*, 28 August 1998, pp. 13–14.

Simmonds, D., *Princess Di: The National Dish* (London: Pluto Press, 1984).

Simons, J. 'The Dialectics of Diana as Empty Signifier', *theory & event* 1:4. http://muse.jhu.edu/journals/theory_&_event/v001/1.4.html.

Simpson, M., *Male Impersonators: Men Performing Masculinity* (London: Cassell, 1994).

Slater, D., 'Marketing Mass Photography', in H. Davis and P. Walton (eds), *Language, Image, Media* (Oxford: Basil Blackwell, 1983), pp. 245–63.

Smart, T., D. Gibbon, and D. Coolican, *Royal Family Album* (London: Colour Library International, 1978).

Smith, D., 'The Revolution of the Flowers', *Gay Times*, October 1997, pp. 7–9, 51–2.

Smith, J., 'Diana was Infantile and Self-indulgent. There, I've Said It', *Independent on Sunday*, 19 April 1998, p. 3.

Smith, J., 'The Frog Princess', in *Misogynies* (London: Faber, 1989), pp. 35–43.

Smith, J., 'To Di For: the Queen of Broken Hearts', *Different for Girls* (London: Chatto and Windus, 1997), pp. 3–17.

Snagge, J., *Our Royal Family: The Record of a Happy Marriage* (London: Odhams Press, n.d.).

Snead, J. (ed. C. MacCabe and C. West), *White Screens Black Images: Hollywood from the Dark Side* (London: Routledge, 1994).

Sofoulis, Z., 'Icon, Referent, Trajectory, World', in Re:Public (ed.), *Planet Diana: Cultural Studies and Global Mourning* (Kingswood: Research Centre in Intercommunal Studies, University of Western Sydney, Nepean, 1997), pp. 13–18.

Spencer, C., 'The Tribute by Earl Spencer', in B. MacArthur (ed.), *Requiem: Memories and Tributes* (London: Pavilion, 1997), pp. 179–82.

Spink, K., *Invitation to a Royal Wedding* (New Malden: Colour Library International Ltd, 1981).

Spurlin, W.J., 'I'd Rather be the Princess than the Queen! Mourning Diana as a Gay Icon', in A. Kear and D.L. Steinberg (eds), *Mourning Diana: Nation, Culture and the Performance of Grief* (London: Routledge, 1999), pp. 155–68.

Starkey, D., 'Diana's Death May Have Signalled the End of the Monarchy', *Sun*, 3 September 1997, p. 10.

Strong, R., 'An Icon for the Meritocratic Age', [*Independent*], rpt. in B. MacArthur (ed.), *Requiem: Memories and Tributes* (London: Pavilion, 1997), pp. 131–5.

Sun, 20 November 1995.

Sun, 22 November 1995.

Sun, 27 June 1997.

Sun, 28 June 1997.

Sun, 3 September 1997.

Sunday Mirror, 'Diana: The People's Princess' Part Two, 2 May 1998.

Sunday Mirror, 2 February 1997.

Sunday Times, Magazine, 21 June 1981.

Sunday Times, 7 June 1992.

Synge, V.M., *Royal Guides: A Story of the 1ˢᵗ Buckingham Palace Company* (London: Girl Guides Association, 1948).

Talbot, G., *The Country Life Book of the Royal Family* (Richmond-upon-Thames: Country Life Books, 1980).

Theweleit, K., *Male Fantasies: Volume 1: Women, Floods, Bodies, History* trans. S. Conway in collaboration with E. Carter and C. Turner (Minneapolis: University of Minnesota Press, 1987).

Times 15 January 1997.

Verma, J., 'Mourning Diana, Asian Style', in A. Kear and D.L. Steinberg (eds), *Mourning Diana: Nation, Culture and the Performance of Grief* (London: Routledge, 1999), pp. 120–5.

Vickers, G., *Debrett's Book of the Royal Wedding* (London: Debretts Peerage/Book Club Associates, 1981).

Vogue, January 1997.

Voice of the *Mirror*, 'Your People Have Spoken ... now YOU must, Ma'am', *Mirror*, 4 September 1997, p. 11.

Wade, J., 'Diana: The Enigma behind the Picture-Perfect Princess of Wales', *Hello!* 462, 14 June 1997, pp. 60–8.

Walkerdine, V., 'The Crowd in the Age of Diana: Ordinary Inventiveness and the Popular Imagination', in A. Kear and D.L. Steinberg (eds), *Mourning Diana: Nation, Culture and the Performance of Grief* (London: Routledge, 1999), pp. 98–107.

Walter, T., 'The Questions People Asked', in T. Walter (ed.), *The Mourning for Diana* (Oxford: Berg, 1999), pp. 19–47.

Wambu, O., 'Introduction', in *Empire Windrush: Fifty Years of Writing About Black Britain* (London: Gollancz, 1998), pp. 19–29.

Ware, V., *Beyond the Pale: White Women, Racism and History* (London: Verso, 1992).

Warner, M., *Monuments and Maidens: The Allegory of the Female Form* ([1985] London: Vintage, 1996).

Warren, R., review of D. Clehane, *Diana: The Secrets of Her Style* at http://www.amazon.com.

Watts, C., 'Unworkable Feeling: Diana, Death and Feminization', *New Formations* 36 (1999), pp. 34–45.

Wheeler, W., 'Together Again After All These Years: Science, Politics and Theology in the New Modernity', in A. Coddington and M. Perryman (eds), *The Moderniser's Dilemma: Radical Politics in the Age of Blair* (London: Lawrence and Wishart, 1998), pp. 175–91.

Whitaker, J., *Diana v. Charles* (London: Signet, 1993).

Whitaker, J., G. Brough and J. Kerr, 'Diana – the Business', *Daily Mirror*, 20 February 1995, pp. 21–3.

Whiting, A., *Family Royal* (London: W.H. Allen, 1982),

Wicke, J., 'Celebrity Material: Materialist Feminism and the Cult of Celebrity', *South Atlantic Quarterly* 93:4 (Fall 1994) pp. 751–78.

Wilding, R., 'Afterimages of Being', in Re:Public (ed.), *Planet Diana: Cultural Studies and Global Mourning* (Kingswood: Research Centre in Intercommunal Studies, University of Western Sydney, Nepean, 1997), pp. 145–8.

Williamson, J., 'Royalty and Representation', in *Consuming Passions: The Dynamics of Popular Cultture* ([1985], London: Marion Boyars, 1986), pp. 75–89.

Wilson, E., 'The Unbearable Lightness of Diana', *New Left Review* 226 (1997), pp. 136–45; reproduced in M. Merck (ed.), *After Diana: Irreverent Elegies* (London: Verso, 1998), pp. 111–26.

Wilson, A.N., *The Rise and Fall of the House of Windsor* (London: Sinclair-Stevenson, 1993).

Winship, J., *Inside Women's Magazines* (London: Pandora, 1987).

Wolfe, L., *Elizabeth and Philip: Our Heiress and Her Consort* (London: Sampson Low, Marston & Co., 1947).

Woman's Own, 28 May 1953.

Wurtzel, E., *Bitch* (London: Quartet, 1998).

Zeldin, T., 'The End of Cynicism', *The Observer*, rpt. in B. MacArthur (ed.), *Requiem: Memories and Tributes* (London: Pavilion, 1997), pp. 142–5.

Index